ARCHAEOLOGY
ESSENTIALS

Theories, Methods, and Practice

COLIN RENFREW & PAUL BAHN

EOLOGY
ITIALS

Theories, Methods, and Practice

with 190 illustrations

Thames & Hudson

© 2007 Thames & Hudson Ltd, London
Text © 2007 Colin Renfrew and Paul Bahn

All Rights Reserved. No part of this publication may be
reproduced or transmitted in any form or by any means,
electronic or mechanical, including photocopy, recording
or any other information storage and retrieval system,
without prior permission in writing from the publisher.

First published in 2007 in paperback in the United States
of America by Thames & Hudson Inc., 500 Fifth Avenue,
New York, New York 10110

thamesandhudsonusa.com

Library of Congress Catalog Card Number 2006901302

ISBN-13: 978-0-500-28637-1
ISBN-10: 0-500-28637-X

Printed and bound in China by Midas Printing Ltd

Contents

Preface

Archaeology Essentials is designed for college students taking an introductory course in archaeology. Today archaeologists might not cast themselves in the romantic and spectacular roles of John Lloyd Stephens and Frederick Catherwood, who revealed to an astonished world the wonders of Maya civilization, or of Howard Carter and Lord Carnarvon, who discovered the extraordinary tomb of the Pharaoh Tutankhamun. But spectacular discoveries do still make the headlines. In 2006 archaeologists announced the excavation of a new burial chamber in the Valley of the Kings, near Luxor in Egypt, the first such discovery there since 1922. However, most archaeologists spend their time engaged in research that rarely makes the news, but is nevertheless vitally important for our understanding of the past. Our aim in this book is to convey some of the excitement of archaeology in the 21st century and to give students a concise and readable account of the ways in which modern archaeologists investigate and understand our remote past.

Archaeology is still often a matter of painstaking excavation of an ancient site, but today very often new technologies are employed so that sometimes excavation can be avoided altogether. Today new technologies and methods for analyzing and evaluating archaeological finds mean that archaeologists can reach conclusions that would have been impossible just 10 or 20 years ago.

This book will introduce students to the new methods and technologies used by archaeologists: from the traditional shovel and trowel to satellite imagery and ground-penetrating radar. New technology has affected the work of archaeologists in the laboratory as well as in the field: we cover, for example the accelerator mass spectrometry methods of radiocarbon dating and the use of genetic evidence.

The story of modern archaeology is not just about technology. There have been enormous advances in the questions archaeologists ask and in the assumptions and theoretical models they apply to archaeological evidence. Some questions, which an earlier generation of archaeologists might have considered closed, have now been opened up for new examination.

In other words, whatever the focus of the college course it is our intention that students will find in this book an authoritative, concise and clear explanation of modern archaeological practice and approaches.

We are grateful to Colin Ridler for proposing *Archaeology Essentials* and to Ian Jacobs with whom we had fruitful discussions about the scope and structure of the book and who has made many useful suggestions. We thank also Ben Plumridge for undertaking the considerable task of putting the volume into shape.

Introduction
the nature and aims of archaeology

About 5300 years ago a 40-year old man made his last journey, on a mountain path in the European Alps. He lay undisturbed until his body was discovered by hikers in September 1991. Archaeologists were able to determine not only his age, but also the contents of his last meal: meat (probably ibex and venison), plants, wheat and plums. The Iceman suffered from arthritis, and analysis of a fingernail showed that he had suffered serious illness 4, 3 and 2 months before he died. At first it was thought that he died from exhaustion in a fog or blizzard. However, later analysis revealed what may be an arrowhead in his left shoulder and cuts on his hands, wrists and ribcage, and traces of blood from four other people on his clothes and weapons, so he may have died a violent death. These observations are just a sample of what archaeologists were able to learn about this long dead man.

The thrill of discovery and the ability of **archaeology** to reveal at least some of the secrets of our past have been the theme of many famous novels and movies: notably Steven Spielberg's Indiana Jones. Many discoveries in archaeology are far less spectacular than that of the Iceman, perhaps a collection of broken pieces of pottery, but these kinds of remains too can tell us a lot about the past through careful collection and analysis of the evidence.

Archaeology is unique in its ability to tell us what we can know about the whole history of humankind from its beginnings over 3 million years ago. Indeed for more than 99 percent of that huge span of time archaeology – the study of past **material culture** – is the only source of information. The archaeological record is the only way that we can answer questions about the **evolution** of our species and the developments in **culture** and society which led to the emergence of the first civilizations and to the more recent societies which are founded upon them.

This book provides a brief introduction to the ways in which archaeologists uncover and collect evidence about our past, how they analyze it (often using sophisticated scientific methods), and how they interpret it (both for fellow scholars and members of the public).

The Discipline of Archaeology

Many archaeologists consider themselves as part of the broader discipline of **anthropology**. Anthropology at its broadest is the study of humanity – our physical characteristics as animals, and our unique non-biological characteristics. Anthropology is thus a broad discipline – so broad that it is often broken down into different fields:

- **Physical** *or* **biological anthropology**: the study of human biological or physical characteristics and how they evolved.
- **Cultural anthropology**: analyzes human culture and society.
- Linguistic anthropology: the study of how speech varies with social factors and over time
- Archaeology: the study of former societies through the remains of their material culture and, in the case of literate cultures such as those of Mesopotamia or Mesoamerica, such written records as have survived

Archaeologists who are interested in the societies of ancient Greece and Rome, their empires and neighbouring territories, consider themselves Classical archaeologists. Like anthropological archaeologists, Classical archaeologists study the material remains of the Greek and Roman worlds, but can also take into account the extensive written records (literature, history, official records and so on) that survive.

Similarly, Biblical archaeologists work in much the same way as anthropological archaeologists, but with reference to the events set out in the Bible.

Archaeology has some aspects in common with both history and with science. Like history, archaeology is concerned with documenting and understanding the human past, but archaeologists operate in a time frame much larger than the periods studied by historians. Conventional historical sources begin only with the introduction of written records around 3000 BC in Western Asia, and much later in most other parts of the world (not until AD 1788 in Australia, for example). The period before written records, and history in the narrow sense, meaning the study of the past using written evidence, is known as **prehistory**. The chart below demonstrates how the period covered by prehistory is much larger than that addresses by history.

Although archaeologists spend much of their time studying artifacts and buildings, it is worth emphasizing that archaeology is about the study of humans, and in that sense, like history is a humanity. But it differs from the study of written history – although it uses written history – in a fundamental way. The material the archaeologist finds does not tell us directly what to think. Historical records make statements, offer opinions, pass judgments (even if those statements and judgments themselves need to be interpreted). The objects that archaeologists discover, on the other hand, tell us nothing directly in themselves. It is *we* today who have to make sense of these things. In this respect the practice of archaeology is rather like a science. The scientist collects data, conducts experiments, formulates a hypothesis (a proposition to account for the data), tests the hypothesis against more data and then devises a model (a description that seems best to summarize the pattern observed in the data). The archaeologist has to develop a picture of the past, just as the scientist has to develop a coherent view of the natural world. It is not found ready made.

Archaeology, in short, is a science as well as a humanity. That is one of its fascinations as a discipline: it reflects the ingenuity of the modern scientist as well as the modern historian. The technical methods of archaeological science are the most obvious, from **radiocarbon dating** to studies of food residues in pots. Equally important are scientific methods of analysis: archaeology is just as much about the analytical concepts of the archaeologist as the instruments in the laboratory.

The Important Questions of Archaeology

Because the evidence of archaeology cannot speak for itself, it is important that archaeologists ask the right questions of the evidence. If the wrong questions are asked, the wrong conclusions will be drawn. For example, early explanations of the hundreds of unexplained mounds found east of the Mississippi river assumed that they could not have been built by the indigenous American Indian peoples of the region. So, it was assumed that the mounds had been built by a mythical and vanished race of Moundbuilders. Thomas Jefferson, later in his career the third President of the United States, decided to test this hypothesis against hard evidence and dug a trench across a mound on his property. He was able to show that the mound had been used as a burial place on many occasions and found no evidence that it could not have been built by the indigenous peoples. In other words, Jefferson asked questions about what the evidence suggested: he did not simply reach a conclusion that fitted his prejudices and assumptions.

If our aim is to learn about the human past, one of the most important tasks of the archaeologist is to ask the right questions about the evidence. Traditional approaches tended to regard the objective of archaeology mainly as reconstruction: piecing together the puzzle. But today it is not simply enough the recreate the material culture of remote periods. We are certainly interested in having a clear picture of how people lived, and how they exploited their environment. But we also want to know *why* they lived that way, why they had certain patterns of behaviour and how their material culture came to take the form it did. We are interested, in short, in explaining change.

How to Use This Book

Because the questions asked by archaeologists are so important we decided to organize this book around some of the most important questions. Chapter 1 looks at the history of archaeology, the kinds of questions asked by archaeologists in the past and the methods they used.

In chapter 2 we ask the question What is Left?: the evidence with which archaeologists work. The next chapter examines the important question Where? Archaeologists can learn a good deal from the **context** in which evidence is found and have developed many techniques for locating and recovering evidence. In chapter 4 the question is When?: how can we know whether something dates from a few hundred years or many thousands of years ago? Chapter 5 examines the fascinating question of How were societies organized? In chapter 6 we look the world in which ancient people lived: What was the environment and what did they eat? Technology was an important factor in changing society and the lives of our ancestors, as was contact with other ancient peoples: the key questions for chapter 7 are How did they make and use tools? And What contact did they have? The next chapter addresses some of the more difficult questions that modern archaeologists are trying to answer: the ways ancient peoples thought about their world and issues of identity. What did they think? And Who were they, what were they like are the questions for chapter 8. An equally difficult question is Why did things change, the subject of chapter 9. In chapter 10 we address the often controversial question: Whose past? The past may be remote in time but it can be very relevant today if it touches on the beliefs, identity and wishes of the descendants who lived long ago.

If you follow the questions examined in this book you will understand how archaeologists work, think, analyze and seek to understand the past. You will also discover that not all questions can be answered or perhaps that there might be more than one answer.

To help you understand how archaeology works, we have provided some special features in this book. Case studies, designed as box features, show you archaeology in action and will help you understand the issues that archaeologists deal with in their research and fieldwork. Key Concept and Key Fact boxes summarize and review important concepts, methods or facts about archaeology. These boxes are usually placed at the end of a section to help you reinforce what you have learned, but sometimes we have positioned them at the beginning of a discussion to help you understand technical concepts as you read about them. At the end of every chapter there is a summary to recap what you have read and a suggested reading list that will guide you to the most important and helpful publications if you want to research any subject further. Archaeological terms in the text that are defined in the glossary are highlighted in bold (e.g. **artifact**) when they first occur in a chapter.

1

The Searchers
the history of archaeology

In this chapter:

The history of **archaeology** is commonly seen as the history of great discoveries: the tomb of Tutankhamun in Egypt, the lost Maya cities of Mexico, the painted caves of the Old Stone Age such as Lascaux in France, or the remains of our human ancestors buried deep in the Olduvai Gorge in Tanzania. But even more than that it is the story of how we have come to look with fresh eyes at the material evidence for the human past, and with new methods to aid us in our task.

It is important to remember that just a century and a half ago, most well-read people in the Western world – where archaeology as we know it today was first developed – believed that the world had been created only a few thousand years earlier (in the year 4004 BC according to the then-standard interpretation of the Bible), and that all that could be known of the remote past had to be gleaned from the earliest historians, notably those of the ancient Near East, Egypt, and Greece. There was no awareness that any kind of coherent history of the periods before the development of writing was possible at all.

But today we can indeed penetrate the depths of the remote past. This is not simply because new discoveries are being made all the time. It is because we have learned to ask some of the right questions, and have developed some of the right methods for answering them. The material evidence of the archaeological record has been lying around for a long time. What is new is our awareness that the methods of archaeology can give us information about the past, even the prehistoric past (before the invention of writing). The history of archaeology is therefore in the first instance a history of ideas, of theory, of ways of looking at the past. Next it is a history of developing research methods, employing those ideas and investigating those questions. And only thirdly is it a history of actual discoveries.

In this chapter and in this book it is the development of the questions and ideas that we shall emphasize, and the application of new research methods. The main thing to remember is that every view of the past is a product of its own time: ideas and theories are constantly evolving, and so are methods. When we describe the archaeological research methods of today we are simply speaking of one point on the trajectory of the subject's evolution. In a few decades or even a few years time these methods will certainly look old-fashioned and out of date. That is the dynamic nature of archaeology as a discipline.

THE SPECULATIVE PHASE

Humans have always speculated about their past, and most **cultures** have their own foundation myths to explain why society is how it is. Most cultures, too, have been fascinated by the societies that preceded them. The Aztecs exaggerated their Toltec ancestry, and were so interested in Teotihuacán, the huge Mexican city abandoned hundreds of years earlier which they mistakenly linked with the Toltecs, that they incorporated ceremonial stone masks from that **site** in the foundation deposits of their own Great Temple. A rather more detached curiosity about the relics of bygone ages developed in several other early civilizations, where scholars and even rulers collected and studied objects from the past.

During the revival of learning in Europe known as the Renaissance (14th to 17th centuries), princes and people of refinement began to form "cabinets of curiosities" in which curios and ancient **artifacts** were displayed rather haphazardly with exotic minerals and all manner of specimens illustrative of what was called "natural history." During the Renaissance also scholars began to study and collect the relics of ancient Greece and Rome. And they began too in more northern lands to study the local relics of their own remote past. At this time these were mainly the field monuments – those conspicuous sites, often made of stone, which immediately attracted attention, such as Stonehenge. Careful scholars, such as the Englishman William Stukeley, made systematic studies of some of these monuments, with accurate plans which are still useful today. Stukeley and his colleagues successfully demonstrated that these monuments had not been constructed by giants or devils, as suggested by local names such as the Devil's Arrows, but by people in antiquity. He was also successful in phasing field monuments, demonstrating that, since Roman roads cut barrows, the former must have been built after the latter.

The First Excavations

In the 18th century more adventurous researchers initiated **excavation** of some of the most prominent sites. The Roman city of Pompeii in Italy was one of the first of these. Buried under meters of volcanic ash after the cataclysmic eruption of nearby Mount Vesuvius, Pompeii was only rediscovered in 1748. Although to begin with the motivation of the excavators was to find valuable ancient masterpieces, it wasn't long before published finds from Pompeii were attracting enormous international attention, influencing styles of furniture and interior decoration, and even inspiring several pieces of romantic fiction. Not until 1860, however, did well-recorded excavations begin.

The credit for conducting what has been called "the first scientific excavation in the history of archaeology" traditionally goes to Thomas Jefferson (later in his career third President of the United States), who in 1784 dug a trench or section across a burial mound on his property in Virginia. Jefferson's work marks the beginning of the end of the Speculative Phase.

In Jefferson's time people were speculating that the hundreds of unexplained mounds known east of the Mississippi river had been built not by the indigenous

"THE FIRST EXCAVATION"

- Thomas Jefferson, later to become President of the United States, conducted the "first scientific excavation" in Virginia in 1784

- By carefully digging a trench across an Indian burial mound he was able to observe different layers and to draw reasoned conclusions from the data

American Indians, but by a mythical and vanished race of "Moundbuilders." Jefferson adopted what today we should call a scientific approach, that is, he tested ideas about the mounds against hard evidence – by excavating one of them. His methods were careful enough to allow him to recognize different layers (or **stratigraphy**) in his trench, and to see that the many human bones present were less well preserved in the lower layers. From this he deduced that the mound had been reused as a place of burial on many separate occasions. Although Jefferson admitted, rightly, that more evidence was needed to resolve the Moundbuilder question, he saw no reason why ancestors of the present-day Indians themselves could not have raised the mounds.

Jefferson was ahead of his time. His sound approach – logical deduction from carefully excavated evidence, in many ways the basis of modern archaeology – was not taken up by any of his immediate successors in North America. In Europe, meanwhile, extensive excavations were being conducted, for instance by the Englishman Richard Colt Hoare, who dug into hundreds of burial mounds in southern Britain during the first decade of the 19th century. None of these excavations, however, did much to advance the cause of knowledge about the distant past, since their interpretation was still within the biblical framework, which insisted on a short span for human existence.

Early excavations: Richard Colt Hoare and William Cunnington direct a dig north of Stonehenge in 1805.

THE BEGINNINGS OF MODERN ARCHAEOLOGY

It was not until the middle of the 19th century that the discipline of archaeology became truly established. Already in the background there were the significant achievements of the newly developed science of geology. The study of the **stratification** of rocks (their arrangement in superimposed layers or strata), established principles which were to be the basis of archaeological excavation, as foreshadowed by Jefferson. It was demonstrated that the stratification of rocks was due to processes which were still going on in seas, rivers, and lakes. This was the principle of "**uniformitarianism**," that geologically ancient conditions were in essence similar to, or "uniform with," those of our own time. This idea could be applied to the human past also, and it marks one of the fundamental notions of modern archaeology: that in many ways the past was much like the present.

The Antiquity of Humankind and the Concept of Evolution

These advances in geology did much to lay the groundwork for what was one of the significant events in the intellectual history of the 19th century (and an indispensable one for the discipline of archaeology): the establishment of the antiquity of humankind. It had become widely agreed that earth's origins extended far back into a remote past, so that the biblical notion of the creation of the world and all its contents just a few thousand years before our own time could no longer be accepted. The possibility of a **prehistory** of humankind, indeed the need for one, was established.

This harmonized well with the findings of Charles Darwin, whose fundamental work, *On the Origin of Species*, published in 1859, established the concept of **evolution** to explain the origin and development of all plants and animals. The idea of evolution itself was not new – earlier scholars had suggested that living things must have changed or evolved through the ages. What Darwin demonstrated was how this change occurred. The key mechanism was, in Darwin's words, "natural selection," or the survival of the fittest. In the struggle for existence, environmentally better-adapted individuals of a particular species would survive (or be "naturally selected") whereas less well-adapted ones would die. The surviving individuals would pass on their advantageous traits to their offspring and gradually the characteristics of a species would change to such an extent that a new species emerged. This was the process of evolution. The implications were clear: that the human species had emerged as part of this same process. The search for human origins in the material record, by the techniques of archaeology, could begin.

Darwin's work on evolution also had an immediate impact on archaeologists who were laying the foundations for the study of artifacts and how they develop

Charles Darwin in a cartoon from the 1860s.

over time. But his influence on social thinkers and anthropologists has been even more significant. The principles of evolution can also be applied to social organization, for culture can be seen as learned and passed on between generations, albeit in a more general way than in biological evolution.

The Three Age System

As we have noted, some archaeological techniques, notably those in the field of excavation, were already being developed. So too was another conceptual device which proved very useful for the progress of European prehistory: the **Three Age System**. As early as 1808, Colt Hoare had recognized a sequence of stone, "brass," and iron artifacts within the barrows he excavated, but this was first systematically studied in the 1830s by the Danish scholar C.J. Thomsen. He proposed that prehistoric artifacts could be divided into those coming from a Stone Age, a Bronze Age, and an Iron Age, and this **classification** was soon found useful by scholars throughout Europe. Later a division in the Stone Age was established between the **Paleolithic** or Old Stone Age and the **Neolithic** or New Stone Age.

These terms were less applicable to Africa, where bronze was not used south of the Sahara, or to the Americas, where bronze was less important and iron was not in use before the European conquest. But it was conceptually significant. The Three Age System established the principle that by studying and classifying prehistoric artifacts, they could be ordered chronologically. Archaeology was moving beyond mere speculation about the past, and becoming instead a discipline involving careful excavation and the systematic study of the artifacts unearthed. Although superseded by modern dating methods, the Three Age System remains one of the fundamental divisions of archaeological materials today.

Ethnography and Archaeology

Another important strand in the thought of the time was the realization that the study by ethnographers of living communities in different parts of the world could be a useful starting point for archaeologists seeking to understand something of the lifestyles of their own early native inhabitants who clearly had comparably simple tools and crafts. For example, as early as the sixteenth century, contact with native Indian communities in North America provided antiquarians and historians with models for tattooed images of Celts and Britons.

And soon ethnographers and anthropologists were themselves producing schemes of human progress. Strongly influenced by Darwin's ideas about evolution, the British anthropologist Edward Tylor, and his American counterpart Lewis Henry Morgan, both published important works in the 1870s arguing that human

Frederick Catherwood's accurate, if somewhat romantic, drawing of Stela A at Copán; at the time of his visit to the site in 1840 Maya glyphs had not been deciphered.

Ephraim Squier.

societies had evolved from a state of savagery (primitive hunting) through barbarism (simple farming) to civilization (the highest form of society). Morgan's work was partly based on his great knowledge of living North American Indians.

Discovering the Early Civilizations

By the 1880s, then, many of the ideas underlying modern archaeology had been developed. But these ideas themselves took shape against a background of major 19th-century discoveries of ancient civilizations in the Old World and the New.

The splendors of ancient Egyptian civilization had already been brought to the attention of an avid public after Napoleon's military expedition there of 1798–1800. It was the discovery by one of his soldiers of the Rosetta Stone that eventually provided the key to understanding Egyptian hieroglyphic writing. Inscribed on the stone were parallel texts written in both Egyptian and Greek scripts. The Frenchman Jean-François Champollion used this bilingual inscription finally to decipher the hieroglyphs in 1822, after 14 years' work. A similar piece of brilliant scholarly detection helped unlock the secrets of cuneiform writing, the script used for many languages in ancient Mesopotamia.

Egypt and the Near East also held a fascination for the American lawyer and diplomat John Lloyd Stephens, but it was in the New World that he was to make his name. His travels in Yucatán, Mexico, with the English artist Frederick Catherwood, and the superbly illustrated books they produced together in the early 1840s, revealed for the first time to an enthusiastic public the ruined cities of the ancient Maya. Unlike contemporary researchers in North America, who continued to argue for a vanished white race of Moundbuilders as the architects of the earthworks there, Stephens rightly believed that the Maya monuments were, in his own words, "the creation of the same races who inhabited the country at the time of the Spanish conquest." Stephens also noted that there were similar hieroglyphic inscriptions at the different sites, which led him to argue for Maya cultural unity – but no Champollion was to emerge to decipher the glyphs until the 1960s.

19th-Century North American Pioneers

In North America, two themes dominated 19th-century archaeology: the enduring belief in a vanished race of Moundbuilders; and the search for "glacial man" – the idea that human fossils and Stone Age tools would be found in the Americas in association with extinct animals, as they had been in Europe. Ephraim Squier, for example, an Ohio newspaperman who excavated over 200 mounds in the 1840s, considered them beyond the capabilities of any native Americans, who were "hunters averse to labor," maintaining the myth of the

Moundbuilders. Their work does still have some use, though, since the plans and records they made are now the best record there is of the many mounds which were destroyed as settlers moved westward.

Samuel Haven, Librarian of the American Antiquarian Society, produced a remarkable synthesis in 1856, *The Archaeology of the United States,* which is considered a foundation stone of modern American archaeology. In it, he argued

Part of a 348-ft long painting illustrating a 19th-century mound excavation. Such excavations were often part of the futile search for a vanished race of Moundbuilders.

Plan of Serpent Mound, Ohio, as prepared by Squier (with the help of Edwin Davis, an Ohio physician) in 1846.

Samuel Haven.

John Wesley Powell.

Cyrus Thomas.

persuasively that the native Americans were of great antiquity, and, through cranial and other physical characteristics, he pointed to their probable links with Asiatic races. Disagreeing strongly with Squier and others, he concluded that the mysterious mounds had been built by the ancestors of living American Indians.

Another scholar, John Wesley Powell, had spent much of his youth digging into mounds and learning geology. Eventually he was appointed director of the U.S. Geographical and Geological Survey of the Rocky Mountain region. He published a wide range of information on the rapidly dwindling native American cultures. Moving to Washington, Powell also headed the Bureau of American Ethnology, an agency he set up to study the North American Indians. A fearless campaigner for native American rights, he recommended the setting up of reservations, and also began the recording of tribal oral histories.

In 1881 Powell recruited Cyrus Thomas to head the Bureau's archaeology program, and to settle the Moundbuilder question once and for all. After 7 years of fieldwork and the investigation of thousands of mounds, Thomas proved that the Moundbuilder race had never existed: the monuments had been erected by the ancestors of modern native Americans.

The Development of Field Techniques

It was only in the late 19th century that a sound methodology of scientific excavation began to be generally adopted. From that time, some major figures stand out who in their various ways have helped create the modern field methods we use today.

General Augustus Lane-Fox Pitt-Rivers, for much of his life a professional soldier, brought long experience of military methods, survey, and precision to

General Pitt-Rivers, excavator of Cranborne Chase, and pioneer in recording techniques. To the right is his meticulous plan of a barrow on Cranborne Chase.

impeccably organized excavations on his estates in southern England. Plans, sections, and even models were made, and the exact position of every object was recorded. He was not concerned with retrieving beautiful treasures, but with recovering all objects, no matter how mundane. He was a pioneer in his insistence on total recording, and his four privately printed volumes, describing his excavations on Cranborne Chase from 1887 to 1898, represent the highest standards of archaeological publication.

A younger contemporary of Pitt-Rivers, Sir William Flinders Petrie was likewise noted for his meticulous excavations and his insistence on the collection and description of everything found, not just the fine objects, as well as on full publication. He employed these methods in his exemplary excavations in Egypt, and later in Palestine, from the 1880s until his death.

Sir Mortimer Wheeler fought in the British army in both world wars and, like Pitt-Rivers, brought military precision to his excavations, notably through techniques such as the grid-square method of dividing and digging a site. He is particularly well known for his work at British hillforts, notably Maiden Castle. Equally outstanding, however, was his achievement as Director-General of Archaeology in India, where he held training schools in modern field methods, and excavated at many important sites.

Flinders Petrie at the Egyptian site of Abydos in 1922.

Sir Mortimer Wheeler, and one of his excavations in India, 1945.

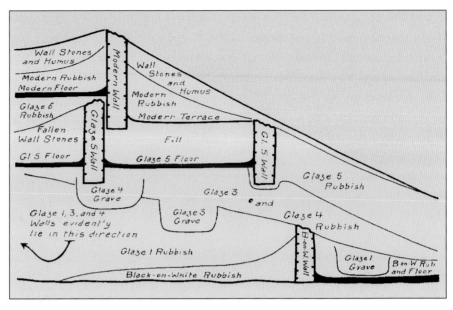

Alfred Kidder and his cross-sectional drawing of the stratigraphy at the Pecos Pueblo site.

Alfred Kidder was the leading Americanist of his time. As well as being a major figure in Maya archaeology, he was largely responsible for putting the Southwest on the archaeological map with his excavations at Pecos Ruin, a large pueblo in northern New Mexico, from 1915 to 1929. His survey of the region, *An Introduction to the Study of Southwestern Archaeology* (1924) has become a classic.

Kidder was one of the first archaeologists to use a team of specialists to help analyze artifacts and human remains. He is also important for his "blueprint" for a regional strategy: (1) reconnaissance; (2) selection of criteria for ranking the remains of sites chronologically; (3) organizing them into a probable sequence; (4) stratigraphic excavation to elucidate specific problems; followed by (5) more detailed regional survey and dating.

KEY EARLY ADVANCES

- The rejection of a literal interpretation of the Biblical account of early human history and the establishment of the antiquity of humankind

- Charles Darwin's theories of evolution and natural selection

- The establishment of the Three Age System which divided prehistory into a Stone Age followed by a Bronze Age and an Iron Age

- The development of archaeological field techniques

CLASSIFICATION AND CONSOLIDATION

As we have seen, well before the end of the 19th century, many of the principal features of modern archaeology had been established and many of the early civilizations had been discovered. There now ensued a period, which lasted until about 1960, which has been described as the "classificatory-historical period." Its central concern was chronology. Much effort went into the establishment of regional chronological systems, and the description of the development of culture in each area.

It was scholars studying the prehistoric societies of Europe and North America who made some of the most significant contributions. In the United States there was a close link between anthropologists and archaeologists studying the American Indians. The anthropologist Franz Boas reacted against the broad evolutionary schemes of his predecessors and demanded much greater attention to the collection and classification of information in the field. Huge inventories of cultural traits, such as pot and basket designs or types of moccasins, were built up. This tied in with the so-called "direct historical approach" of the archaeologists, who attempted to trace modern Indian pottery and other styles "directly" back into the distant past. By the 1930s the number of separate regional sequences was so great that a group of scholars led by W.C. McKern devised what became known as the "**Midwestern Taxonomic System**," which correlated sequences in the Midwest by identifying similarities between artifact collections.

Professor Gordon Childe at the site of the Neolithic settlement at Skara Brae, Orkney, in 1930.

Meanwhile, Gordon Childe, a brilliant Australian based in Britain and a leading thinker and writer about European prehistory, had almost single-handedly been making comparisons of this sort between prehistoric sequences in Europe. Both his methods and the Midwestern Taxonomic System were designed to order the material, to answer the question: To what period do these artifacts date? and also: With which other materials do they belong? This latter question usually carried with it an assumption which Gordon Childe made explicit: that a constantly recurring collection or "assemblage" of artifacts (a "culture" in his terminology) could be attributed to a particular group of people. This approach thus offered the hope of answering, in a very general sense, the question: Who did these artifacts belong to?

But Childe went beyond merely describing and correlating the culture sequences and attempted to account for their origin. In the late 19th century scholars had argued that all the attributes of civilization, from stone architecture to metal weapons, had spread or "diffused" to Europe from the Near East by trade or migration of people. With the much greater range of evidence available to him, Childe modified this approach and argued that Europe had undergone some indigenous development – but he nevertheless attributed the major cultural changes to Near Eastern influences.

Later Childe went on to try and answer the much more difficult question: Why had civilization arisen in the Near East? Himself influenced by Marxist ideas and the relatively recent Marxist revolution in Russia, he proposed that there had been a Neolithic Revolution which gave rise to the development of farming, and later an Urban Revolution which led to the first towns and cities. Childe was one of the few archaeologists of his generation bold enough to address this whole broad issue of why things happened or changed in the past. Most of his contemporaries were more concerned with establishing chronologies and cultural sequences. But after World War II scholars with new ideas began to challenge conventional approaches.

The Ecological Approach

One of the most influential new thinkers in North America was the anthropologist Julian Steward. Like Childe he was interested in explaining cultural change, but he brought to the question an anthropologist's understanding of how living cultures work. Moreover he highlighted the fact that cultures do not interact simply with each other but with the environment as well. Steward christened the study of ways in which adaptation to the environment could cause cultural change "**cultural ecology**." Perhaps the most direct archaeological impact of these ideas can be seen in the work of Gordon Willey, one of Steward's graduate associates, who carried out a pioneering investigation in the Virú Valley, Peru, in the late 1940s. This study of 1500 years of pre-Columbian occupation involved a combination of observations from detailed maps and aerial photographs, survey at ground level, and excavation and surface potsherd collection to establish dates for the hundreds of prehistoric sites identified. Willey then plotted the geographical distribution of these sites in the valley at different periods and set the results against the changing local environment.

Quite independently of Steward, however, the British archaeologist Grahame Clark developed an ecological approach with even more direct relevance for archaeological fieldwork. Breaking away from the artifact-dominated "culture history" approach of his contemporaries, he argued that by studying how human populations adapted to their environments we can understand many aspects of ancient society. Collaboration with new kinds of specialists was essential: for example, specialists who could identify animal bones or plant remains in the archaeological record could help build up a picture not only of what prehistoric environments were like, but what foods prehistoric peoples ate.

The Rise of Archaeological Science

The other striking development of the period immediately after World War II was the rapid development of scientific aids for archaeology. We have already seen how pioneers of the ecological approach forged an alliance with specialists from the environmental sciences. Even more important, however, was the application to archaeology of the physical and chemical sciences.

The greatest breakthrough came in the field of dating. In 1949 the American chemist Willard Libby announced his invention of **radiocarbon dating**. It was not until well over a decade later that the full impact of this momentous technical achievement began to be felt, but the implications were clear: here at last archaeologists might have a means of directly determining the age of undated sites and finds anywhere in the world without complicated cross-cultural comparisons. Traditionally, prehistoric Europe had been dated by supposed contacts with early Greece and hence (indirectly) with ancient Egypt, which could itself be dated historically. The radiocarbon method now promised a completely independent chronology for ancient Europe. It also meant that to establish a date was no longer one of the main end products of research. It was still important, but it could now be done much more efficiently, allowing the archaeologist to go on to ask more challenging questions than merely chronological ones.

Archaeological applications for scientific techniques now include plant and animal studies, and methods for analyzing human remains and artifacts. Over the past decade developments in biochemistry and molecular genetics have led to the emergence of the new disciplines of molecular archaeology and archaeogenetics. Sensitive techniques in the field of chemistry are beginning to allow the precise

KEY DEVELOPMENTS

- The early 20th-century establishment of regional chronologies and sequences of artifacts

- Gordon Childe's bold questioning of why things happened or changed in the past

- The post-World War II development of an environmental or ecological explanation for past change

- Increasing collaboration with specialists in other disciplines such as animal or plant studies

- The development of scientific aids for archaeology, notably radiocarbon dating identification of organic residues and are giving fresh insights into both diet and nutrition. The study of DNA, both modern and ancient, has offered novel approaches to the study of human evolution, and is now beginning to give the study of plant and animal domestication a systematic, molecular basis.

A TURNING POINT IN ARCHAEOLOGY

The 1960s mark a turning point in the development of archaeology. By this time some archaeologists were dissatisfied with the way research in the subject was being conducted. These dissatisfactions were not so much with excavation techniques, or with the newly developed scientific aids in archaeology, but with the way conclusions were drawn from them – how archaeologists explain things.

The fundamental cause for dissatisfaction with the traditional archaeology was that it never seemed to explain anything, other than in terms of migrations of peoples and supposed "influences." Already in 1948 the American archaeologist Walter W. Taylor had argued for an approach which would take into consideration the full range of a culture system. And in 1958, Gordon Willey and Philip Phillips argued for a greater emphasis on the social aspect, for a broader study of the general processes at work in culture history (a "processual interpretation").

That was all very well, but what would it mean in practice?

The Birth of the New Archaeology

In the United States the answer was provided, at least in part, by a group of younger archaeologists, led by Lewis Binford, who set out to offer a new approach to the problems of archaeological interpretation, which was soon dubbed "the **New Archaeology**." Binford and his colleagues argued against the approach which tried to use archaeological data to write a kind of "counterfeit history." They maintained that the potential of the archaeological evidence was much greater than had been realized for the investigation of social and economic aspects of past societies. Their view of archaeology was more optimistic than that of many of their predecessors.

They also argued that archaeological reasoning should be made explicit. Conclusions should be based not simply on the personal authority of the scholar making the interpretation, but on an explicit framework of logical argument. Thus conclusions, if they are to be considered valid, must be open to testing.

These processual archaeologists sought to explain rather than simply to describe, and to do so, as in all sciences, by seeking to make valid generalizations. They tried to avoid the rather vague talk of the "influences" of one culture

PROCESSUAL ARCHAEOLOGY: KEY CONCEPTS

In the early days of the New Archaeology, its principal exponents were very conscious of the limitations of the older, traditional archaeology. The following contrasts were among those which they often emphasized:

The Nature of Archaeology: Explanatory vs Descriptive
Archaeology's role was now to *explain* past change, not simply to reconstruct the past and how people had lived. This involved the use of *explicit* theory.

Explanation: Culture process vs Culture history
Traditional archaeology was seen to rely on historical explanation: the New Archaeology, drawing on the *philosophy of science*, would think in terms of culture process, of how changes in economic and social systems take place. This implies *generalization*.

Reasoning: Deductive vs Inductive
Traditional archaeologists saw archaeology as resembling a jigsaw puzzle: the task was one of "piecing together the past." Instead, the appropriate procedure was now to formulate *hypotheses*, constructing *models*, and deducing their consequences.

Validation: Testing vs Authority
Hypotheses were to be tested, and conclusions should not be accepted on the basis of the authority or standing of the research worker.

Research Focus: Project design vs Data accumulation
Research should be designed to answer specific *questions* economically, not simply to generate more information which might not be relevant.

Choice of Approach: Quantitative vs Simply qualitative
Quantitative data allowed computerized statistical treatment, with the possibility of *sampling* and *significance testing*. This was often preferred to the purely verbal traditional approach.

Scope: Optimism vs Pessimism
Traditional archaeologists often stressed that archaeological data were not well suited to the reconstruction of *social organization* or *cognitive systems*. The New Archaeologists were more positive and argued that it would never be known how hard these problems were until archaeologists had tried to solve them.

upon another, but rather to analyze a culture as a system which could be broken down into subsystems (like technology, trade, or ideology) which could be studied in their own right. They placed much less emphasis on artifact **typology** and classification.

In order to fulfill these aims, the New Archaeologists to a large extent turned away from the approaches of history towards those of the sciences. There was a great willingness to employ more sophisticated quantitative techniques and to draw on ideas from other disciplines, notably geography.

In their enthusiasm to use a battery of new techniques, the New Archaeologists drew also on a range of previously unfamiliar vocabularies which their critics tended to dismiss as jargon. Indeed in recent years, several critics have reacted against some of those aspirations to be scientific. But there can be no doubt that archaeology will never be the same again. Most workers today, even the critics of the early New Archaeology, implicitly recognize its influence when they agree that it is indeed the goal of archaeology to explain what happened in the past as well as to describe it. Most of them agree too that in order to do good archaeology it is necessary to make explicit, and then to examine, our underlying assumptions.

The Postprocessual Debate of the 1980s and 1990s

Post-modernist currents of thought in the 1980s and 1990s encouraged a great diversity of approaches to the past. While many field archaeologists were relatively untouched by theoretical debates, and the processual tradition established by the New Archaeology rolled on, there were several new approaches, sometimes collectively termed "postprocessual," which dealt with interesting and difficult questions.

Influential arguments, some of them first advanced by the archaeologist Ian Hodder and his students, have stressed that there is no single, correct way to undertake archaeological inference, and that the goal of objectivity is unattainable. However, this well-justified critique of the scientism of the early New Archaeology sometimes overlooks more recent developments in scientific methodology. It can also lead to charges of relativism, where one person's view has to be regarded as good as another's, and where, in interpretive matters, "anything goes," and where the borderlines between archaeological research and fiction (or science-fiction) may be difficult to define.

For its early proponents, postprocessual archaeology represented so radical a critique of processual archaeology as to establish a new beginning in archaeological theory. However, others saw "postprocessualism" as simply a development of

POSTPROCESSUAL ARCHAEOLOGY: KEY INFLUENCES

Postprocessualism is a collective term for a number of approaches to the past, all of which have roots in the post-modernist current of thought that developed in the 1980s and 1990s.

The *neo-Marxist* element has a strong commitment to social awareness: that it is the duty of the archaeologist not only to describe the past, but to use such insights to change the present world. This contrasts quite strikingly with the aspirations towards objectivity of many processual archaeologists.

The *post-positivist* approach rejects the emphasis on the systematic procedures of scientific method which are such a feature of processual archaeology, sometimes seeing modern science as hostile to the individual, as forming an integral part of the "systems of domination" by which the forces of capitalism exert their "hegemony."

The *phenomenological* approach lays stress on the personal experiences of the individual and on the way in which encounters with the material world and with the objects in it shape our understanding of the world. In landscape archaeology, for example, the archaeologist sets out to experience the humanly shaped landscape as it has been modified and formed by human activities.

The *praxis* approach lays stress upon the central role of the human "agent" and upon the primary significance of human actions (praxis) in shaping social structure. Many social norms and social structures are established and shaped by habitual experience (and the notion of *habitus* similarly refers to the unspoken strategy-generating principles employed by the individual which mediate between social structure and practice). The role of the individual as a significant agent is thus emphasized.

The *hermeneutic* (or interpretive) view rejects generalization, another feature of processual archaeology. Emphasis is laid, rather, upon the uniqueness of each society and culture and on the need to study the full context of each in all its rich diversity. A related view stresses that there can be no single correct interpretation: each observer or analyst is entitled to their own opinion about the past. There will therefore be a diversity of opinions, and a wide range of perspectives – which is why the emphasis is on interpretive archaeologies (plural).

some of the ideas and theoretical problems introduced by the New Archaeology. To these critics it brought in a variety of approaches from other disciplines, so that the term "postprocessual" was a shade arrogant in presuming to supersede what it might quite properly claim to complement. The term "interpretive archaeologies" (plural) has been suggested as a more positive label than "post-processual."

In recent times, the majority of postprocessual archaeologists have taken a less aggressively anti-scientific tone, and the emphasis has instead been upon the use of a variety of personal and often humanistic insights to develop a range of different fields and interests, recognizing the varied perspectives of different social groups. Ian Hodder's work at the early farming site of Çatalhöyük in Turkey provides a good example of this approach in action. It is now recognized that there is no single or coherent postprocessual archaeology, but rather a whole series of interpretive approaches and interests.

One of the strengths of the interpretive approach is to bring into central focus the actions and thoughts of individuals in the past. It argues that in order to understand and interpret the past, it is necessary to "get inside the minds" and think the thoughts of the people in question. This might seem a logical goal when examining symbolic systems (for example figurative artworks employing a complex iconography) but there is in reality no easy way to get into other people's minds, especially past minds.

Whatever the methodological problems, the consequence of the various debates has been to broaden the range of archaeological theory in a positive manner and to emphasize the symbolic and cognitive aspects of human endeavor in a way that the early New Archaeology failed to do.

The Widening Field

The postprocessual archaeologists are certainly right in arguing that our own interpretation and presentation of the past involve choices which depend less on an objective assessment of the data than on the feelings and opinions of the researchers and of the clients whom they aim to please. The great national museum in the United States, the Smithsonian Institution in Washington D.C., found it almost impossible to mount an exhibition in 1995 dealing with the destruction of Hiroshima 50 years earlier, without exciting the anger both of ex-servicemen and of liberals respectful of Japanese sensibilities.

It is evident that archaeology cannot avoid being caught up in the issues of the day, social and political as well as intellectual. An example is the influence of feminist thinking and the growth of feminist archaeology, which overlaps with the relatively new field of gender studies. A pioneer in the emphasis of the importance of women in prehistory was Marija Gimbutas. Her research in the Balkans led her to create a vision of an "Old Europe" associated with the first farmers whose central focus was (or so she argued) a belief in a great Mother Goddess figure. Although many feminist archaeologists today would take issue with certain aspects of Gimbutas' approach, she has certainly helped foster the current debate on gender roles.

In an article published in 1984, Margaret Conkey and Janet Spector drew attention to the androcentrism (male bias) of the discipline of archaeology. As Margaret Conkey pointed out, there existed a need "to reclaim women's experience as valid, to theorize this experience, and to use this to build a program of political action."

The deeply pervasive nature of androcentric thinking in most interpretations of the past should not be underestimated: the gender-specific terminology of "Man the Toolmaker," even when swept away with every reference to "mankind" corrected to "humankind," does in fact conceal further, widely held assumptions or prejudices – for instance that Paleolithic stone tools were mainly made by men rather than women, for which there is little or no evidence.

The box overleaf describes some of the more high-profile female archaeologists who have made important contributions to the discipline, but feminist archaeologists can with justice point to the imbalances between female and male professionals among archaeologists today; the goal of "political action" may be seen as justified by current social realities. In the 1990s feminist concern over androcentrism became one voice among many questioning the supposed objectivity and political neutrality of archaeology.

Comparable questions have continued to emerge in the developing indigenous archaeologies in the territories of former colonies, now freed from the previous imperial power. The appropriate policy for cultural heritage management, and indeed the very nature of the cultural heritage itself, are often contested among competing interest groups, sometimes along ethnic lines. Marginalized groups, such as the Australian Aborigines, have sought to achieve more influence in the definition and management of the heritage, and have often found their interests overlooked and misunderstood.

While some aspects of archaeology at the beginning of the new millennium were inevitably controversial, they were also in some ways very positive. They emphasized the value and importance of the past for the contemporary world, and

WOMEN PIONEERS OF ARCHAEOLOGY

The story of many early women archaeologists was one of exclusion and lack of recognition or promotion – or even employment. Furthermore, many brilliant academic women accepted that, after marriage, their career would no longer be a professional one, and supported the academic work of their husband with little public recognition. This has remained so until the present time, so the achievements of the following pioneers, spanning the 19th and 20th centuries, stand out all the more.

Harriet Boyd Hawes

This well-educated American majored in Classics and was fluent in Greek. Just after graduating, in her early twenties, she spent several seasons riding around Crete on muleback, in dangerous territory, alone or in the company of a woman friend, looking for prehistoric sites. In 1901 she discovered the Bronze Age site of Gournia – the first Minoan town site ever unearthed – which she excavated for the next three years, supervising a hundred local workmen. She published her findings in exemplary fashion in a lavishly illustrated report that is still consulted today.

Gertrude Caton-Thompson

A wealthy British researcher who followed courses in prehistory and anthropology at Cambridge, Caton-Thompson subsequently became well known for her pioneering inter-disciplinary project of survey and excavation in the Fayum of Egypt; and later, perhaps most famously, at Great Zimbabwe, where her excavations in 1929 unearthed datable artifacts from a stratified context, and confirmed that the site represented a major culture of African origin.

Dorothy Garrod

In 1937 Dorothy Garrod became the first woman professor in any

Dorothy Garrod, one of the first to study the prehistoric Near East systematically.

subject at Cambridge, and probably the first woman prehistorian to achieve professorial status anywhere in the world. Her excavations at Zarzi in Iraq and Mount Carmel in Palestine provided the key to a large section of the Near East, from the Middle Paleolithic to the Mesolithic, and found fossil human remains crucial to our knowledge of the relationship between Neanderthals and *Homo sapiens sapiens*. With her discovery of the Natufian culture, the predecessor of the world's first farming societies, she posed a series of new problems still not fully resolved today.

Anna O. Shepard

An American who studied archaeology as well as a wide range of hard sciences, Shepard subsequently became a specialist in ceramics, as well as Mesoamerican and Southwestern archaeology. She was one of the pioneers of petrographic analysis of archaeological pottery, focusing on sherd paste, paint, and temper.

Harriet Boyd Hawes (in 1892), discoverer of the Minoan town site of Gournia, Crete.

Gertrude Caton-Thompson – her work at Great Zimbabwe confirmed that the site was the work of a major African culture.

Anna O. Shepard was an acknowledged expert in the ceramics of the American Southwest and Mesoamerica.

Kathleen Kenyon was a great excavator and worked at two of the most important and complex sites in the Near East, Jericho and Jerusalem.

Tatiana Proskouriakoff – her work on Maya glyphs contributed greatly to their final decipherment.

She published extensively on the technology of New World pottery, and wrote a standard work, *Ceramics for the Archaeologist.*

Kathleen Kenyon
A formidable British archaeologist, Kenyon trained on Roman sites in Britain under Mortimer Wheeler, and adopted his method, with its close control over stratigraphy. She subsequently applied this approach in the Near East at two of the most complex and most excavated sites in Palestine: Jericho and Jerusalem. aAt Jericho, in 1952–58, she found evidence that pushed back the date of occupation to the end of the Ice Age, and uncovered the walled village of the Neolithic farming community, commonly referred to as "the earliest town in the world."

Tatiana Proskouriakoff
Born in Siberia, Proskouriakoff moved with her family to Pennsylvania in 1916. Unemployed after graduating as an architect in 1930, she ended up working as a museum artist in the University of Pennsylvania. A visit to the Maya site of Piedras Negras led her to devote the rest of her life to Maya architecture, art, and hieroglyphs.

Mary Leakey
A cigar-smoking, whisky-drinking, British archaeologist who, together with her husband Louis, transformed their chosen field. They worked for almost half a century at many sites in East Africa, carrying out meticulous excavations, most notably at Olduvai Gorge, Tanzania, and at Laetoli, where she excavated the famous trails of fossilized hominid footprints, made 3.7 million years ago.

Mary Leakey worked for almost half a century at various early hominid sites in East Africa, transforming our knowledge of human development.

they led to the realization that the cultural heritage is an important part of the human environment, and in some ways as fragile as the natural environment. They imply, then, that the archaeologist has an important role to play in achieving a balanced view also of our present world, which is inescapably the product of the worlds which have preceded it. The task of interpretation is now seen as very much more complex than it once seemed.

SUMMARY

- The history of archaeology is a history of new ideas, methods, and discoveries. Modern archaeology took root in the 19th century with the acceptance of three key concepts: the great antiquity of humanity, Darwin's principle of evolution, and the Three Age System for ordering material culture.

- Many of the early civilizations, especially in the Old World, had been discovered by the 1880s, and some of their ancient scripts deciphered. This was followed by a long phase of consolidation – of improvements in fieldwork and excavation and the establishment of regional chronologies.

- After World War II the pace of change in the discipline quickened. New ecological approaches sought to help us understand human adaptation to the environment. New scientific techniques introduced among other things reliable means of dating the prehistoric past. The New Archaeology of the 1960s and 1970s turned to questions not just of what happened when, but why, in an attempt to explain processes of change. Meanwhile, pioneer fieldworkers studying whole regions opened up a truly world archaeology in time and space – in time back from the present to the earliest toolmakers, and in space across all the world's continents.

- More recently a diversity of theoretical approaches, often grouped under the label postprocessual, highlighted the variety of possible interpretations and the sensitivity of their political implications.

- Precisely how archaeologists are continuing to push back the frontiers of knowledge about our planet's human past forms the subject of the rest of this book.

FURTHER READING

Good introductions to the history of archaeology include:

Bahn, P.G. (ed.). 1996. **The Cambridge Illustrated History of Archaeology.** CAMBRIDGE UNIVERSITY PRESS: CAMBRIDGE & NEW YORK.

Daniel, G. & Renfrew, C. 1988. **The Idea of Prehistory.** EDINBURGH UNIVERSITY PRESS: EDINBURGH; COLUMBIA UNIVERSITY PRESS: NEW YORK.

Fagan, B.M. 1996. **Eyewitness to Discovery.** OXFORD UNIVERSITY PRESS: OXFORD & NEW YORK.

Johnson, M. 1999. **Archaeological Theory, an Introduction.** BLACKWELL: OXFORD.

Lowenthal, D. 1985. **The Past is a Foreign Country.** CAMBRIDGE UNIVERSITY PRESS: CAMBRIDGE & NEW YORK.

Trigger, B.G. 1989. **A History of Archaeological Thought.** CAMBRIDGE UNIVERSITY PRESS: CAMBRIDGE & NEW YORK.

Willey, G.R. & Sabloff, J.A. 1993. **A History of American Archaeology.** (3rd ed.) FREEMAN: NEW YORK.

2 What is Left?
the variety of the evidence

In this chapter:

The relics of past human activity are all around us. Some of them were deliberate constructions, built to last, like the pyramids of Egypt, the Great Wall of China, or the temples of Mesoamerica and India. Others, like the remains of the Maya irrigation systems of Mexico and Belize, are the visible relics of activities whose aim was not primarily to impress the observer, but which still command respect today for the scale of the enterprise they document.

Most of the remains of **archaeology** are far more modest, however. They are the discarded garbage from the daily activities of human existence: the food remains, the bits of broken pottery, the fractured stone tools, the debris that everywhere is formed as people go about their daily lives.

In this chapter we define the basic archaeological terms, briefly survey the scope of the surviving evidence and look at the great variety of ways in which it has been preserved for us. From the frozen soil of the Russian steppes, for instance, have come the wonderful finds of Pazyryk, those great chieftains' burials where wood and textiles and skins are splendidly preserved. From the dry caves of Peru and other arid environments have come remarkable textiles, baskets, and other remains that often perish completely. And by contrast, from wetlands, whether the swamps of Florida or the lake villages of Switzerland, further organic remains are being recovered, this time preserved not by the absence of moisture, but by its abundant presence to the exclusion of air.

Extremes of temperature and of humidity have preserved much. So too have natural disasters. The volcanic eruption that destroyed Pompeii and Herculaneum in Italy is the most famous of them, but there have been others, such as the eruption of the Ilopango volcano in El Salvador in the 2nd century AD, which buried land surfaces and settlement remains in a large part of the southern Maya area.

Unfortunately most archaeological **sites** are not in areas subjected to extremes of climate or volcanic activity, and levels of preservation can vary enormously. Our knowledge of the early human past is dependent in this way on the human activities and natural processes that have formed the archaeological record, and on those further processes that determine, over long periods of time, what is left and what is gone for ever. Today we can hope to recover much of what *is* left, and to learn from it by asking the right questions in the right way.

BASIC CATEGORIES OF ARCHAEOLOGICAL EVIDENCE

The evidence studied by archaeologists very often includes **artifacts** – objects used, modified, or made by people. But equally important is the study of organic and environmental remains – known as "**ecofacts**" – that, although not made by humans, can still be very revealing about many aspects of past human activity.

Much archaeological research concentrates on the analysis of these artifacts and ecofacts that are found together on *sites*, which in turn are most productively studied together with their surrounding landscapes and grouped together into *regions*. Some of these different scales at which archaeologists operate, as well as the terminology they use, are illustrated above and opposite.

Artifacts are humanly made or modified portable objects, such as stone tools, pottery, and metal weapons. But artifacts provide evidence to help us answer all the key questions – not just technological ones – addressed in this book. A single clay vessel or pot can be analyzed in a number of different ways. The clay may be tested to produce a date for the vessel and thus perhaps a date for the location where it was found. It could also be tested to find the source of the clay and thus give evidence for the range and contacts of the group that made the vessel. Pictorial decoration on the pot's surface could help to form or be related to a sequence of design styles (a **typology**), and it could tell us something about ancient beliefs, particularly if it shows gods or other figures. And analysis of the vessel's shape and any food or other residues found in it can yield information about the pot's use, perhaps in cooking, as well as about ancient diet.

Some researchers broaden the meaning of the term "artifact" to include all humanly modified components of a site or landscape, such as hearths, postholes, and storage pits – but these non-portable artifacts are more usefully described as **features**. Simple features such as postholes may themselves, or in combination with remains of hearths, floors, ditches, etc., give evidence for complex features or structures, defined as buildings of all kinds, from houses and granaries to palaces and temples.

Non-artifactual organic and environmental remains or *ecofacts* include human skeletons, animal bones, and plant remains, but also soils and sediments – all of which may shed light on past human activities. They are important because they can indicate, for example, what people ate or the environmental conditions under which they lived.

SMALL REGION

Areas with soils suitable for first farmers

Rhine R.

Sites

1 : 400,000

GROUP OF SITES in association with river

Merzbach R.

1 : 40,000

INDIVIDUAL SITE (SMALL VILLAGE)

Early phase house (*structure*)

Refuse pit (*feature*) containing organic remains (*ecofacts*)

Path (*feature*)

Silo (small *structure*)

Later phase house (*structure*)

1 : 4000

Different scales and terminology used in archaeology, from the continental region (opposite page, top left) to the individual structure (right). In this representation of the pattern of settlement of Europe's first farmers (5th millennium BC), the archaeologist might study – at the broader scale – the interesting association between sites and light, easily worked soils near rivers. At the smaller scale, the association – established by excavation – of houses with other houses and with structures such as silos for grain storage raises questions, for example, about social organization and permanence of occupation at this period.

INDIVIDUAL STRUCTURE (HOUSE)

Scatter of *artifacts*

Postholes (*features*)

1 : 400

Artifacts and features are found *in association with* the structure

Archaeological *sites* may be thought of as the huge variety of places where artifacts, features, structures, and organic and environmental remains are found together. For working purposes we can simplify this still further and define sites as places where significant traces of human activity are identified. Thus a village or

KEY CONCEPTS: TYPES OF EVIDENCE

- *Artifacts:* portable objects used, modified or made by humans
- *Ecofacts:* organic and environmental remains not made by humans
- *Features:* non-portable artifacts
- *Sites:* places where artifacts, ecofacts, and features are found together

town is a site, and so too is an isolated monument like Serpent Mound in Ohio. Equally, a surface scatter of stone tools or potsherds may represent a site occupied for no more than a few hours, whereas a Near Eastern **tell** or mound is a site indicating human occupation over perhaps thousands of years.

The Importance of Context

In order to reconstruct past human activity at a site it is crucially important to understand the **context** of a find, whether artifact, ecofact, or feature. A find's context consists of its immediate **matrix** (the material surrounding it, usually some sort of sediment such as gravel, sand, or clay), its *provenience* (horizontal and vertical position within the matrix), and its **association** with other finds (occurrence together with other archaeological remains, usually in the same matrix). In the 19th century the demonstration that stone tools were often associated with the bones of extinct animals in a sealed matrix helped establish the idea of the great antiquity of humankind.

Increasingly since then archaeologists have recognized the importance of identifying and accurately recording associations between remains on sites. This is why it is such a tragedy when looters dig up sites indiscriminately looking for rich finds, without recording matrix, provenience, or associations. All the contextual information is lost. A looted vase may be an attractive object for a collector, but far more could have been learnt about the society that produced it had archaeologists been able to record where it was found (in a tomb, ditch, or house?) and in association with what other artifacts or organic remains (weapons, tools or animal bones?). Much information about the Mimbres people of the American Southwest has been lost forever because looters bulldozed their sites, hunting for the superbly painted – and highly sought after – bowls made by the Mimbres 1000 years ago.

When modern (or ancient) looters disturb a site, perhaps shifting aside material they are not interested in, they destroy that material's *primary context*. If archaeologists subsequently excavate that shifted material, they need to be able to recognize that it is in a *secondary context*. This may be straightforward for, say, a Mimbres site, looted quite recently, but it is much more difficult for a site disturbed in antiquity.

KEY CONCEPTS: CONTEXT

- *Matrix:* the material surrounding a find (an artifact, ecofact, or feature)

- *Provenience:* the exact position of a find within the matrix

- *Association:* a find's relationship with other finds

- Without context, an artifact loses much of its archaeological value

Nor is disturbance confined to human activity: archaeologists dealing with the tens of thousands of years of the Old Stone Age or **Paleolithic** period know well that the forces of nature – encroaching seas or ice sheets, wind and water action – invariably destroy primary context. A great many of the Stone Age tools found in European river gravels are in a secondary context, transported by water action far from their original, primary context.

FORMATION PROCESSES

In recent years archaeologists have become increasingly aware that a whole series of **formation processes** may have affected both the way in which finds came to be buried and what happened to them after they were buried. The study of these processes is called *taphonomy.*

A useful distinction has been made between *cultural formation processes* and non-cultural or *natural formation processes.* Cultural formation processes involve the deliberate or accidental activities of human beings as they make or use artifacts, build or abandon buildings, plow their fields and so on. Natural formation processes are natural events that govern both the burial and the survival of the archaeological record. The sudden fall of volcanic ash that covered Pompeii is an exceptional example; a more common one would be the gradual burial of artifacts or features by wind-borne sand or soil. Likewise the transporting of stone tools by river action, referred to above, or the activities of animals – burrowing into a site or chewing bones and pieces of wood – are also examples of natural formation processes.

At first sight these distinctions may seem of little interest to the archaeologist. In fact they are vital to the accurate reconstruction of past human activities. It can be important to know whether certain archaeological evidence is the product of human or non-human (cultural or natural) activity. If, for example, you are trying to reconstruct human woodworking activities by studying cutmarks on timber, then you should learn to recognize certain kinds of marks made by beavers using their teeth and to distinguish these from cutmarks made by humans using stone or metal tools.

Let us take an even more significant example. For the earliest phases of human existence in Africa, at the beginning of the Old Stone Age or Paleolithic period,

Early humans as mighty hunters (left) or mere scavengers (right)? Our understanding of formation processes governs the way in which we interpret associations of human tools with animal bones from the fossil record in Africa.

theories about our primitive hunting ability have been based on the association between stone tools and animal bones found at archaeological sites. The bones were assumed to be those of animals hunted and slaughtered by early humans who made the tools. But studies of animal behavior and cutmarks on animal bones suggest that in many cases the excavated bones are the remains of animals hunted and largely eaten by other predatory animals. The humans with their stone tools would have come upon the scene as mere scavengers, at the end of a pecking order of different animal species. By no means everyone agrees with this scavenging hypothesis. The point to emphasize here is that the issue can best be resolved by improving our techniques for distinguishing between cultural and natural formation processes – between human and non-human activity. Many studies are now focusing on the need to clarify how to differentiate cutmarks on bones made by stone tools from those made by the teeth of animal predators. Modern experiments using replica stone tools to cut meat off bones are one helpful approach. Other kinds of **experimental archaeology** can be most instructive about some of the formation processes that affect physical preservation of archaeological material (see box opposite).

The remainder of this chapter is devoted to a more detailed discussion of the different cultural and natural formation processes.

CULTURAL FORMATION PROCESSES – HOW PEOPLE HAVE AFFECTED WHAT SURVIVES IN THE ARCHAEOLOGICAL RECORD

We may separate these processes rather crudely into two kinds: those that reflect the original human behavior and activity before a find or site became buried; and those (such as plowing or looting) that came after burial. Now of course most major archaeological sites are formed as the result of a complex sequence of use, burial, and reuse repeated many times over, so that a simple two-fold division of cultural formation processes may not be so simple to apply in practice. Nevertheless, since one of our main aims is to reconstruct original human behavior and activity, we must make the attempt.

EXPERIMENTAL ARCHAEOLOGY

One effective way to study formation processes is through long-term experimental archaeology. An excellent example is the experimental earthwork constructed on Overton Down, southern England, in 1960.

The earthwork consists of a substantial chalk and turf bank, 21 m (69 ft) long, 7 m (25 ft) wide, and 2 m (6 ft 7 in) high, with a ditch cut parallel to it. The aim of the experiment has been to assess not only how the bank and ditch alter through time, but also what happens to materials such as pottery, leather, and textiles that were buried in the earthwork in 1960. Sections (trenches) have been – or will be – cut across the bank and ditch at intervals of 2, 4, 8, 16, 32, 64, and 128 years (in real time, 1962, 1964, 1968, 1976, 1992, 2024, and 2088): a considerable commitment for all concerned.

On this timescale, the project is still at a relatively early stage. But preliminary results are interesting. In the 1960s the bank dropped some 25 cm (10 in) in height and the ditch silted up quite rapidly. Since

The bank and ditch as cut in 1960, together with the changes revealed by sections cut across the earthwork in 1962 and 1976.

the mid-1970s, however, the structure has stabilized. As for the buried materials, tests after 4 years showed that pottery was unchanged and leather little affected, but textiles were already becoming weakened and discolored.

The 1992 excavations revealed that preservation was better in the chalk bank, which is less biologically active, than in the turf core where textiles and some wood

had completely disappeared. The structure itself had changed little since 1976, though there was considerable reworking and transport of fine sediment by earthworms.

The experiment has already shown that many of the changes that interest archaeologists occur within decades of burial, and that the extent of these changes can be far greater than had hitherto been suspected.

Original human behavior is often reflected archaeologically in at least four major activities: for example, in the case of a tool (see diagram overleaf) there may be

1 *acquisition* of the raw material;
2 *manufacture*;
3 *use*; and finally
4 *disposal* or *discard* when the tool is worn out or broken. (The tool may of course be reworked and recycled, i.e. repeating stages 2 and 3.)

Similarly a food crop such as wheat will be acquired (harvested), manufactured (processed), used (eaten), and discarded (digested and the waste products excreted) – here we might add a common intermediate stage of *storage* before use. From the archaeologist's point of view the critical factor is that remains can enter the archaeological record at any one of these stages – a tool may be lost or thrown

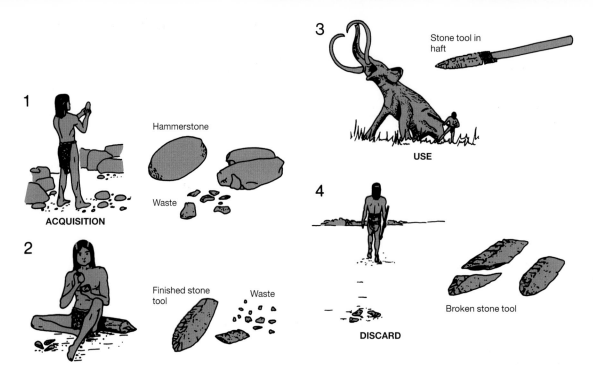

1 ACQUISITION

Hammerstone

Waste

2 MANUFACTURE

Finished stone tool

Waste

3 USE

Stone tool in haft

4 DISCARD

Broken stone tool

An artifact, a stone tool in this case, may have entered the archaeological record at any one of these four stages in its life cycle. The archaeologist's task is to determine which stage is represented by the find in question.

out as inferior quality during manufacture, a crop may be accidentally burnt and thus preserved during processing. In order accurately to reconstruct the original activity it is therefore crucial to try to understand which of the stages we are looking at. It may be quite easy to identify, say, the first stage for stone tools, because stone quarries can often be recognized by deep holes in the ground with piles of associated waste flakes and blanks which survive well. But it is much more difficult to know beyond reasonable doubt whether a sample of charred plant remains comes from, say, a threshing area or an occupation area – and this may also make it difficult to reconstruct the true plant diet, since certain activities may favor the preservation of certain species of plant.

Deliberate burial of valuables is another major aspect of original human behavior that has left its mark on the archaeological record. In times of conflict or war people often deposit prized possessions in the ground, intending to reclaim them at a later date but sometimes for one reason or another failing to do so. These **hoards** are a prime source of evidence for certain periods, such as the European Bronze Age, for which hoards of metal goods are common, or later Roman Britain, which has yielded buried treasures of silver and other precious metals. The archaeologist, however, may not find it easy to distinguish between hoards originally intended to be recovered and valuables buried with no reclamation intended, perhaps to placate supernatural powers (placed for example at a particularly dangerous part of a crossing over a bog).

How archaeologists set about trying to demonstrate belief in supernatural powers and an afterlife will be seen in Chapter 8. Here we may note that, in addition to hoards, the major source of evidence comes from *burial of the dead*, whether in simple graves, elaborate burial mounds, or giant pyramids, usually with grave-goods such as ceramic vessels or weapons, and sometimes with painted tomb-chamber walls, as in ancient Mexico or Egypt. The Egyptians indeed went so far as to mummify their dead – to preserve them, they hoped, for eternity – as did the Incas of Peru, whose kings were kept in the Temple of the Sun at Cuzco and brought outside for special ceremonies.

Human destruction of the archaeological record might be caused by burials of the kind just described being dug into earlier deposits. But people in the past deliberately or accidentally obliterated traces of their predecessors in innumerable other ways. Rulers, for instance, often destroyed monuments or erased inscriptions belonging to previous chiefs or monarchs. Some human destruction meant to obliterate has inadvertently preserved material for the archaeologist to find. Burning, for example, may not always destroy. It can often improve the chances of survival of a variety of remains such as of plants: the conversion into carbon greatly increases the powers of resistance to the ravages of time. Clay daubing and adobe usually decay, but if a structure has been fired, the mud is baked to the consistency of a brick. In the same way thousands of clay writing tablets from the Near East have been baked accidentally or deliberately in fires and thus preserved. Timbers too may char and survive in structures, or at least leave a clear impression in the hardened mud.

Today human destruction of the archaeological record continues at a frightening pace, through land drainage, plowing, building work, looting, etc. In Chapter 10 we discuss how this affects archaeology generally and what the potential implications are for the future.

NATURAL FORMATION PROCESSES – HOW NATURE AFFECTS WHAT SURVIVES IN THE ARCHAEOLOGICAL RECORD

We saw above how natural formation processes such as river action can disturb or destroy the primary context of archaeological material. Here we will focus on that material itself, and the natural processes that cause decay or lead to preservation. Practically any archaeological material can survive in exceptional circumstances. Usually, however, inorganic materials survive far better than organic ones.

Inorganic Materials

The most common inorganic materials to survive archaeologically are stone, clay, and metals.

Stone tools survive extraordinarily well – some are over 2 million years old. Not surprisingly they have always been our main source of evidence for human activities during the Old Stone Age, even though wooden and bone tools (which are less likely to be preserved) may originally have equalled stone ones in importance. Stone tools sometimes come down to us so little damaged or altered from their primary state that archaeologists can examine microscopic patterns of wear on their cutting edges and learn, for example, whether the tools were used to cut wood or animal hides. This is now a major branch of archaeological inquiry.

Fired clay, such as pottery and baked mud-brick or adobe, is virtually indestructible if well fired. It is therefore again not surprising that for the periods after the introduction of pottery making (some 16,000 years ago in Japan, and 9000 years ago in the Near East and parts of South America) ceramics have traditionally been the archaeologist's main source of evidence. As we saw at the beginning of this chapter, pots can be studied for their shape, surface decoration, mineral content, and even the food or other residues left inside them. Acid soils can damage the surface of fired clay, and porous or badly fired clay vessels or mud brick can become fragile in humid conditions. However, even disintegrated mud brick can help to assess rebuilding phases in, for instance, Peruvian villages or Near Eastern tells.

Metals such as gold, silver, and lead survive well. Copper, and bronze with a low-quality alloy, are attacked by acid soils, and can become so oxidized that only a green deposit or stain is left. Oxidation is also a rapid and powerful agent of destruction of iron, which rusts and may similarly leave only a discoloration in the soil.

The sea is potentially very destructive. Underwater remains can be broken and scattered by currents, waves, or tidal action. On the other hand, the sea can cause metals to be coated with a thick, hard casing of metallic salts from the objects

KEY CONCEPTS: SURVIVAL OF INORGANIC MATERIALS

- Stone tools, fired clay, and some metals such as gold, silver, and lead, survive very well in nearly all environments

- Some metals, such as copper, can corrode depending on the soil conditions, and iron rarely survives in an uncorroded state

- Although inorganic materials, particularly stone tools and pottery, are very often found at archaeological sites, these objects may well have been equalled or superseded in abundance and importance by objects that usually do not survive, such as wooden tools or baskets themselves; this helps to preserve the artifacts. If the remains are simply taken out of the water and not treated, the salts react with air, and give off acid which destroys the remaining metal. But the use of **electrolysis** – placing the object in a chemical solution and passing a weak current through it – leaves the metal artifact clean and safe. This is a standard procedure in underwater archaeology and is used on all types of objects from cannons to the finds recovered from the *Titanic*.

Organic Materials

Survival of organic materials is determined largely by the matrix (the surrounding material) and by climate (local and regional) – with the occasional influence of natural disasters such as volcanic eruptions, which are often far from disastrous for archaeologists.

The *matrix*, as we saw earlier, is usually some kind of sediment or soil. These vary in their effects on organic material; chalk, for example, preserves human and animal bone well (in addition to inorganic metals). Acid soils destroy bones and wood within a few years, but will leave telltale discolorations where postholes or hut foundations once stood. Similar brown or black marks survive in sandy soils, as do dark silhouettes which used to be skeletons.

But the immediate matrix may in exceptional circumstances have an additional component such as metal ore, salt, or oil. Copper can favor the preservation of organic remains, perhaps by preventing the activity of destructive micro-organisms. The prehistoric copper (and salt) mines of central and southeast Europe have many remains of wood, leather, and textiles.

A combination of salt and oil ensured the preservation of a woolly rhinoceros at Starunia, Poland, with skin intact, and the leaves and fruits of tundra vegetation around it. The animal had been carried by a strong current into a pool saturated with crude oil and salt from a natural oil seep, which prevented decomposition: bacteria could not operate in these conditions, while salt had permeated the skin and preserved it. Similarly, the asphalt pits of La Brea, Los Angeles, are world famous for the large quantities and fine condition of the skeletons of a wide range of prehistoric animals and birds recovered from them.

Climate plays an important role too in the preservation of organic remains. Occasionally the "local climate" of an environment such as a cave preserves finds. Caves are natural "conservatories" because their interiors are protected from outside climatic effects, and (in the case of limestone caves) their alkaline conditions permit excellent preservation. If undisturbed by floods or the trampling feet of animals and people, they can preserve bones and even such fragile remains as footprints.

More usually, however, it is the regional climate that is important. *Tropical climates* are the most destructive, with their combination of heavy rains, acid soils, warm temperatures, high humidity, erosion, and wealth of vegetation and insect life. Tropical rainforests can overwhelm a site remarkably quickly, with roots that dislodge masonry and tear buildings apart, while torrential downpours gradually destroy paint and plasterwork, and woodwork rots away completely. Archaeologists in southern Mexico, for example, constantly have to battle to keep back the jungle. On the other hand, jungle conditions can be positive, in that they hinder looters from easily reaching even more sites than they do already.

Temperate climates, as in much of Europe and North America, are not good, as a rule, for the preservation of organic materials; their relatively warm but variable temperatures and fluctuating rainfall combine to accelerate the processes of decay. In some circumstances, however, local conditions can counteract these processes. At the Roman fort of Vindolanda, near Hadrian's Wall in northern England, over 1300 letters and documents, written in ink on wafer-thin sheets of birch and alderwood, have been found. The fragments, dating to about AD 100, have survived because of the soil's unusual chemical condition: clay compacted between layers in the site created oxygen-free pockets (the exclusion of oxygen is vital to the preservation of organic materials), while chemicals produced by bracken, bone, and other remains effectively made the land sterile in that locality, thus preventing disturbance by vegetation and other forms of life.

Natural disasters sometimes preserve sites, including organic remains, for the archaeologist. The most common are violent storms, such as that which covered the coastal **Neolithic** village of Skara Brae, Orkney Islands, with sand, the mudslide that engulfed the prehistoric village of Ozette on America's Northwest Coast (see box on p. 54), or volcanic eruptions such as that of Vesuvius, which buried and

KEY CONCEPTS: SURVIVAL OF ORGANIC MATERIALS

The main factors which determine survival are:

- Matrix: the conditions and make-up of the soil or sediment surrounding the material (which only in special circumstances preserve organic material)

- Climate: the local and regional weather conditions, which in turn affect soils, erosion, flora, and fauna

- Natural disasters, such as volcanic eruptions, and extremes of dry, cold, and wet climates preserved Roman Pompeii under a blanket of ash. Another volcanic eruption, this time in El Salvador in about AD 595, deposited a thick and widespread layer of ash over a densely populated area of Maya settlement. Work here has uncovered a variety of organic remains at the site of Cerén, including palm and grass roofing, mats, baskets, stored grain and even preserved agricultural furrows.

Apart from these special circumstances, the survival of organic materials is limited to cases involving extremes of moisture: that is, very dry, frozen, or waterlogged conditions.

Preservation of Organic Materials: Extreme Conditions

Dry Environments.   Great aridity or dryness prevents decay through the shortage of water, which ensures that many destructive micro-organisms are unable to flourish. Archaeologists first became aware of the phenomenon in Egypt (see Tutankhamun box, overleaf), where much of the Nile Valley has such a dry atmosphere that bodies of the predynastic period (before 3000 BC) have survived intact, with skin, hair, and nails, without any artificial mummification or coffins – the corpses were simply placed in shallow graves in the sand. Rapid drying out, plus the draining qualities of the sand, produced such spectacular preservative effects that they probably suggested the practice of mummification to the later Egyptians of the dynastic period.

The pueblo dwellers of the American Southwest (c. AD 700–1400) buried their dead in dry caves and rockshelters where, as in Egypt, natural desiccation took place: these are not therefore true, humanly created mummies, although they are often referred to as such. The bodies survive, sometimes wrapped in fur blankets or tanned skins, and in such good condition that it has been possible to study hair styles. Clothing (from fiber sandals to string aprons) also remains, together with a wide range of goods such as basketry, feathered ornaments, and leather. Some far earlier sites in the same region also contain organic remains: Danger Cave, Utah (occupied from 9000 BC onward), yielded wooden arrows, trap springs, knife handles, and other wooden tools, while caves near Durango, Colorado, had preserved maize cobs, squashes, and sunflower and mustard seeds. Plant finds of this type have been crucial in helping to reconstruct ancient diet.

The coastal dwellers of central and southern Peru lived – and died – in a similarly dry environment, so that it is possible today to see the tattoos on their desiccated bodies, and admire the huge and dazzlingly colorful textiles from cemeteries at Ica and Nazca, as well as basketry and featherwork, and also maize cobs and other items of food. In Chile, the oldest deliberately made mummies have been found at Chinchorro, preserved again by the aridity of the desert environment.

DRY PRESERVATION: THE TOMB OF TUTANKHAMUN

The arid conditions that prevail in Egypt have helped preserve a wide range of ancient materials, ranging from numerous written documents on papyrus (made of the pith of a Nile water plant) to two full-size wooden boats buried beside the Great Pyramid at Giza. But the best-known and most spectacular array of objects was that discovered in 1922 by Howard Carter and Lord Carnarvon in the tomb at Thebes of the pharaoh Tutankhamun, dating to the 14th century BC.

Tutankhamun had a short reign and was relatively insignificant in Egyptian history, a fact reflected in his burial, a poor one by pharaonic standards. But within the small tomb, originally built for someone else, was a wealth of treasure. For Tutankhamun was buried with everything he might need in the next life. The entrance corridor and the four chambers were crammed with thousands of individual grave-goods. They include objects of precious metal, like the jewelry and famous gold mask, and food and clothing. But wooden objects, such as statues, chests, shrines, and two of the three coffins, make up a large part of the tomb's contents.

The grave furniture was not all originally intended for Tutankhamun. Some of it had been made for other members of his family, and then hastily adopted when the young king died unexpectedly. There were also touching items, such as a chair the king had used as a child, and a simple reed stick mounted in gold labeled as "A reed which His Majesty cut with his own hand." Even wreaths and funerary bouquets had survived in the dry conditions, left on the second and third coffins by mourners.

The outermost of Tutankhamun's three coffins was made of cypress wood, overlaid with gold foil.

A floral collar found remarkably well preserved among the contents of the tomb of Tutankhamun.

A cutaway view of the tomb and its treasures, as found in 1922.

A slightly different phenomenon occurred in the Aleutian Islands, off the west coast of Alaska, where the dead were kept and naturally preserved in volcanically warmed caves that were extremely dry. Here the islanders seem to have enhanced the natural desiccation by periodically drying the bodies by wiping or suspension over a fire; in some cases they removed the internal organs and placed dry grass in the cavity.

Cold Environments.   Natural refrigeration can hold the processes of decay in check for thousands of years. Perhaps the first frozen finds to be discovered were the numerous remains of mammoths encountered in the permafrost (permanently frozen soil) of Siberia, a few with their flesh, hair, and stomach contents intact. The unlucky creatures probably fell into crevices in snow, and were buried by silt in what became a giant deep-freeze. The best known are Beresovka, recovered in 1901, and baby Dima, found in 1977. Preservation can be still so good that dogs will eat the meat and they have to be kept well away from the carcasses.

The most famous frozen archaeological remains are those from the burial mounds of steppe nomads at Pazyryk in the Altai, southern Siberia, dating to the Iron Age, about 400 BC. They comprise pits dug deep into the ground, lined with logs, and covered with a low cairn of stones. They could only have been dug in the warm season, before the ground froze solid. Any warm air in the graves rose and deposited its moisture on the stones of the cairn; moisture also gradually infiltrated down into the burial chambers, and froze so hard there during the harsh winter that it never thawed during subsequent summers, since the cairns were poor conductors of heat and shielded the pits from the warming and drying effects of wind and sun. Consequently, even the most fragile materials have survived intact – despite the boiling water that had to be used by excavators to recover them.

The Pazyryk bodies had been placed inside log coffins, with wooden pillows, and survived so well that their spectacular tattoos can still be seen. Clothing included linen shirts, decorated caftans, aprons, stockings, and headdresses of felt and leather. There were also rugs, wall-coverings, tables laden with food, and horse carcasses complete with elaborate bridles, saddles, and other trappings. A further well-preserved burial has been found in the region, containing a female accompanied by six horses and grave-goods including a silver mirror and various wooden objects.

Similar standards of preservation have also been encountered in other regions such as Greenland and Alaska. More southerly regions can produce the same effect at high altitude, for instance the Inca-period tomb at Cerra El Plomo in the Andes, which contained the naturally freeze-dried corpse of a boy wearing a camelid-wool poncho; or the 5300-year-old Iceman found preserved in the ice in the Alps near the border between Italy and Austria (see box overleaf).

Frozen conditions in southern Siberia helped to preserve many remarkable finds from the burial mounds of steppe nomads at Pazyryk dating from about 400 BC, including this tattoo pattern on the torso and arms of a chieftain.

COLD PRESERVATION: THE ICEMAN

Ötztaler Alps
ITALY

The world's oldest fully preserved human body was found in September 1991 by German hikers near the Similaun glacier, in the Ötztaler Alps of South Tyrol. They spotted a human body, its skin yellowish-brown and desiccated, at an altitude of 3200 m (10,500 ft). The Iceman is the first prehistoric human ever found with his everyday clothing and equipment, and presumably going about his normal business; other similarly intact bodies from prehistory have been either carefully buried or sacrificed.

The body was placed in a freezer in Austria, but subsequent investigation determined that the corpse – called Similaun Man, Ötzi, or simply the "Iceman" – had lain c. 90 m (300 ft) inside Italy, and he has been housed there, in a museum in Bolzano, since 1998. Fifteen radiocarbon dates have been obtained from the body, the

artifacts, and the grass in the boots: they are all in rough agreement, averaging at 3300 BC.

According to the first investigators, the Iceman was probably overcome by exhaustion on the mountain – perhaps caught in a fog or a blizzard. After death, he was dried out by a warm autumn wind, before becoming encased in ice. Since the body lay in a depression, it was protected from the movement of the glacier above it for 5300 years, until a storm from the Sahara laid a layer of dust on the ice that absorbed sunlight and finally thawed it out.

He was a dark-skinned male, aged in his mid- to late 40s. Only about 1.56–1.6 m (5ft 2 in) tall, his size and stature fit well within the measurement ranges of Late Neolithic populations of Italy and Switzerland. Preliminary analysis of his DNA confirms his links to northern Europe.

The corpse currently weighs only about 54 kg (120 lb). His teeth are very worn, especially the front incisors, suggesting that he ate coarse ground grain, or that he regularly used them as a tool. When found he was bald, but hundreds of curly brownish-black human hairs, about 9 cm (3.5 in) long, were recovered from the vicinity of the body and on the clothing fragments. These had fallen out after death and it is possible he had a beard.

A body scan has shown that the brain, muscle tissues, lungs, heart, liver, and digestive organs are in excellent condition, though the lungs are blackened by smoke, probably from open fires, and he has hardening of the arteries and blood vessels. Traces of meat have been found in his colon, and his final meal seems to have consisted of meat (probably ibex

The equipment and clothing of the Iceman are a virtual time-capsule of everyday life – over 70 objects were found associated with him.

Calf leather belt and pouch, with 3 flint tools, a bone awl, and organic material (for tinder)

Dagger: flint blade with ashwood haft in woven grass sheath

Leather loincloth

Leather leggings

Coat of tanned domestic goat hide

Copper axe with yew haft and leather binding

Shoes: bearskin soles with deerskin uppers; filled with grass

Yew long bow (unfinished)

Hazel and larchwood frame for a fur backpack

Bearskin cap

Deerskin quiver with 14 arrows (only 2 finished) of viburnum and dogwood, an antler point and 2 fragments, coiled string, and 2 bundles of animal sinews

Cape of woven grass or reeds

Sewn birchbark containers (1 with evidence of fire)

and venison), wheat, plants, and plums.

Traces of chronic frostbite were noted in one little toe and eight of his ribs were fractured, though these were healed or healing when he died. A fracture to his left arm and severe damage to the left pelvic area occurred during his recovery from the ice.

Groups of tattoos, mostly short parallel vertical blue lines were discovered on both sides of his lower spine, on his left calf and right ankle, and a blue cross on his inner right knee. These marks may be therapeutic, aimed at relieving the arthritis which he had in his neck, lower back, and right hip.

His nails had dropped off, but one fingernail was recovered. Its analysis revealed not only that he undertook manual labor, but also that he experienced periods of reduced nail growth corresponding to episodes of serious illness – 4, 3, and 2 months before he died. The fact that he was prone to periodic crippling disease supported the view that he fell prey to adverse weather and froze to death. However, recent work has revealed what appears to be an arrowhead lodged in the Iceman's left shoulder, cuts on his hands, wrists, and ribcage, and traces of blood from four other people on his clothes and weapons, which may indicate some kind of violent death.

The items found with him constitute a unique "time-capsule" of everyday life, many made of organic materials that were preserved by the cold and ice. A great variety of woods and a range of sophisticated techniques of working with leather and grasses were used to create the collection of 70 objects, which add a new dimension to our knowledge of the period.

Waterlogged Environments. A useful distinction in land archaeology (as opposed to archaeology beneath the sea) can be drawn between dryland and wetland sites. The great majority of sites are "dry" in the sense that moisture content is low and preservation of organic remains is poor. Wetland sites include all those found in lakes, swamps, marshes, fens, and peat bogs. In these situations organic materials are effectively sealed in a wet and airless environment which favors their preservation, as long as the waterlogging is more or less permanent up to the time of **excavation**. (If a wet site dries out, even only seasonally, decomposition of the organic materials can occur.)

It has been estimated that on a wet site often 75–90 percent, sometimes 100 percent, of the finds are organic. Little or none of this material, such as wood, leather, textiles, basketry, and plant remains of all kinds, would survive on most dryland sites. It is for this reason that archaeologists are turning their attention more and more to the rich sources of evidence about past human activities to be found on wet sites. Growing threats from drainage and peatcutting in the wetlands, which form only about 6 percent of the world's total land area, give this work an added urgency.

Wetlands vary a great deal in their preservative qualities. Acidic peat bogs preserve wood and plant remains, but may destroy bone, iron, and even pottery. The famous lake sites of the Alpine regions of Switzerland, Italy, France, and southern Germany on the other hand preserve most materials well. Sometimes other forces can help to preserve waterlogged remains, such as the mudslide that buried the Ozette site in Washington State (see box overleaf).

WET PRESERVATION: THE OZETTE SITE

A special kind of waterlogging occurred at the Ozette site, Washington, on the U.S. Northwest Coast. About AD 1750, a huge mudslide buried part of a whale-hunting settlement. The village lay protected for two centuries – but not forgotten, for the descendants of the village kept the memory of their ancestors' home alive. Then the sea began to strip away the mud, and it seemed as if the site would fall prey to looters. Local people called on the government to excavate the site and to protect the remains. Richard Daugherty was appointed to organize the excavation. As the mud was cleared with high-pressure hoses, a wealth of organic material came to view.

Several cedarwood long houses, up to 21 m (68 ft 3 in) in length and 14 m (45 ft 6 in) wide, were found, with adzed and carved panels

Pieces of preserved wood in one of the Ozette houses.

(painted with black designs including wolves and thunderbirds), roof-support posts, and low partition walls. These houses contained hearths, cooking platforms, sleeping benches, and mats.

Over 50,000 artifacts were recovered in a fine state of preservation – almost half in wood or other plant material. The most spectacular was a block of red cedar,

a meter high, carved in the form of a whale's dorsal fin. Even ferns and cedar leaves had survived, together with an abundance of whale bones.

The project was an excellent example of cooperation between archaeologists and indigenous peoples. The Makah Indians value the contribution made by archaeologists to the understanding of their past, and have built a museum to display the finds.

Richard Daugherty with the carved cedar representation of the dorsal fin of a whale. It was inlaid with over 700 sea-otter teeth arranged in the shape of a thunderbird holding a serpent in its claws.

A Makah Indian crew member cleans a basket found on the site.

Peat bogs, nearly all of which occur in northern latitudes, are some of the most important environments for wetland archaeology. The Somerset Levels in southern England, for example, have been the scene not only of excavations in the early 20th century to recover the well-preserved Iron Age lake villages of Glastonbury and Meare, but of a much wider campaign in the last few decades that has unearthed numerous wooden trackways (including the world's "oldest road," a 6000-year-old 1.6-km (1-mile) stretch of track), and many details about early woodworking skills, and the ancient environment. On the continent of Europe, and in Ireland, peat bogs have likewise preserved many trackways – sometimes with evidence for the wooden carts that ran along them – and other fragile remains. Other types of European wetlands, such as coastal marshes, have yielded dugout logboats, paddles, even fish-nets and fish-weirs.

Bog bodies, however, are undoubtedly the best-known finds from the peat bogs of northwest Europe. Most of them date from the Iron Age. The degree of preservation varies widely, and depends on the particular conditions in which the corpses were deposited. Most individuals met a violent death and were probably either executed as criminals or killed as a sacrifice before being thrown into the bog. The best-preserved examples, such as Denmark's Tollund Man, were in a truly remarkable state, with only the staining caused by bogwater and tannic acid as an indication that they were ancient rather than modern. Within the skin, the bones have often disappeared, as have most of the internal organs, although the stomach and its contents may survive. In Florida, prehistoric human brains have even been recovered.

Occasionally, waterlogged conditions can occur inside burial mounds. The oak-coffin burials of Bronze Age northern Europe, and most notably those of Denmark dating to about 1000 BC, had an inner core of stones packed round the tree-trunk coffin, with a round barrow built above. Water infiltrated the inside of the mound and by combining with tannin from the tree trunks, set up acidic conditions which destroyed the skeleton but preserved the skin (discolored like the bog bodies), hair, and ligaments of the bodies inside the coffins, as well as their clothing and objects such as birch-bark pails.

A somewhat similar phenomenon occurred with the ships that the Vikings used as coffins. The Oseberg ship in Norway, for example, held the body of a Viking queen of about AD 800, and was buried in clay, covered by a packing of stones and a layer of peat that sealed it in and ensured its preservation.

Lake-dwellings have rivaled bog bodies in popular interest ever since the discovery of wooden piles or house supports in Swiss lakes well over a century ago. The range of preserved material is astonishing, not simply wooden structures, artifacts, and textiles but, at Neolithic Charavines in France for example, even nuts, berries, and other fruits.

Perhaps the greatest contribution to archaeology that lake-dwellings and other European wetland sites have made in recent years, however, is to provide abundant well-preserved timber for the study of tree rings, the annual growth rings in trees, for dating purposes. In Chapter 4 we explore the breakthrough this has brought about in the establishment of an accurate tree-ring chronology for parts of northern Europe stretching back thousands of years.

Another rich source of waterlogged and preserved timbers in land archaeology can be found in the old waterfronts of towns and cities. Archaeologists have been particularly successful in uncovering parts of London's Roman and medieval waterfront, but such discoveries are not restricted to Europe. In the early 1980s New York City archaeologists excavated a well-preserved 18th-century ship that had been sunk to support the East River waterfront there. Underwater archaeology itself, in rivers and lakes and especially beneath the sea, is not surprisingly the richest source of all for waterlogged finds (see pp. 89–90).

The major archaeological problem with waterlogged finds, and particularly wood, is that they deteriorate rapidly when they are uncovered, beginning to dry and crack almost at once. They therefore need to be kept wet until they can be treated or freeze-dried at a laboratory. Conservation measures of this kind help to explain the enormous cost of both wetland and underwater archaeology. It has been estimated that "wet archaeology" costs four times as much as "dry archaeology." But the rewards, as we have seen above, are enormous.

The rewards in the future, too, will be very great. Florida, for example, has about 1.2 million ha (3 million acres) of peat deposits, and on present evidence these probably contain more organic artifacts than anywhere else in the world. So far the wetlands here have yielded the largest number of prehistoric watercraft from any one region, together with totems, masks, and figurines dating as far back as 5000 BC. In the Okeechobee Basin, for instance, a 1st-millennium BC burial platform has been found, decorated with a series of large carved wooden totem posts, representing an array of animals and birds. After a fire, the platform had collapsed into its pond. Yet it is only recently that wet finds in Florida have come to us from careful excavation rather than through the drainage that is destroying large areas of peat deposits and, with them, untold quantities of the richest kinds of archaeological evidence.

SUMMARY

- The archaeological evidence available to us depends on a number of important factors:

  - What people, past and present, have done to it (cultural formation processes).

  - What natural conditions such as soil and climate have preserved or destroyed (natural formation processes). Inorganic materials usually survive far better than organics, but the latter can be well preserved in a range of special environments – the dry, the cold and the waterlogged.

  - Our ability to find, recognize, recover, and conserve it.

- We can do nothing about the first two factors, being at the mercy of the elements and previous human behavior. But the third factor, which is the subject of this book, is constantly improving, as we understand better the processes of decay and destruction, and design research strategies and technical aids to make the most of what archaeological evidence actually survives.

FURTHER READING

Good introductions to the problems of differential preservation of archaeological materials can be found in:

Binford, L.R. 2002. **In Pursuit of the Past: Decoding the Archaeological Record.** UNIVERSITY OF CALIFORNIA PRESS: BERKELEY & LONDON.
Coles, B. & J. 1989. **People of the Wetlands: Bogs, Bodies and Lake-Dwellers.** THAMES & HUDSON: LONDON & NEW YORK.
Nash, D.T. and Petraglia, M.D. (eds.). 1987. **Natural Formation Processes and the Archaeological Record. British Archaeological Reports, International Series 352:** OXFORD.

Purdy, B.A. (ed.) 2001. **Enduring Records. The Environmental and Cultural Heritage of Wetlands.** OXBOW BOOKS: OXFORD.
Schiffer, M.B. 1996. **Formation Processes of the Archaeological Record.** UNIVERSITY OF UTAH PRESS: SALT LAKE CITY.

3

Where?
survey and excavation of sites and features

In this chapter:

Traditionally, archaeologists are known for finding and excavating **sites**, but today, while sites and their **excavation** do remain of paramount importance, the focus has broadened. Archaeologists have become aware that there is a great range of "off-site" or "non-site" evidence, from scatters of **artifacts** to **features** such as plowmarks and field boundaries, that provides important information about the past. The study of entire landscapes by regional survey, for example, is now a major part of archaeological fieldwork.

It should also not be forgotten that suitable evidence for study often comes from new work at sites already the subject of fieldwork. Much potentially rich and rewarding material also lies locked away in museum and institution vaults, waiting to be analyzed by imaginative modern techniques. It is only recently, for example, that the plant remains discovered in Tutankhamun's tomb in the 1920s have received thorough analysis. Yet it remains true that the great majority of archaeological research is still dependent on the collection of new material by fresh fieldwork. The main way that archaeologists find this new material – in other words new sites and features – is by **reconnaissance survey**, either on the ground or from the air.

In the early days of **archaeology** the next step would have been to excavate. But when archaeologists excavate a site, digging through the layers of evidence, uncovering features and removing artifacts that may have been lying undisturbed for thousands of years, it is important to remember that this is essentially a destructive act – there is just one chance to record exactly what is found and the "experiment" can never be repeated. Excavation is also very expensive and after the digging the excavators must be prepared to put considerable time, effort, and money into the conservation and storage of their finds, and into the interpretation and publication of their results. Non-destructive means of assessing the layout of sites and features, using, for example, site **surface survey** or **remote sensing** devices, have therefore taken on a new importance, often providing enough information for archaeologists to interpret features at a site, and making large-scale excavation unnecessary. Although excavation does remain a very important aspect of archaeology, archaeologists are becoming increasingly aware that it should not be undertaken lightly, and that it is only absolutely vital where sites would otherwise be destroyed by modern development or natural erosion.

Before any archaeological fieldwork begins, archaeologists try to make explicit what their objectives are and what their plan of campaign will be. This procedure is commonly called devising a **research design**, which broadly has four stages (listed in the box overleaf). There is seldom if ever a straightforward progression through these stages. In real life the research strategy will constantly be refined as

KEY CONCEPTS: RESEARCH DESIGN

1 *Formulation of a research strategy* to resolve a particular question or test a hypothesis or idea;

2 *Collecting and recording of evidence* against which to test that idea, usually by the organization of a team of specialists and conducting of fieldwork;

3 *Processing and analysis* of that evidence and its interpretation in the light of the original idea to be tested;

4 *Publication* of the results in articles, books etc.

evidence is collected and analyzed. All too often, and inexcusably, publication may be neglected. But in the best planned research the overall objective – the broad question or questions to be answered – will stand even if the strategy for achieving it alters.

In this chapter we are focussing on stage 2 of the research process – on the methods and techniques archaeologists use to obtain evidence against which to test their ideas. We will distinguish between *methods used in the discovery* of archaeological sites and non-site features or artifact scatters, which include a variety of ground-based and aerial survey techniques, and those employed *once those sites and features have been identified*, which include detailed survey and selective excavation at individual sites.

The Great Wall of China, over 2000 km (1250 miles) long, was begun in the 3rd century BC. Like the pyramids of Egypt, it has never been lost to posterity.

LOCATING ARCHAEOLOGICAL SITES AND FEATURES

One major task of the archaeologist is to locate and record the whereabouts of sites and features. In this section we will be reviewing some of the principal techniques used to locate sites. But we should not forget that many monuments have never been lost to posterity: the massive pyramids of Egypt have always been known to succeeding generations, as has the Great Wall of China. Their exact function or purpose may indeed have aroused controversy down the centuries, but their presence, the fact of their existence, was never in doubt.

And not all those sites that were once lost were discovered by archaeologists. No one has ever made a precise count, but a significant number of sites known today were found by accident, from the decorated French cave of Lascaux, and more recently Cosquer, the underwater entrance to which was discovered by a deep-sea diver in 1985, to the amazing terracotta army of China's first emperor, unearthed in 1974 by farmers digging for a well, as well as the countless underwater wrecks first spotted by fishermen, sponge-gatherers, and sport-divers. Construction workers building new roads, subways, dams, and office blocks have made their fair share of discoveries too.

Nevertheless it is archaeologists who have systematically attempted to record these sites, and it is archaeologists who seek out the full range of sites and features, large or small, that make up the great diversity of past landscapes. How do they achieve this?

A practical distinction can be drawn between site identification conducted at ground level (**ground reconnaissance**) and identification from the air or from space (**aerial reconnaissance**), although any one field project will usually employ both types of reconnaissance.

Ground Reconnaissance

Methods for identifying individual sites include consultation of documentary sources and place-name evidence, but primarily actual fieldwork, whether the monitoring of building developers' progress in **salvage archaeology**, or reconnaissance survey in circumstances where the archaeologist is more of a free agent.

Documentary Sources.   In the nineteenth century, Homer's account of the Trojan Wars in his narrative poem the *Iliad* fired the imagination of German banker Heinrich Schliemann, sending him on a quest for the city of Troy; with remarkable luck and good judgement he successfully identified it in western Turkey. A more recent success story of the same kind was the location and excavation by Helge and Anne Stine Ingstad of the Viking settlement of L'Anse aux Meadows in Newfoundland, thanks in large part to clues contained in the medieval Viking sagas. Much of modern biblical archaeology concerns itself with the search in the Near East for evidence of the places – as well as the people and events – described in the Old and New Testaments. Treated objectively as one possible source of information about Near Eastern sites, the Bible can be a rich source of documentary material, but there is certainly the danger that belief in the absolute religious truth of the texts can cloud an impartial assessment of their archaeological validity.

Much research in biblical archaeology involves attempting to link named biblical sites with archaeologically known ones. Place-name evidence, however, can also lead to actual discoveries of new archaeological sites. In southwest Europe, for example, many prehistoric stone tombs have been found thanks to old names printed on maps that incorporate local words for "stone" or "tomb."

Cultural Resource Management and Salvage Archaeology.   In this specialized work – discussed more fully in Chapter 10 – the role of the archaeologist is to locate and record sites, in some cases before they are destroyed by new roads, buildings, or dams, or by peatcutting and drainage in wetlands. In the USA a large number of sites are located and recorded in inventories under Cultural Resource Management

(CRM) laws every year. Proper liaison with a developer should allow archaeological survey to take place in advance along the projected line of road or in the path of development. Important sites thus discovered may require excavation, and in some cases can even cause construction plans to be altered. Certain archaeological remains unearthed during the digging of subways in Rome and Mexico City, for instance, were incorporated into the final station architecture.

Reconnaissance Survey.   How does the archaeologist set about locating sites, other than through documentary sources and salvage work? A conventional and still valid method is to look for the most prominent remains in a landscape, particularly surviving remnants of walled buildings, and burial mounds such as those in eastern North America or Wessex in southern Britain. But many sites are visible on the surface only as a scatter of artifacts and thus require more thorough survey – what we may call reconnaissance survey – to be detected.

Furthermore in recent years, as archaeologists have become more interested in reconstructing the full human use of the landscape, they have begun to realize that there are very faint scatters of artifacts that might not qualify as sites, but which nevertheless represent significant human activity. Some scholars have therefore suggested that these "off-site" or "non-site" areas (that is, areas with a low density of artifacts) should be located and recorded, which can only be done by systematic survey work involving careful sampling procedures (see below). This approach is particularly useful in areas where people leading a mobile way of life have left only a sparse archaeological record, as in much of Africa.

Reconnaissance survey has become important for another major reason: the growth of regional studies. Thanks to the pioneering researches of scholars such as Gordon Willey in the Virú Valley, Peru, and William T. Sanders in the Basin of Mexico, archaeologists increasingly seek to study settlement patterns – the distribution of sites across the landscape within a given region. The significance of this work for the understanding of past societies is discussed further in Chapter 5. Here we may note its impact on archaeological fieldwork: it is rarely enough now simply to locate an individual site and then to survey it and/or excavate it in isolation from other sites. Whole regions need to be explored, involving a program of reconnaissance survey.

In the last few decades, reconnaissance survey has developed from being simply a preliminary stage in fieldwork (looking for appropriate sites to excavate) to a more or less independent kind of inquiry, an area of research in its own right which can produce information quite different from that achieved by digging. In some cases excavation may not take place at all, perhaps because permission to dig was not forthcoming, or because of a lack of time or funds – modern excavation is slow and costly, whereas survey is cheap, quick, relatively non-destructive, and requires only maps, compasses, and tapes. Usually, however, archaeologists deliberately choose a surface approach as a source of regional data in order to investigate specific questions that interest them and that excavation could not answer.

Reconnaissance survey encompasses a broad range of techniques: no longer just the identification of sites and the recording or collection of surface artifacts, but sometimes also the sampling of natural and mineral resources such as stone and clay. Much survey today is aimed at studying the spatial distribution of human activities, variations between regions, changes in population through time, and relationships between people, land, and resources.

Reconnaissance Survey in Practice. For questions formulated in regional terms, it is necessary to collect data on a regional scale, but in a way which provides a maximum of information for a minimum of cost and effort. First, the region to be surveyed needs to be defined: its boundaries may be either natural (such as a valley or island), cultural (such as the extent of an artifact style), or purely arbitrary, though natural boundaries are the easiest to establish.

The area's history of development needs to be examined, not only to familiarize oneself with previous archaeological work and with the local materials but also to assess the extent to which surface material may have been covered or removed by natural processes. There is little point, for example, in searching for prehistoric material in sediments only recently laid down by river action. Other factors may have affected surface evidence as well. In much of Africa, for example, great animal herds or burrowing animals will often have disturbed surface material, so that the archaeologist may be able to examine only very broad distribution patterns. Geologists and environmental specialists can generally provide useful advice.

This background information will help determine the intensity of surface coverage of the survey. Other factors to take into consideration are the time and resources available, and how easy it is actually to reach and record an area. Arid (dry) and semi-arid environments with little vegetation are among the best for this type of work, whereas in equatorial rainforest survey may be limited to soil exposures along river banks, unless time and labor permit the cutting of trails. Many regions, of course, contain a variety of landscapes, and more than one strategy for survey is often needed. Moreover, it must be remembered that some archaeological phases (with easily distinguishable artifacts or pottery styles, for example) are more "visible" than others, and that mobile **hunter-gatherer** or pastoral communities leave a very different – and generally sparser – imprint on the landscape than do agricultural or urban communities. All these factors must be taken into account when planning the search patterns and recovery techniques.

There are two basic kinds of reconnaissance survey: the *unsystematic* and the *systematic*. The former is the simpler, involving walking across each part of the area (for example, each plowed field), scanning a strip of ground, collecting or examining artifacts on the surface, and recording their location together with that of any surface features. It is generally felt, however, that the results may be biased and misleading. Walkers have an inherent desire to find material, and will therefore tend to concentrate on those areas that seem richer, rather than obtaining a sample representative of the whole area that would enable the archaeologist to assess the varying distribution of material of different periods or types. On the other hand, the method is flexible, enabling the team to focus greater efforts on the areas that have proved most likely to contain sites or finds.

Much modern survey is done in a *systematic* way, employing either a grid system or a series of equally spaced transects (straight paths) across the area. The area to be searched is divided into sectors, and these are walked systematically. Because of the constraints of time and money, it is often not possible to survey the entirety of an area in this way, so archaeologists have to employ a *sampling strategy* (see box opposite) where only certain sectors or transects are picked to be searched. Systematic survey also makes it easier to plot the location of finds since an exact position is always known.

For example, from 1992 to 1998 the Sydney Cyprus Survey Project, led by Bernard Knapp and Michael Given of the University of Glasgow, undertook an intensive archaeological survey in a 65-sq. km (25-sq. mile) area in the northern Troodos Mountains of Cyprus. This is an area famed for its copper sulphide ore deposits, exploited as early as the Bronze Age. The project examined the human transformation of the landscape over a period of 5000 years and placed it in its regional context. A first requirement for the systematic intensive survey strategy was good maps. Enlarged aerial photographs were used to create a base map of the entire survey region. The main survey approach was a transect survey with the aim of obtaining a broad **systematic sample** of the area; areas with extensive evidence of early industrial, agricultural, or settlement activities and locales with high densities of artifacts were investigated more closely. It took the team around 6 years to survey just 10 percent of the area.

Results tend to be more reliable from long-term projects that cover a region repeatedly, since the visibility of sites and artifacts can vary widely from year to year or even with the seasons, thanks to vegetation and changing land-use. In addition, members of field crews inevitably differ in the accuracy of their observations, and in their ability to recognize and describe sites (the more carefully we look, and the more experience we have, the more we see); this factor can never be totally eliminated, but

SAMPLING STRATEGIES

Archaeologists cannot usually afford the time and money necessary to investigate the whole of a large site or all sites in a given region, so they need to **sample** the area being researched. In a ground reconnaissance survey this will involve using one of the methods described below to choose a number of smaller areas to be searched, with the objective being to draw reliable conclusions about the whole area. The way archaeologists use sampling is similar to the way it is employed in public opinion polls, which make generalizations about the opinions of millions of people using samples of just a few thousand. Surprisingly often the polls are more or less right. This is because the structure of sampled populations is well known – for example, we know their ages and occupations. We have much less background information to work with in archaeology, so must be more careful when we extrapolate generalizations from a sample. But as with opinion polls, in archaeological work the larger and better designed the sample, the more likely the results are to be valid.

Some sites in a given region, however, may be more accessible than others, or more prominent in the landscape, which may prompt a more informal sampling strategy. Long years of experience in the field will also give some archaeologists an intuitive "feel" for the right places to undertake work.

Types of Sampling
The simplest form is a **simple random sample**, where the areas to

be sampled are chosen using a table of random numbers. However, the nature of random numbers results in some areas being allotted clusters of squares, while others remain untouched – the sample is, therefore, inherently biased.

One answer is the **stratified random sample**, where the region or site is divided into its natural zones (strata, hence the technique's name), such as cultivated land and forest, and squares are then chosen by the same random-number procedure, except that each zone has the number of squares proportional to its area. Thus, if forest comprises 85 percent of the area, it must be allotted 85 percent of the squares.

Another solution, **systematic sampling**, entails the selection of a grid of equally spaced locations – e.g. choosing every other square. By adopting such a regular spacing one runs the risk of missing (or hitting) every single example in an equally regular pattern of distribution – this is another source of potential bias.

A more satisfactory method is to use a **stratified unaligned systematic sample**, which combines the main elements from all three techniques just described. In collecting artifacts from the surface of a large tell or mound site at Girik-i-Haciyan in Turkey, Charles Redman and Patty Jo Watson used a grid of 5-m squares, but orientated it along the site's main N-S/E-W axes, and the samples were selected with reference to these axes. The strata chosen were blocks of 9 squares (3 x 3), and one square in each block was picked for excavation by selecting its N-S/E-W coordinates from a table of random numbers. This method ensures an

unbiased set of samples, more evenly distributed over the whole site.

Transects vs Squares
In large-scale surveys, *transects* (straight paths) are sometimes preferable to squares. This is particularly true in areas of dense vegetation such as tropical rainforest. It is far easier to walk along a series of paths than to locate accurately and investigate a large number of randomly distributed squares. In addition, transects can easily be segmented into units, whereas it may be difficult to locate or describe a specific part of a square; and transects are useful not merely for finding sites but also for recording artifact densities across the landscape. On the other hand, squares have the advantage of exposing more area to the survey, thus increasing the probability of intersecting sites. A combination of the two methods is often best: using transects to cover long distances, but squares when larger concentrations of material are encountered.

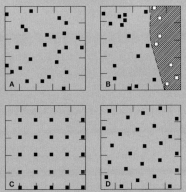

Types of sampling: (A) simple random; (B) stratified random; (C) systematic; (D) stratified unaligned systematic.

repeated coverage can help to counter its effects. The use of standardized recording forms makes it easy to put the data into a computer at a later stage.

Finally, it may be necessary or desirable to carry out small excavations to supplement or check the surface data (particularly for questions of chronology, contemporaneity, or site function), or to test hypotheses which have arisen from the survey. The two types of investigation are complementary, not mutually exclusive. Their major difference can be summarized as follows: excavation tells us a lot about a little of a site, and can only be done once, whereas survey tells us a little about a lot of sites, and can be repeated.

Extensive and Intensive Survey.   Surveys can be made more extensive by combining results from a series of individual projects in neighboring regions to produce very large-scale views of change in landscape, land-use, and settlement through time – though, as with individual members of a field crew, the accuracy and quality of different survey projects may vary widely. Alternatively survey can be made more intensive by aiming at total coverage of a single large site or site-cluster. It is a paradox that some of the world's greatest and most famous archaeological sites have never, or only recently, been studied in this way, since attention has traditionally focused on the grand monuments themselves rather than on any attempt to place them within even a local context. At Teotihuacán, near Mexico City, a major mapping project initiated in the 1960s has added hugely to our knowledge of the area around the great pyramid-temples (the work is described on pp. 74–75).

KEY CONCEPTS: LOCATING SITES USING GROUND RECONNAISSANCE

- *Documentary Sources:* mainly of use in locating Classical, biblical, and relatively recent sites

- *Cultural Resource Management:* sites in areas that may be under threat from development are located, recorded, and sometimes excavated prior to their destruction

- Reconnaissance Survey: Surveys can be either **unsystematic** (where archaeologists randomly search an area on foot for artifacts or evidence of features) or, more commonly, **systematic** (where archaeologists walk an area using carefully laid out grid systems or transects). A **sampling strategy**, where only a representative part of an area is actually searched, is often used to save time and money. Small-scale excavations can be undertaken to check survey results

Ground reconnaissance survey has a vital place in archaeological work, and one that continues to grow in importance. In modern projects, however, it is usually supplemented (and often preceded) by reconnaissance from the air, one of the most important advances made by archaeology in the 20th century. In fact, the availability of air photographs can be an important factor in selecting and delineating an area for ground reconnaissance.

Aerial Reconnaissance

It must be stressed that aerial reconnaissance, particularly aerial photography, is not merely or even mainly used for the discovery of sites, being more crucial to their recording and interpretation, and to monitoring changes in them through time. Nevertheless, air photography – together with remote sensing from space – has been responsible for a large number of discoveries, and continues to find more sites every year.

Aerial Photography. The first major archaeological applications of this technique occurred at the start of the 20th century with photographs of the Roman town of Ostia taken from a balloon. World War I gave the technique a great impetus when archaeologists in England discovered the clarity that air photographs taken from aircraft and balloons could provide in their plan view of prehistoric monuments. From these beginnings aerial photography developed into one of the archaeologist's most valued aids, able to detect sites, roads, field-systems, and even underwater sites such as ancient harbors.

Archaeologists use aircraft to search the ground for traces of former sites and past landscapes. Photographs are usually oblique and taken by hand-held cameras. Such oblique photography is a selective process, involving archaeological judgment, in contrast to the unselective view obtained by vertical survey. Single-frame shots of

(Below left) Aerial photographs are of two types: oblique and vertical. Obliques are easier to view and understand than verticals but may present more difficulty to the interpreter who must transform the information to plan views.

(Below) Oblique aerial photograph taken in 1922 of the vicinity of Monk's Mound, Cahokia (center right), revealing other features in the vicinity of the mound.

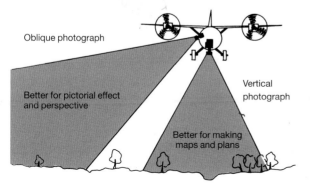

Oblique photograph

Better for pictorial effect and perspective

Vertical photograph

Better for making maps and plans

a site or feature are usual, although stereoscopic pairs of oblique photographs considerably assist subsequent interpretation. Oblique aerial photographs show sites in the context of the landscape and can also be used for preparing archaeological maps.

How Sites Show from the Air.   Those who take and use aerial photographs must understand the means by which the evidence is made visible in order to determine the type of feature that has been recorded. Conventionally, features photographed from the air are often described according to the way they are revealed, rather than by the archaeological reality they represent, thus "earthworks," "soil-marks," or "crop-marks."

Earthworks is a term used to describe banks and associated ditches, or stone-walled features – in fact, any feature that can be seen in relief. These features are usually revealed from the air as shadow marks – an effect that is dependent on the lighting and weather conditions at the time of photography. They also show in relief when viewed as a stereoscopic pair. Such features may also be seen by the differences in vegetation supported by banks and ditches, by differential melting or drifting of snow, or by retention of water in ditches in times of flood. Time of day and time of year are thus important in the discovery and recording of such sites.

Soil-marks reveal the presence of buried ditches, banks, or foundations by the changes in subsoil color caused when a plowshare catches and turns over part of the buried feature, bringing it to the surface. Most soil-marked sites are being destroyed by modern cultivation. They are mostly visible in photographs taken in winter months. Bare soil will sometimes also reveal features through differential moisture retention – damp marks – or by differences in thermal properties that affect the melting of snow and frost.

Earthwork seen from the air: the Iron Age hillfort of Maiden Castle, southern England, whose complex ramparts are thrown into relief by shadows cast by massive earthen banks. The air photograph also highlights an interesting earlier feature: a shallow Neolithic ditch running across the middle of the fort.

Winter plowing has scraped the chalk foundations of this Gallo-Roman villa in France. This process of destruction has in fact revealed the plan of its main structures against the dark soil.

Crop-marks develop when a buried wall or ditch either stunts or boosts crop growth by affecting the availability of moisture and nutrients through changing the depth of soil. Suitable crops, such as wheat, barley, and some root vegetables, provide a perfect medium for revealing features in the underlying soil. This response to buried features is very delicate and dependent on variables such as the type and condition of soil, weather during the growing season, crop type, and agricultural practices. Thus features can stand out strongly in one year and be invisible the next. Knowledge of recent and past land-use in an area can be particularly valuable when assessing the potential of apparently blank modern fields. Some features simply do not produce crop-marked evidence.

Crop-marks clearly reveal two concentric rings of ditches defining an enclosure at Merzien, Sachsen-Anhalt, Germany. Both ditch circuits are interrupted and may therefore be of Neolithic date.

How crop-marks are formed: crops grow taller and more thickly over sunken features such as ditches (1), and show stunted growth over buried walls (2). Such variations may not be obvious at ground level, but are often visible from the air, as different colored bands of vegetation.

Map of the area around Danebury, an Iron Age hillfort in southern England (6th–2nd centuries BC), created from aerial survey, with details of ancient fields, tracks, and enclosures.

Photo Interpretation and Mapping. Interpretation is the process by which features photographed from the air, such as soil-marks, are analyzed in order to deduce the types of archaeological structures causing them. Given that the visibility of features varies from year to year, photos taken over several years need to be studied to compile an accurate plan. Such plans may guide excavation to key points in a structure, place field-collected data in context, or themselves be used as the starting point for new research.

Aerial photos can also be employed to produce a map of known features within a region. In Britain, Roger Palmer used thousands of individual photographs of a 450-sq. km (175-sq. mile) territory around the Iron Age hillfort of Danebury to produce accurate maps. These show that the site lay within very complex agricultural landscapes, with at least 8 other hillforts in the area. Crop- and soil-marks revealed the presence of 120 ditched farming enclosures, hundreds of acres of small fields, regularly arranged, and 240 km (150 miles) of linear ditches and boundary works, many of which were roughly contemporaneous with Danebury to judge from their forms and/or surface finds. Many such records are drawn on to transparent sheets that are overlaid on to maps showing topographical or other information, but more up-to-date systems have converted such information as part of computerized **Geographic Information Systems** (GIS, see below).

Recent Developments in Aerial Photography. New technology is having an impact on aerial photography in different ways. Computer enhancement of pictures can improve their sharpness and contrast. Digital manipulation of images has also been developed and enables a single image, from an oblique or vertical photograph, to be transformed to match the map of the area. Computer programs also exist which allow several images to be transformed and then combined. This is especially useful in cases where a site may lie in two modern fields from which crop-marked information has been recorded in different years. Such plan-form images may help subsequent photo interpretation and mapping. Use of aerial data as a GIS layer may lead to fruitful results from analyses in conjunction with topographic and other archaeological information.

New World archaeological projects now routinely use the commercially available and cost-effective black-and-white aerial photographs. The 9 x 9 in negatives can be enlarged considerably before showing grain and thus quite small features such as walls, pits, etc. can be clearly seen. Digital cameras may be used to advantage to acquire images of larger-scale structures and systems, more common in arid and jungle zones.

Satellite Photography.   Photographs taken from satellites or the space shuttle have a limited application to archaeology, since their scale is often huge (though this is getting better), but images from the LANDSAT (Earth Resources Technology) satellites have proved useful. Scanners record the intensity of reflected light and the infrared radiation from the earth's surface, and convert these electronically into photographic images. LANDSAT images have been used to trace large-scale features such as ancient levee systems in Mesopotamia and an ancient riverbed running from the deserts of Saudi Arabia to Kuwait, as well as sediments around Ethiopia's Rift Valley that are likely to contain hominid fossil beds. Space Imaging Radar (which can reveal features beneath 5 m (16 ft) of sand) has been used from the space shuttle to locate ancient riverbeds beneath the deserts of Egypt and hundreds of kilometers of long-abandoned caravan routes in Arabia, many of which converged on a spot in Oman, that may be the lost city of Ubar.

The most remarkable archaeological application so far, however, has been in Mesoamerica. Using false-color LANDSAT imagery, in which natural colors are converted into more sharply contrasting hues, NASA scientists working with archaeologists in 1983 found an extensive network of Maya farmed fields and settlements in the Yucatán peninsula of Mexico. In this expensive experiment, costing $250,000, Maya ruins showed up in false color as tiny dots of blue, pink, and light red – blue for ancient reservoirs cut out of the limestone surface, pink and light red for vegetation on and adjacent to the sites. By looking for examples of blue dots next to pink and light red ones, archaeologists were able to pinpoint 112 sites. They visited 20 by helicopter in order to verify their conclusions.

The project also found an unknown city with twin pyramids, dating to the Classic Maya phase of AD 600–900; and relocated the major city of Oxpemul which had been discovered in the early 1930s but was then lost again in the thick jungle.

Recently, the vast ruins of the 1000-year-old temple complex of Angkor in northern Cambodia, which cover an area of about 260 sq. km (100 sq. miles) and

A satellite image of the huge ancient site of Angkor in Cambodia.

are shrouded in dense jungle and surrounded by land-mines, have been the subject of new studies using high-resolution radar imagery obtained from the space shuttle. The resulting dark squares and rectangles on the images are stone moats and reflecting pools around the temples. The main temple complex of Angkor Wat is readily visible as a small square bounded with black. The most important discovery for archaeologists so far has been the network of ancient canals surrounding the city (visible as light lines) which irrigated rice fields and fed the pools and moats. They were probably also used to transport the massive stones needed for constructing the complex.

The application of these new techniques to archaeology is only just beginning. So long as they remain expensive, conventional air photography will continue to dominate aerial reconnaissance; but advanced airborne remote sensing techniques will no doubt become cheaper and more widespread in the future.

KEY CONCEPTS: LOCATING SITES USING AERIAL RECONNAISSANCE

- *Aerial Photography:* aerial photographs can be either oblique (better for pictorial effect and perspective) or vertical (better for maps and plans). Features visible from the air are classed as either earthworks, soil-marks, or crop-marks
- *Satellite Photography:* useful only at the largest scales, for example mapping very large sites or tracing ancient irrigation systems

Geographic Information Systems

A significant new development in archaeological mapping is the use of GIS (Geographic Information Systems), described in one official report as "the biggest step forward in the handling of geographic information since the invention of the map." A GIS combines a database with powerful digital mapping tools; in other words, GIS are designed for the collection, storage, retrieval, analysis, and display of spatial data. A true GIS also incorporates the ability to carry out a statistical analysis of site distribution, and to generate new information.

A GIS may include an enormous amount of topographical and environmental data on relief, communications, hydrology etc. To make all this information easier to handle, it is normal to divide it into different map layers, each representing a single variable (see the illustration at right). Archaeological data may themselves be split into several layers, most often so that each layer represents a discrete time slice. As long as they can be spatially located, many different types of data can be integrated in a GIS. These can include site plans, satellite images, aerial photographs, geophysical survey, as well as maps.

The ability to incorporate satellite and aerial photographs can be particularly valuable for site reconnaissance as they can provide detailed and current land-use information. Many topographic data already exist in the form of digital maps which can be taken directly into a GIS. Use can also be made of a handheld Global Positioning System (GPS) to provide a longitude and latitude for a position on the ground. These are extremely useful where a region is unmapped, or where the maps are old or inaccurate. Although most archaeological applications have so far focused on landscape survey, there is also no reason why a GIS should not be used at a finer scale to examine spatial relationships within an individual site.

Once data are stored within a GIS it is relatively straightforward to generate maps on demand, and to query the database to select particular categories of site to be displayed. Individual map layers, or combinations of layers, can be selected according to the subject under investigation.

One of the earliest, and most widespread, uses of GIS within archaeology has been the construction of *predictive models* of site locations. Most of the development of these techniques has taken place within North American archaeology, where the enormous spatial extent of some archaeological landscapes means that it is not always possible to survey them comprehensively. The underlying premise of all predictive models is that particular kinds of archaeological sites tend to occur in the same kinds of place. For example, certain settlement sites tend to occur close to sources of fresh water and on southerly aspects because these provide ideal conditions in which humans can live (not too cold, and within easy walking distance of a

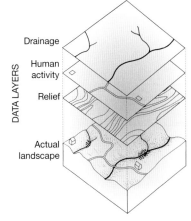

Diagram showing some possible GIS data layers.

water source). Using this information it is possible to model how likely a given location is to contain an archaeological site from the known environmental characteristics of that location. In a GIS environment this operation can be done for an entire landscape producing a predictive model map for the whole area.

An example was developed by the Illinois State Museum for the Shawnee National Forest in southern Illinois. It predicts the likelihood of finding a prehistoric site anywhere within the 91 sq. km (35 sq. miles) of the forest by using the observed characteristics of the 68 sites which are known from the 12 sq. km (4.6 sq. miles) which have been surveyed. A GIS database was constructed for the entire area and the characteristics of the known sites were compared with the characteristics of the locations known not to contain sites. This resulted in a model which can be used to predict the likelihood that any location with known environmental characteristics will contain a prehistoric site.

ASSESSING THE LAYOUT OF SITES AND FEATURES

Finding and recording sites and features is the first stage in fieldwork, but the next stage is to make some assessment of site size, type, and layout. These are crucial factors for archaeologists, not only for those who are trying to decide whether, where, and how to excavate, but also for those whose main focus may be the study of settlement patterns, site systems, and landscape archaeology without planning to carry out any excavation.

We have already seen how aerial photographs may be used to plot the layout of sites as well as helping to locate them in the first place. What are the other main methods for investigating sites without excavating them?

Site Surface Survey

The simplest way to gain some idea of a site's extent and layout is through a site surface survey – by studying the distribution of surviving features, and recording and possibly collecting artifacts from the surface.

The Teotihuacán Mapping Project, for instance, used site surface survey to investigate the layout and orientation of the city, which had been the largest and most powerful urban center in Mesoamerica in its heyday from AD 200 to 650. The layout and orientation of the city had intrigued scholars for decades; however, they considered the grandiose pyramid-temples, plazas, and the major avenue – an area now known as the ceremonial center – to be the entire extent of the metropolis. It was not until the survey conducted by the Teotihuacán Mapping Project that the outer limits, the great east-west axis, and the grid plan of the city were discovered and defined.

Fortunately, structural remains lay just beneath the surface, so that the team were able to undertake the mapping from a combination of aerial and surface survey, with only small-scale excavation to test the survey results. Millions of potsherds were collected, and over 5000 structures and activity areas recorded. Teotihuacán had been laid out on a regular plan, with four quadrants orientated on the great north-south "Street of the Dead" and another major avenue running east-west across it. Construction had occurred over several centuries, but always following the master plan.

Archaeological and topographic map of Teotihuacán produced by the Teotihuacán Mapping Project. The survey grid system of 500-m squares is oriented to the north–south axis of the city, in particular the central "Street of the Dead" (dividing W1 and E1 on the map). (Below) Aerial view of the city.

For artifacts and other objects collected or observed during site surface survey, it may not be worth mapping their individual locations if they appear to come from badly disturbed secondary contexts. Or there may simply be too many artifacts realistically to record all their individual proveniences. In this latter instance the archaeologist will probably use sampling procedures for the selective recording of surface finds. However, where time and funds are sufficient and the site is small enough, collection and recording of artifacts from the total site area may prove possible.

For example, a site surface survey was conducted at the Bronze Age city of Mohenjodaro in Pakistan. Here, a team of archaeologists from Pakistan, Germany, and Italy investigated the distribution of craft-working debris and found, to their surprise, that craft activities were not confined to a specific manufacturing zone within the city, but were scattered throughout the site, representing assorted small-scale workshops.

Reliability of Surface Finds. Archaeologists have always used limited surface collection of artifacts as one way of trying to assess the date and layout of a site prior to excavation. However, now that surface survey has become not merely a preliminary to excavation but in some instances a substitute for it – for cost and time reasons – a vigorous debate is taking place in archaeology about how far surface traces do in fact reflect distributions below ground.

We would logically expect single-period or shallow sites to show the most reliable surface evidence of what lies beneath. Equally one might predict that multi-period, deep sites such as Near Eastern village mounds would show few if any traces on the surface of the earliest and deepest levels. However, this is by no means always true – for example, at Tell Halula in northern Syria, a survey was

CORONA satellite image of the Halula district, showing the location of the tell and the boundary of the sampling area.

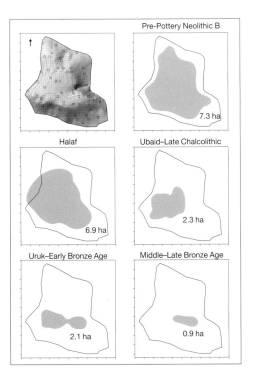

Pre-Pottery Neolithic B

7.3 ha

Halaf

6.9 ha

Ubaid–Late Chalcolithic

2.3 ha

Uruk–Early Bronze Age

2.1 ha

Middle–Late Bronze Age

0.9 ha

Plan of Tell Halula showing the layout of collection squares, plus outline plans of the tell showing the changing location and size of settlement during 5 of the 10 occupation phases.

carried out by an Australian team in 1986, involving the collection of artifacts such as potsherds and stone tools from the surface using stratified random sampling procedures based on a grid system. Forty-six squares in this grid were sampled, amounting to 4 percent of the 12.5-ha (31-acre) site area. Typological analysis of the artifacts made it possible to identify 10 major occupation phases, representing 15 different cultural periods.

Those who support the validity of surface survey, while agreeing that there is bound to be a quantitative bias in favor of the most recent periods on the surface, nevertheless point out that one of the surprises for most survey archaeologists is how many of their sites, if collected with care, are truly multi-period, reflecting many phases of a site's use, not just the latest one. The reasons for this are not yet entirely clear, but they certainly have something to do with the kind of formation processes discussed in Chapter 2 – from erosion and animal disturbance to human activity such as plowing.

The relationship between surface and subsurface evidence is undoubtedly complex and varies from site to site. It is therefore wise wherever possible to try to determine what really does lie beneath the ground, perhaps by digging test pits (usually meter squares) to assess a site's horizontal extent, ultimately by more thorough excavation (see below). There are, however, a whole battery of **subsurface detection** devices that can be used before – or indeed sometimes instead of – excavation, which of course is destructive as well as expensive.

Subsurface Detection

Probes. The most traditional technique is that of probing the soil with rods or borers, and noting the positions where they strike solids or hollows. Metal rods with a T-shaped handle are the most common, but augers – large corkscrews with a similar handle – are also used, and have the advantage of bringing samples of soil to the surface, clinging to the screw. Many archaeologists routinely use hand-held probes that yield small, solid cores. Probing of this type was used, for example, by Chinese archaeologists to plot the 300 pits remaining to be investigated near the first emperor's buried terracotta army. However, there is always a risk of damaging fragile artifacts or features.

One notable advance in this technique was developed by Carlo Lerici in Italy in the 1950s for Etruscan tombs of the 6th century BC. Having detected the precise location of a tomb through aerial photography and **soil resistivity** (see below), he would bore down into it a hole 8 cm (3 in) in diameter, and insert a long tube with a periscope head and a light, and also a tiny camera attached if needed. Lerici examined some 3500 Etruscan tombs in this way, and found that almost all were completely empty, thus saving future excavators a great deal of wasted effort. He also discovered over 20 with painted walls, thus doubling the known heritage of Etruscan painted tombs at a stroke.

Shovel-Test Pits (STPs). To gain a preliminary idea of what lies beneath the surface, small pits may often be dug into the ground at consistent distances from each other; in Europe these are usually in the form of meter-squares, but in some parts of North America small round holes are dug, about the diameter of a dinner-plate and less than a meter deep. These pits help show what an area has to offer, and help identify the extent of a possible site, while analysis and plotting of the material retrieved from them by sieving of the soil can produce maps showing areas with high concentrations of different kinds of artifacts.

Probing the Pyramids. Modern technology has taken this kind of work even further, with the development of the endoscope and miniature TV cameras. In a project reminiscent of Lerici's, a probe was carried out in 1987 of a boat pit beside the Great Pyramid of Cheops (Khufu), in Egypt. This lies adjacent to another pit, excavated in 1954, that contained the perfectly preserved and disassembled parts of a 43-m (141-ft) long royal cedarwood boat of the 3rd millennium BC. The $250,000 probe revealed that the unopened pit does indeed contain all the dismantled timbers of a second boat but that the pit was not airtight – thus dashing hopes of analyzing the "ancient" air to see whether carbon dioxide in the atmosphere had increased over the millennia, and which component of the air preserves antiquities so efficiently.

Projects of this kind are beyond the resources of most archaeologists. But in future, funds permitting, probes of this type could equally well be applied to other

Egyptian sites, to cavities in Maya structures, or to the many unexcavated tombs in China. The Great Pyramid itself has recently been the subject of probes by French and Japanese teams who believe it may contain as yet undiscovered chambers or corridors. Using ultrasensitive microgravimetric equipment – which is normally employed to search for deficiencies in dam walls, and can tell if a stone has a hollow behind it – they detected what they think is a cavity some 3 m (10 ft) beyond one of the passage walls. However, test drilling to support this claim has not been completed and all tests are carefully monitored by the Egyptian authorities until their potential contribution to Egyptology has been established.

Ground-Based Remote Sensing

Probing techniques are useful, but inevitably involve some disturbance of the site. There are, however, a wide range of non-destructive techniques ideal for the archaeologist seeking to learn more about a site before – or without – excavation. These are geophysical sensing devices which can be either active (i.e. they pass energy of various kinds through the soil and measure the response in order to "read" what lies below the surface); or passive (i.e. they measure physical properties such as magnetism and gravity without the need to inject energy to obtain a response).

Electromagnetic Methods. A method which employs radio pulses is called ground-penetrating (or probing) radar (GPR). An emitter sends short pulses through the soil, and the echoes not only reflect back any changes in the soil and sediment conditions encountered, such as filled ditches, graves, walls, etc., but also measure the depth at which the changes occur on the basis of the travel time of the pulses. Three-dimensional maps of buried archaeological remains can then be produced from data processing and image-generation programs (see "time-slices" below).

In the field, the technique usually employs a single surface radar antenna which transmits very short pulses of electromagnetic energy (radar waves) down into the ground. A receiver records reflections from the discontinuities encountered, whether these are natural changes in soil horizons or properties, or buried archaeological features. The time it takes radar waves to travel from the surface source to the discontinuity and back to the receiver is measured in nanoseconds (i.e. billionths of a second), and since the wave velocity can be estimated, this indicates the distance involved.

In archaeological exploration and mapping, the radar antenna is generally dragged along the ground at walking speed in transects, sending out and receiving many pulses per second. In the early years of this method, the reflections were printed on paper and interpreted visually, and thus relied heavily on the experience and ability of the operator who had to guess what the buried feature might be from often indecipherable images. Inevitably this led to uncertainties and inconclusive results, with some notable successes and failures. Now, however, the method has greatly improved, and the reflection data can be stored digitally, which enables sophisticated data processing and analysis to be carried out, producing clean, crisp reflection records which are easier to interpret. Powerful computers and software programs make it possible to store and process large three-dimensional sets of GPR data, and computer advances now permit automated data and image processing which can help to interpret complicated reflection profiles.

One such advance is the use of "time-slices" or "slice-maps." Thousands of individual reflections are separated into horizontal slices, each of which corresponds to a specific estimated depth in the ground, and can reveal the general shape and location of buried features at each depth. A variety of colors (or shades of gray) are used to make a visual image that the brain can interpret more easily – e.g. areas with little or no subsurface reflection may be colored blue, those with high reflection may be red. Each slice therefore becomes like a horizontal excavation, and illustrates many buried components of the site. In fact, the slices do not need to be horizontal, and can be programmed to follow stratigraphic layers, and to have any orientation or thickness required.

For example, in the Forum Novum, an ancient Roman marketplace located about 100 km (62 miles) north of Rome, British archaeologists from the University

Amplitude slice-maps from the Forum Novum site, Italy. The top slice, at 0–10 ns (nanosecond, equivalent to 0–50 cm) reveals a Y-shaped anomaly, reflecting two gravel roads. As the slices go deeper, the Roman walls begin to emerge very clearly, showing a well-organized plan of rooms, doors, and corridors. The deepest slice shows the actual floor levels of the rooms and the objects preserved on them.

of Birmingham and the British School of Archaeology in Rome needed a fuller picture of an unexcavated area than they had been able to obtain from aerial photographs and other techniques such as resistivity (see below). A series of GPR slices of the area revealed a whole series of walls, individual rooms, doorways, courtyards – in short, produced an architectural layout of the site which means that future excavation can be concentrated on a representative sample of the structures, thus avoiding a costly and time-consuming uncovering of the whole area.

Electrical Resistivity.   A commonly used method that has been employed on archaeological sites for several decades, particularly in Europe, is *electrical resistivity*. The technique derives from the principle that the damper the soil the more easily it will conduct electricity, i.e. the less resistance it will show to an electric current. A resistivity meter attached to electrodes in the ground can thus measure varying degrees of subsurface resistance to a current passed between the electrodes. Silted up ditches or filled-in pits retain more moisture than stone walls or roads and will therefore display lower resistivity than stone structures.

The technique works particularly well for ditches and pits in chalk and gravel, and masonry in clay. It involves first placing two "remote" probes, which remain stationary, in the ground. Two "mobile" probes, fixed to a frame that also supports the meter, are then inserted into the earth for each reading. A new development is "resistivity profiling," which involves the measurement of earth resistance at increasing depths by widening the probe spacings and thus building up a vertical "pseudosection" across a site.

Magnetic Survey Methods.   These are among the most widely used methods of survey, being particularly helpful in locating fired clay structures such as hearths and pottery kilns; iron objects; and pits and ditches. Such buried features all produce slight but measurable distortions in the earth's magnetic field. The reasons for this vary according to the type of feature, but are based on the presence of iron, even if only in minute amounts. For example, grains of iron oxide in clay, their magnetism randomly orientated if the clay is unbaked, will line up and become permanently fixed on the direction of the earth's magnetic field when heated to about 700°C (1292°F) or more. The baked clay thus becomes a weak permanent magnet, creating an anomaly in the surrounding magnetic field. Anomalies caused by pits and ditches, on the other hand, occur because the so-called magnetic susceptibility of their contents is greater than that of the surrounding subsoil.

All the magnetic instruments (see box overleaf) can produce informative site plans which help to delimit archaeological potential. Common means of presentation are contour, dot density, and gray-scale maps, all also used to display resistivity

METHODS FOR MEASURING MAGNETISM

The main instruments for tracing buried features using magnetic methods are magnetometers. Metal detectors can detect metals and some soil features as well.

The **proton precession magnetometer** consists of a sensor (a bottle of water) encircled by an electrical coil, mounted on a staff and connected by a cable to a small portable box of electronics. The device can detect small but sharp differences in magnetic field intensity caused by buried objects and features.

Proton magnetometers are usually employed using a grid divided into squares 1 m to 3 m on a side. Unfortunately their rate of operation is somewhat slow. Other drawbacks which they share with all other kinds of magnetometer include the fact that the operator cannot wear any iron: all buckles, watches, bootnails, metal pens, etc.

Results of a magnetometer survey of the site of Stanton Drew in Somerset. This revealed the existence of a wooden henge structure consisting of nine concentric rings of timbers that had completely disappeared above ground.

must be kept several meters away; there must be no wire fences or corrugated sheeting nearby.

Proton magnetometers are also susceptible to interference from overhead cables. In a small, crowded country such as Japan, where sites are never far from electrified rail lines or other direct current power lines, two magnetometers have to be used simultaneously in order to overcome the "noise" that causes fluctuations in the magnetic field.

Fluxgate magnetometers have the advantage of sensors which give a continuous reading, but they are more complex to set up and operate – this is a directional instrument, and all measurements must be made with the sensor pointing in precisely the same direction (usually by hanging it vertically).

The most favored type of fluxgate magnetometer, the fluxgate gradiometer, uses two sensors in a light, self-contained instrument which produces a continuous output, and records differences in magnetic intensities on a meter. This can be combined with automatic trace recording and computer processing – consequently it can do fast, accurate surveys of large areas. A survey team using two fluxgate magnetometers can provide detailed coverage of at least 2 ha (5 acres) per day. Such rapidity, and the responsiveness of such instruments to a wide range of archaeological features, has led to their increased use in archaeological

evaluations, for instance in advance of the building of roads. Along one stretch of the future M3 highway in England, it found 8 sites in 10 km (6.2 miles).

The caesium magnetometer is a highly sensitive portable magnetometer that can detect minute magnetic variations, down to about one millionth of the earth's magnetic field. It is being increasingly used to detect weakly magnetized features such as postholes, and more deeply buried sites. Mounted on wheels, it can achieve rates of ground coverage comparable to fluxgate gradiometer surveys.

Metal detectors use both magnetism and conductivity – they respond to the high electrical conductivity of all metals and to the high magnetic susceptibility of ferrous metals. There are two main instruments. The soil conductivity meter comprises a radio transmitter and receiver in continuous operation, and detects subsurface features by measuring the distortion of the transmitted field caused by changes in the conductivity or susceptibility of the soil. Metals, for example, produce strong anomalies, while pits produce weak ones. The pulsed induction meter can find metal objects and magnetic soil anomalies such as pits by applying pulses of magnetic field to the ground from a transmitter coil – the larger the coil, the deeper the penetration. Similar devices are also employed in underwater archaeology.

KEY CONCEPTS: ASSESSING THE LAYOUT OF SITES AND FEATURES

- *Site Surface Survey:* the study of the distribution of surviving features at a site (such as earthworks or traces of structures), and the recording and sometimes collecting of artifacts (often pottery or stone tools) from the surface

- *Subsurface Detection:* the use of probes and shovel-test pits (and sometimes miniature TV cameras and endoscopes) to find and map subsurface features

- *Ground-Based Remote Sensing:* the use of non-destructive techniques, such as ground-penetrating radar and magnetometry, to find and map subsurface features

survey results. In the case of magnetic survey, the contour map has contour lines that join all points of the same value of the magnetic field intensity – this successfully reveals separate anomalies, such as tombs in a cemetery. In dot-density mapping, individual magnetometer readings are plotted as dots on a plan, with shading dependent on the magnetic intensity, the blacker areas therefore represent the highest anomalies in the local magnetic field. This makes it easier to pick up regular features, even where changes may be slight.

So far, we have discovered sites and mapped as many of their surface and subsurface features as possible. But, despite the growing importance of survey, the only way to check the reliability of surface data, confirm the accuracy of the remote sensing techniques, and actually see what remains of these sites is to excavate them. Furthermore, survey can tell us a little about a large area, but only excavation can tell us a great deal about a relatively small area.

EXCAVATION

Excavation retains its central role in fieldwork because it yields the most reliable evidence for the two main kinds of information archaeologists are interested in: (1) human activities at a particular period in the past; and (2) changes in those activities from period to period. Very broadly we can say that contemporary activities take place *horizontally in space*, whereas changes in those activities occur *vertically through time*. It is this distinction between horizontal "slices of time" and vertical sequences through time that forms the basis of most excavation methodology.

In the horizontal dimension archaeologists demonstrate that activities occurred at the same time by proving through excavation that artifacts and features are found in association in an undisturbed **context**. Of course, as we saw in Chapter 2, there are many formation processes that may disturb this primary context. One of the main purposes of the survey and remote sensing procedures outlined in the earlier sections is to select for excavation sites, or areas within sites, that are reasonably undisturbed. On a single-period site such as an East African early human camp site this is vital if human behavior at the camp is to be reconstructed at all accurately. But on a multi-period site, such as a long-lived European town or Near Eastern village mound, finding large areas of undisturbed deposits will be almost impossible. Here archaeologists have to try to reconstruct during and after excavation just what disturbance there has been and then decide how to interpret it. Clearly, adequate records must be made as excavation progresses if the task of interpretation is to be undertaken with any chance of success. In the vertical dimension archaeologists analyze changes through time by the study of **stratigraphy**.

Stratigraphy

As we saw in Chapter 1, one of the first steps in understanding the great antiquity of humankind was the recognition by geologists of the process of **stratification** – that layers or strata are laid down, one on top of the other, according to processes that still continue. Archaeological strata (the layers of cultural or natural debris visible in the side of any excavation) accumulate over much shorter periods of time than geological ones, but nevertheless conform to the same *law of superposition*. Put simply, this states that where one layer overlies another, the lower was deposited first. Hence, an excavated vertical profile showing a series of layers constitutes a sequence that has accumulated through time.

Chapter 4 explores the significance of this for dating purposes. Here we should note that the law of superposition refers only to the sequence of deposition, not to the age of the material in the different strata. The contents of lower layers are indeed usually older than those of upper layers, but the archaeologist must not simply assume this. Pits dug down from a higher layer or burrowing animals (even earthworms) may introduce later materials into lower levels. Moreover, occasionally strata can become inverted, as when they are eroded all the way from the top of a bank to the bottom of a ditch.

In recent years, archaeologists have developed an ingenious and effective method of checking that artifacts – so far mostly of stone or bone – discovered in a particular deposit are contemporaneous and not intrusive. They have found that in a surprising number of cases flakes of stone or bone can be fitted back together again: reassembled in the shape of the original stone block or pieces of bone from which they came. At the British **Mesolithic** (Middle Stone Age) site of Hengistbury Head, for example, reanalysis of an old excavation showed that two groups of flint flakes, found in two different layers, could be refitted. This cast doubt on the stratigraphic separation of the two layers, and demolished the original excavator's argument that the flints had been made by two different groups of people. As well as clarifying questions of stratification, these refitting or conjoining exercises are transforming archaeological studies of early technology (Chapter 7).

The complexity of stratification varies with the type of site. This hypothetical section through an urban deposit indicates the kind of complicated stratigraphy, in both vertical and horizontal dimensions, that the archaeologist can encounter. There may be few undisturbed stratified layers. The chances of finding preserved organic material increase as one approaches the water table, near which deposits may be waterlogged.

modern disturbance

present ground surface

natural soil level

drain

intact stratification

preserved organic material

wall foundations

water table

Stratigraphy, then, is the study and validating of stratification – the analysis in the vertical, time dimension of a series of layers in the horizontal, space dimension (although in practice few layers are precisely horizontal).

What are the best excavation methods for retrieving this information?

Methods of Excavation

Excavation is both costly and destructive, and therefore never to be undertaken lightly. Wherever possible non-destructive approaches outlined earlier should be used to meet research objectives in preference to excavation. But assuming excavation is to proceed, and the necessary funding and permission to dig have been obtained, what are the best methods to adopt?

It goes without saying that all excavation methods need to be adapted to the research question in hand and the nature of the site. It is no good digging a deeply stratified urban site, with hundreds of complex structures, thousands of intercutting pits, and tens of thousands of artifacts, as if it were the same as a shallow **Paleolithic** open site, where only one or two structures and a few hundred artifacts may survive. On the Paleolithic site, for example, it may be possible to uncover all the structures and record the exact position, vertically and horizontally – i.e. the *provenience* – of each and every artifact. On the urban site there is no chance of doing this, given time and funding constraints. Instead, we have to adopt a sampling strategy, and only key artifacts such as coins (important for dating purposes: see Chapter 4) will have their provenience recorded with three-dimensional precision, the remainder being allocated simply to the layer and perhaps the grid-square in which they were found (sites are usually divided up into grid-squares, just like maps are, in order to aid in accurate recording; naturally, the size and number of the grid squares will depend on the type, size and likely depth of the site).

It should be noted, however, that we have already reintroduced the idea of the vertical and horizontal dimensions. These are as crucial to the methods of excavation as they are to the principles behind excavation. Broadly speaking we can divide excavation techniques into:

1   those that emphasize the vertical dimension, by cutting into deep deposits to reveal stratification;

2   those that emphasize the horizontal dimension, by opening up large areas of a particular layer to reveal the spatial relationships between artifacts and features in that layer.

Most excavators employ a combination of both strategies, but there are different ways of achieving this. All presuppose that the site has first been surveyed and a grid of squares laid down over it.

The **Wheeler box-grid** – developed from the work of General Pitt-Rivers, as noted in Chapter 1 – seeks to satisfy both vertical and horizontal requirements by retaining intact balks of earth between the squares of the grid, as can be clearly seen in the picture at right, so that different layers can be traced and correlated across the site in vertical profiles. Once the general extent and layout of the site have been ascertained, some of the balks can be removed and the squares joined into an open excavation to expose any features (such as a mosaic floor) that are of special interest.

Advocates of **open-area excavation** criticize this method, arguing that the balks are invariably in the wrong place or wrongly orientated to illustrate the relationships required from sections, and that they prevent the distinguishing of spatial patterning over large areas. It is far better, these critics say, not to have such permanent or semi-permanent balks, but to open up large areas and only to cut vertical sections (at whatever angle is necessary to the main site grid) where they are needed to elucidate particularly complex stratigraphic relationships. Apart from these "running sections," the vertical dimension is recorded by accurate three-dimensional measurements as the dig proceeds and reconstructed on paper after the end of the excavation. The introduction since Wheeler's day of more advanced recording methods, including field computers, makes this more demanding open-area method feasible, and it has become the norm, for instance, in much of British archaeology. The open-area method is particularly effective where single-period deposits lie near the surface, as for instance with remains of Native American or European Neolithic long houses. Here the time dimension may be represented by lateral movement (a settlement rebuilt adjacent to, not on top of, an earlier one)

Box-grid excavation trenches at Anuradhapura's Abhayagiri Buddhist monastery, Sri Lanka.

Open-area excavation at Sutton Hoo, eastern England. A large area, 32 x 64 m, was uncovered to establish the perimeters of two burial mounds. Detailed stratigraphy was then studied in smaller squares. Immediately below the topsoil lay early medieval features, recorded using overhead color photographs to emphasize soil variations, and plotted on site plans at scales of 1:10 and 1:100.

The American Indian site of Koster, in the Illinois River Valley: large horizontal areas were uncovered to locate living floors and activity zones. However, so that the vertical dimension could be analyzed at this deep site, vertical sections were cut as steps as the excavation descended. At this complex site 14 occupation levels were identified, dating from *c.* 7500 BC to AD 1200.

and it is essential to expose large horizontal areas in order to understand the complex pattern of rebuilding. Large open-area excavations are often undertaken in salvage or rescue operations when land is going to be destroyed – otherwise farmers are naturally opposed to stripping large areas of plow-disturbed soil. The box-grid method is still widely used in parts of South Asia where it was introduced by Wheeler in the 1940s. It remains popular as it enables large numbers of untrained workers in individual boxes to be easily supervised by small numbers of staff.

No single method, however, is ever going to be universally applicable. The rigid box-grid, for instance, has rarely been employed to excavate very deep sites, such as Near Eastern tells, because the trench squares rapidly become uncomfortable and dangerous as the dig proceeds downward. One solution commonly adopted is **step-trenching**, with a large area opened at the top which gradually narrows as the

KEY CONCEPTS: EXCAVATION

- Excavation yields evidence of contemporary activities (which are found horizontally through space) and changes through time (which are found vertically in sequences)

- Stratigraphy is the study of archaeological layers found during excavations. The law of superposition states that where one layer overlies another, the lower was deposited first. This forms the basis of the way archaeologists investigate changes through time

- Excavation methods should be adapted to the site and particular questions that need to be answered. The two main strategies are the Wheeler box-grid and open-area excavation; a combination of both is often used. A sampling strategy of some kind can be required to save time and money dig descends in a series of large steps. This technique was used effectively at the Koster site, Illinois.

Whatever the method of excavation, a dig is only as good as its methods of recovery and recording. Since excavation involves destruction of much of the evidence, it is an unrepeatable exercise. Well-thought-out recovery methods are essential, and careful records must be kept of every stage of the dig.

Underwater Archaeology

One special category of both survey and excavation is constituted by *underwater archaeology*, which is generally considered to have been given its first major impetus during the winter of 1853–54, when a particularly low water level in the Swiss lakes laid bare enormous quantities of wooden posts, pottery, and other artifacts. From the earliest investigations, using crude diving-bells, it has developed into a valuable complement to work on land. It encompasses a wide variety of sites, including wells, sink holes, and springs (e.g. the great sacrificial well at Chichén Itzá, Mexico); submerged lakeside settlements; and marine sites ranging from shipwrecks to sunken harbors and drowned cities.

The invention in recent times of miniature submarines, other submersible craft, and above all of scuba diving gear has been of enormous value, enabling divers to stay underwater for much longer, and to reach sites at previously impossible depths. As a result, the pace and scale of discovery have greatly increased. More than 1000 shipwrecks are known in shallow Mediterranean waters, but recent explorations using deep-sea submersibles, such as miniature unmanned submarines (remotely operated vehicles – ROV) with sonar, high-powered lighting, and video cameras, have begun to find Roman wrecks at depths of up to 850 m (2790 ft), and two Phoenician wrecks packed with amphorae discovered off the coast of Israel are the oldest vessels ever found in the deep sea.

Underwater Reconnaissance.   Geophysical methods are as useful for finding sites underwater as they are for locating land sites. For example, in 1979 it was magnetometry combined with **side-scan sonar** that discovered the *Hamilton* and the *Scourge*, two armed schooners sunk during the War of 1812 at a depth of 90 m (295 ft) in Lake Ontario, Canada. Nevertheless, in regions such as the Mediterranean the majority of finds have resulted from methods as simple as talking to local sponge-divers, who collectively have spent thousands of hours scouring the seabed.

Underwater Excavation.   Excavation underwater is complex and expensive (not to mention the highly demanding post-excavation conservation and analytical work that is also required). Once underway, the excavation may involve shifting vast quantities of sediment, and recording and removing bulky objects as diverse as storage

Three methods of geophysical underwater survey. (1) The proton magnetometer is towed well behind the survey boat, detecting iron and steel objects (e.g. cannons, steel hulls) that distort the earth's magnetic field. (2) Side-scan sonar transmits sound waves in a fan-shaped beam to produce a graphic image of surface (but not sub-surface) features on the seafloor. (3) The sub-bottom profiler emits sound pulses that bounce back from features and objects buried beneath the seafloor.

Underwater excavation techniques: at left, the lift bag for raising objects; center, measuring and recording finds in situ; right, the air lift for removing sediment.

jars (amphorae), metal ingots, and cannons. George Bass, founder of the Institute of Nautical Archaeology in Texas, and others have developed many helpful devices, such as baskets attached to balloons to raise objects, and air lifts (suction hoses) to remove sediment. If the vessel's hull survives at all, detailed drawings must be made so that specialists can later reconstruct the overall form and lines, either on paper or in three dimensions as a model or full-size replica. In some rare cases, like that of England's *Mary Rose* (a 16th-century AD warship that sank off Portsmouth), preservation is sufficiently good for the remains of the hull to be raised – funds permitting.

Nautical archaeologists have now excavated more than 100 sunken vessels, revealing not only how they were constructed but also many insights into shipboard life, cargoes, trade routes, early metallurgy, and glassmaking. For example, a Basque whaling ship, the *San Juan*, which had sunk in Red Bay, Labrador, in 1565, was excavated in the 1980s from a specially equipped barge, anchored above the site, that contained a workshop, storage baths for artifacts, a crane for lifting timbers, and a compressor able to run 12 air lifts for removing silt. Salt water was heated on board and pumped down through hoses direct to the divers' suits to maintain body warmth in the near-freezing conditions. An important technique devised during the project was the use of latex rubber to mold large sections of the ship's timbers in position underwater, thereby reproducing accurately the hull shape and details such as toolmarks and wood grain. The remains of the vessel were also raised in pieces to the surface for precise recording, but the latex molds eliminated the need for costly conservation of the original timbers, which were reburied on-site.

Model, at a scale of 1:10, to show how the *San Juan*'s surviving timbers may have fitted together.

Structural plan of the wreck on the harbor bottom (2-m grid squares).

Recovery and Recording of the Evidence

As we saw above, different sites have different requirements. We should aim to recover and plot the three-dimensional provenience of every artifact from a shallow single-period Paleolithic or Neolithic site, an objective that is simply not feasible for the urban archaeologist. On both types of site, a decision may be made to save time by using mechanical diggers to remove topsoil, but thereafter the Paleolithic or Neolithic specialist will usually want to screen or sieve as much excavated soil as possible in order to recover tiny artifacts, animal bones, and plant remains. The urban archaeologist on the other hand will only be able to adopt sieving much more selectively, as part of a sampling strategy, for instance where plant remains can be expected to survive, as in a latrine or garbage pit.

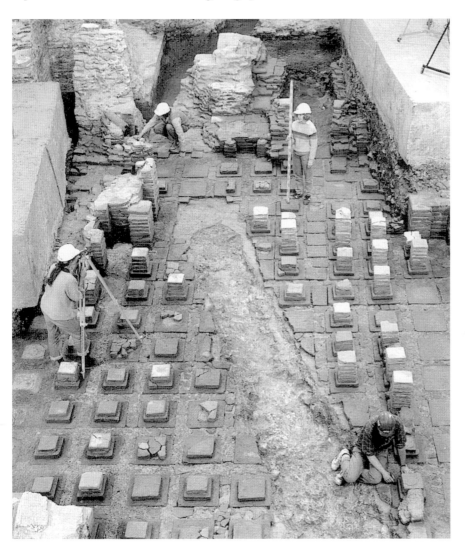

The Roman baths at Huggin Hill in London. A Museum of London archaeologist uses a theodolite (a surveying instrument) to measure the accurate position of a column base on which another archaeologist holds a survey rod (range pole). Their measurements will later form the basis for a detailed plan.

Once an artifact has been recovered, and its provenience recorded, it must be given a number which is entered in a catalog book or field computer and on the bag in which it is to be stored. Day-to-day progress of the dig is recorded in site notebooks, or on data sheets preprinted with specific questions to be answered (which helps produce uniform data suitable for later analysis by computer).

Unlike artifacts, which can be removed for later analysis, features and structures usually have to be left where they were found (or *in situ*), or destroyed as the excavation proceeds to another layer. It is thus imperative to record them, not simply by written description in site notebooks, but by accurately scaled drawings and photography. The same applies to vertical profiles (sections), and for each horizontally exposed layer good overhead photographs taken from a stand or tethered balloon are also essential.

It is the site notebooks, scaled drawings, photographs and computer data – in addition to recovered artifacts, animal bones, and plant remains – that form the total record of the excavation, on the basis of which all interpretations of the site will be made. This post-excavation analysis will take many months, perhaps years, often much longer than the excavation itself. However, some preliminary analysis, particularly sorting and classification of the artifacts, will be made in the field during the course of the excavation.

Processing and Classification

Like excavation itself, the processing of excavated materials in the field laboratory is a specialized activity that demands careful planning and organization. For example, an archaeologist excavating a wet site will need experts in the conservation of waterlogged wood, and facilities for coping with such material.

Two important aspects of field laboratory procedure are cleaning of artifacts and sorting and classifying them. In both cases the archaeologist always needs to consider in advance what kinds of questions the newly excavated material might be able to answer. Thorough cleaning of artifacts, for example, is a traditional part of excavations worldwide. But many of the new scientific techniques discussed later in this book make it quite evident that artifacts should *not* necessarily be cleaned thoroughly before a specialist has had a chance to study them. For instance, we now know that food residues are often preserved in pots and possible blood residues on stone tools. The chances of such preservation need to be assessed before evidence is destroyed.

Nevertheless most artifacts eventually have to be cleaned to some degree if they are to be sorted and classified. Initial sorting is into broad categories such as stone tools, pottery, and metal objects. These categories are then subdivided or classified,

INDIVIDUALS	ATTRIBUTES	ARTIFACTS	Attribute patterning reflects individual behavior patterns
GROUPS	ARTIFACTS	SUBASSEMBLAGES	Artifact patterning reflects group behavior patterns
COMMUNITIES	SUBASSEMBLAGES	ASSEMBLAGES	Subassemblage patterning reflects community behavior patterns
SOCIETIES	ASSEMBLAGES	ARCHAEOLOGICAL CULTURES	Assemblage patterning reflects societal behavior patterns

Terms used in archaeological classification, from attributes (shape, decoration) of a pot to the complete archaeological culture: a diagram developed by the American archaeologist James Deetz. The columns at left and right give the inferred human meaning of the terms. The extent to which one can draw behavioral inferences from such classification is discussed in Chapter 9.

so as to create more manageable groups that can later be analyzed. Classification is commonly done on the basis of three kinds of characteristics or *attributes*:

1 surface attributes (including decoration and color);
2 shape attributes (dimensions as well as shape itself);
3 technological attributes (primarily raw material).

Artifacts found to share similar attributes are grouped together into artifact types – hence the term **typology**, which simply refers to the creation of such types.

Typology dominated archaeological thinking until the 1950s, and still plays an important role. The reason for this is straightforward. Artifacts make up a large part of the archaeological record, and typology helps archaeologists create order in this mass of evidence. As we saw in Chapter 1, C. J. Thomsen demonstrated early on that artifacts could be ordered in a Three Age System or sequence of stone, bronze, and iron. This discovery underlies the continuing use of typology as a method of dating (Chapter 4). Typology has also been used as a means of defining archaeological entities at a particular moment in time: groups of artifact (and building) types at a particular time and place are termed *assemblages*, and groups of assemblages have been taken to define *archaeological cultures*. These definitions are also long established, but, as we shall see later, the difficulty comes when one tries to translate this terminology into human terms and to relate an archaeological "culture" with an actual group of people in the past.

This brings us back to the purpose of classification. Types, assemblages, and cultures are all concepts designed to put order into disordered evidence – they are artificial. The trap that former generations of scholars fell into was to allow these concepts to determine the way they thought about the past, rather than using them merely as one means of giving shape to the evidence. We now recognize more clearly that different classifications are needed for the different kinds of questions we want to ask. A student of ceramic technology would base a classification on variations in raw material and methods of manufacture, whereas a scholar studying the various functions of pottery for storage, cooking etc. might classify the vessels according to shape and size. Our ability to construct and make good use of new classifications has been immeasurably enhanced by computers, which allow archaeologists to compare the association of different attributes on hundreds of objects at once.

In conclusion, it cannot be stressed too strongly that all the effort put into survey, excavation, and post-excavation analysis will have been largely wasted unless the results are published.

SUMMARY

- Although many sites are found either by accident or during modern development, the archaeologist has a barrage of ground and aerial reconnaissance techniques available with which to find new sites.

- Until the present century, individual sites were the main focus of archaeological attention, but today archaeologists study whole regions, often employing sampling techniques to bring ground reconnaissance survey within the scope of individual research teams. Having located sites within those regions, and mapped them (often using GIS), archaeologists can then turn to a whole battery of remote sensing site survey devices able to detect buried features without excavation.

- Remote sensing methods almost all involve either passing energy into the ground and locating buried features from their effect on that energy or measuring the intensity of the earth's magnetic field. In either case, they depend on contrast between the buried features and their surroundings. Many of the techniques are costly in both equipment and time, but they are often cheaper and certainly less destructive than random trial trenches. They allow archaeologists to be more selective in deciding which parts of a site, if any, should be fully excavated.

- Excavation itself relies on methods designed to elucidate the horizontal extent of a site in space, and the vertical stratification representing changes through time. Good recording methods are essential, together with a well-equipped field laboratory for processing and classifying the finds. Classification based on selected attributes (decoration, shape, material) of each artifact is the fundamental means of organizing the excavated material, usually into types – hence typology. But classification is only a means to an end, and different schemes are needed for the different questions archaeologists want to address.

- However, little of the material retrieved during survey and excavation will be of much use unless it can be dated in some way. In the next chapter we turn to this crucial aspect of archaeology.

FURTHER READING

Useful introductions to methods of survey and excavation can be found in the following:

Collis, J. 2001. **Digging up the Past: An Introduction to Archaeological Excavation.** SUTTON: STROUD.

Gaffney, V. & Gater, J. 2003. **Revealing the Buried Past. Geophysics for Archaeologists.** TEMPUS: STROUD.

Hester, T.N., Shafer, H.J., & Feder, K.L. 1997. **Field Methods in Archaeology. (7th ed.)** MAYFIELD: PALO ALTO, CALIF. (AMERICAN METHODS.)

McIntosh, J. 1999. **The Practical Archaeologist.** (2nd ed.). Facts on File: NEW YORK; THAMES & HUDSON: LONDON. Wheatley, D. & Gillings, M. 2002. **Spatial Technology and Archaeology. The Archaeological Applications of GIS.** ROUTLEDGE: LONDON.

Zimmerman, L.J. & Green, W. (eds.). 2003. **The Archaeologist's Toolkit** (7 vols.). ALTAMIRA PRESS: WALNUT CREEK.

4

When?
dating methods & chronology

All human beings experience time. An individual experiences a lifetime of perhaps 70 years or so. That person, through the memories of his or her parents and grandparents, may also indirectly experience earlier periods of time, back over more than 100 years. The study of history gives us access to hundreds more years of recorded time. But it is only **archaeology** that opens up the almost unimaginable vistas of thousands and even a few millions of years of past human existence. This chapter will examine the various ways in which we, as archaeologists, date past events within this great expanse of time.

Relative and Absolute Dating. It might seem surprising that in order to study the past it is not always essential to know precisely how long ago (in years) a particular period or event occurred. It is often very helpful simply to know whether one event happened before or after another. By ordering **artifacts**, deposits, societies, and events into sequences, earlier before later, we can study developments in the past without knowing how long each stage lasted or how many years ago such changes took place. This idea that something is older (or younger) relative to something else is the basis of **relative dating**.

Ultimately, however, we want to know the full or absolute age in years before the present of different events or parts of a sequence – we need methods of **absolute dating**. Absolute dates help us find out how quickly changes such as the introduction of agriculture occurred, and whether they occurred simultaneously or at different times in different regions of the world. Only in the last 50 years or so have independent means of absolute dating become available, transforming archaeology in the process. Before then, virtually the only reliable absolute dates were historical ones, such as the date of the reign of the ancient Egyptian pharaoh Tutankhamun.

Measuring Time. How do we detect the passage of time? We can all observe its passing through the alternating darkness and light of nights and days, and then through the annual cycle of the seasons. In fact, for most of human history these were the only ways of measuring time, other than by the human lifespan. As we shall see, some dating methods still rely on the annual passage of the seasons. Increasingly, however, dating methods in archaeology have come to rely on other physical processes, many of them not observable to the human eye. The most significant of these is the use of radioactive clocks.

Some degree of error, usually expressed as an age-bracket which can stretch over several centuries or even millennia, is inevitable when using any dating technique. But while the science behind dating methods is being ever more refined, the main source of errors remains the archaeologist – by poor choice of samples to be dated, by contaminating those samples, or by misinterpreting results.

Dating Conventions.   To be meaningful, our timescale in years must relate to a fixed point in time. In the Christian world, this is by convention taken as the birth of Christ, supposedly in the year AD 1 (there is no year 0), with years counted back before Christ (BC) and forward after Christ (AD or *Anno Domini*, which is Latin for "In the Year of Our Lord"). However, this is by no means the only system. In the Muslim world, for example, the basic fixed point is the date of the Prophet's departure from Mecca (AD 622 in the Christian calendar). As a result of these differences some scholars prefer to use the terms "Before the Common Era" (BCE) and "in the Common Era" (CE) instead of BC and AD.

Scientists who derive dates from radioactive methods want a neutral international system, and have chosen to count years back from the present (BP). But since scientists too require a firm fixed point to count from, they take BP to mean "before 1950" (the approximate year of the establishment of the first radioactive method, radiocarbon). This may be convenient for scientists, but can be confusing for everyone else (a date of 400 BP is not 400 years ago but AD 1550, currently over 450 years ago). It is therefore clearest to convert any BP date for the last few thousand years into the BC/AD system.

For the **Paleolithic** period, however (stretching back two or three million years before 10,000 BC), archaeologists use the terms "BP" and "years ago" interchangeably, since a difference of 50 years or so between them is irrelevant. For this remote epoch we are dating **sites** or events at best only to within several thousand years of their "true" date. If even the most precise dates for the Paleolithic give us glimpses of that epoch only at intervals of several thousand years, clearly archaeologists can never hope to reconstruct a conventional history of Paleolithic events. On the other hand, Paleolithic archaeologists can gain insights into some of the broad long-term changes that shaped the way modern humans evolved – insights that are denied archaeologists working with shorter periods of time, where in any case there may be too much "detail" for the broader pattern to be apparent.

The way in which archaeologists carry out their research therefore depends very much on the precision of dating obtainable for the period of time in question.

RELATIVE DATING

The first, and in some ways the most important, step in much archaeological research involves ordering things into sequences. The things to be put into sequence can be archaeological deposits in a stratigraphic **excavation**. Or they can be artifacts as in a typological sequence. Changes in the earth's climate also give rise to local, regional, and global environmental sequences – the most notable being the sequence of global fluctuations during the Ice Age. All these sequences can be used for relative dating.

STRATIGRAPHY: ORDERING ARCHAEOLOGICAL LAYERS

Stratigraphy, as we saw in Chapter 3, is the study of **stratification** – the laying down or depositing of strata or layers (also called deposits) one above the other. From the point of view of relative dating, the important principle is that the underlying layer was deposited first and therefore earlier than the overlying layer. A succession of layers provides a relative chronological sequence, from earliest (bottom) to latest (top).

Good stratigraphic excavation at an archaeological site is designed to obtain such a sequence. Part of this work involves detecting whether there has been any human or natural disturbance of the layers since they were originally deposited (such as rubbish pits dug down by later occupants of a site into earlier layers, or animals burrowing holes). Armed with carefully observed stratigraphic informa-tion, the archaeologist can hope to construct a reliable relative chronological sequence for the deposition of the different layers.

But of course what we mostly want to date are not so much the layers or deposits themselves as the materials that humans have left within them – artifacts, struc-tures, organic remains – which ultimately reveal past human activities at the site. Here the idea of **association** is important. When we say that two objects were found in association within the same archaeological deposit, we generally mean that they became buried at the same time. Provided that the deposit is a sealed one, without stratigraphic intrusions from another deposit, the associated objects can be said to be no more recent than the deposit itself. A sequence of sealed deposits thus gives a sequence – and relative chronology – for the time of burial of the objects found associated in those deposits.

This is a crucial concept to grasp, because if one of those objects can later be given an absolute date – say a datable coin or a piece of charcoal that can be dated by radiocarbon in the laboratory – then it is possible to assign that absolute date not only to the charcoal but to the sealed deposit and the other objects associated with it as well. A series of such dates from different deposits will give an absolute chronology for the whole sequence. It is this interconnecting of stratigraphic sequences with absolute dating methods that provides the most reliable basis for dating archaeological sites and their contents. The example shown overleaf is Mortimer Wheeler's drawing of a section across an ancient mound in the Indus Valley (modern Pakistan). The site has been disturbed by more recent pits, but the sequence of layers is still visible, and the Harappan seal, of known age and found in an undisturbed context in layer 8, helps to date that layer and the wall next to it.

EXAMPLE OF
TRUE STRATIFICATION

PRESENT SURFACE OF TELL

PRECINCT WALL OF BUDDHIST MONASTERY

MODERN TREE-PIT

SPOIL PIT

WALL OF HARAPPAN HOUSE

SPOIL PIT

HARAPPAN SEAL
3RD MILLENNIUM B.C.

ANNA
1910 A.D.

KUSHAN COIN
2ND CENTURY A.D.

Stratigraphy in action: a section across a mound or tell in the Indus Valley. Attention to stratigraphy is crucial because, as with the coins and the seal here, not everything found at the same level is always equally old.

But there is another important point to consider. So far we have dated, relatively and with luck absolutely, the time of burial of the deposits and their associated material. As we have observed, however, what we want ultimately to reconstruct and date are the past human activities and behavior that those deposits and materials represent. If a deposit is a rubbish pit with pottery in it, the deposit itself is of interest as an example of human activity, and the date for it is the date of human use of the pit. This will also be the date of final burial of the pottery – but it will *not* be the date of human use of that pottery, which could have been in circulation tens or hundreds of years earlier, before being discarded with other rubbish in the pit. It is necessary therefore always to be clear about which activity we are trying to date, or can reliably date in the circumstances.

TYPOLOGICAL SEQUENCES: COMPARING OBJECTS

When we look at the artifacts, buildings, or any of the human creations around us, most of us can mentally arrange them into a rough chronological sequence. One kind of aircraft looks older than another, one set of clothes looks more "old-fashioned" than the next. How do archaeologists exploit this ability for relative dating?

Archaeologists define the form of an artifact such as a pot by its specific attributes of material, shape, and decoration. Several pots with the same attributes constitute a pot **type**, and **typology** groups artifacts into such types. Underlying the notion of relative dating through typology are two other ideas.

The first is that the products of a given period and place have a recognizable style: through their distinctive shape and decoration they are in some sense characteristic of the society that produced them. The archaeologist or anthropologist can often recognize and classify individual artifacts by their style, and hence assign them to a particular place in a typological sequence.

The second idea is that the change in style (shape and decoration) of artifacts is often quite gradual, or evolutionary. This idea came from the Darwinian theory of the **evolution** of species, and was used by 19th-century archaeologists who applied a very convenient rule, that "like goes with like." In other words, particular artifacts (e.g. bronze daggers) produced at about the same time are often alike, but those produced several centuries apart will be different as a result of centuries of change. It follows, then, that when studying a series of daggers of unknown date, it is logical first to arrange them in a sequence in such a way that the most closely similar are located beside each other. This is then likely to be the true chronological sequence, because it best reflects the principle that "like goes with like." In the diagram below, designs of automobiles and prehistoric European axes have been arranged in a relative chronological sequence; however, the rate of change (a century for the automobile, millennia for the axe) has to be deduced from absolute dating methods.

For many purposes, the best way to assign a relative date to an artifact is to match it with an artifact already recognized within a well-established typological system. Pottery typologies usually form the backbone of the chronological system, and nearly every area has its own well-established ceramic sequence. One example is the very extensive ceramic sequence for the ancient societies of the American Southwest, a part of which is shown in the diagram overleaf. If such a typology is tied into a stratigraphic sequence of deposits that can be dated by radiocarbon or other absolute means, then the artifacts in the typological sequence can themselves be assigned absolute dates in years.

Different types of artifact change in style (decoration and shape) at different rates, and therefore vary in the chronological distinctions that they indicate.

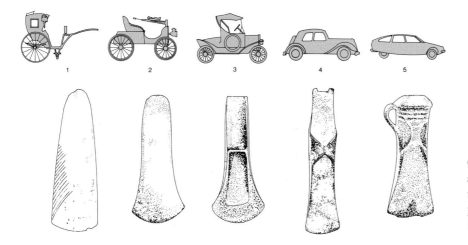

Gradual changes in design are evident in the history of the automobile and of the prehistoric European axe – (1) stone; (2–5) bronze.

PHASE	DECORATION	SHAPE

SACATON
AD 1000–1175

SANTA
CRUZ
AD 875–1000

GILA
BUTTE
AD 800–875

SNAKETOWN
AD 750–800

SWEETWATER
AD 700–750

ESTRELLA
AD 650–700

Pottery typology, as exemplified by this 500-year sequence of Hohokam bowl styles from the American Southwest.

Usually, with pottery, surface decoration changes most rapidly (often over periods of just a few decades) and is therefore the best attribute to use for a typological sequence. On the other hand, the shape of a vessel or container may be most strongly influenced by a practical requirement, such as water storage, which need not alter for hundreds of years.

Other artifacts, such as metal weapons or tools, can change in style quite rapidly, and so may be useful chronological indicators. By contrast stone tools, such as **hand-axes**, are often very slow to change in form and therefore rarely make useful indicators of the passage of time (and are more useful in making general distinctions between much longer periods).

Seriation: Comparing Assemblages of Objects

The insights of the principle that "like goes with like" have been developed further to deal with associations of finds (assemblages) rather than with the forms of single objects taken in isolation. The technique of **seriation** allows assemblages of artifacts to be arranged in a succession or serial order, which is then taken to indicate their ordering in time, or their relative chronology.

The great pioneer of Egyptian archaeology, Sir Flinders Petrie, was one of the first to develop a technique for arranging the graves of a cemetery in relative order by considering carefully and systematically the associations of the various pottery forms found within them. His lead in the late 19th century was taken up half a century later by American scholars who realised that the frequency of a particular ceramic style, as documented in the successive layers of a settlement, is usually small to start with, rises to a peak as the style gains popularity, and then declines again (which diagrammatically produces a shape like a battleship viewed from above, known as a "battleship curve"). Using this insight they were able to compare the pottery assemblages from different sites in the same area, each with a limited stratigraphic sequence, and arrange these sites into chronological order so that the ceramic frequencies would conform to the pattern of rising to a maximum and then declining.

The diagram opposite shows how this technique has been applied to changes in the popularity of three tombstone designs found in central Connecticut cemeteries dating from 1700 to 1860. The fluctuating fortunes of each design produce characteristic and successive battleship curves – as elsewhere in New England, the Death's head design (peak popularity 1710–1739) was gradually replaced by the Cherub (peak 1760–1789) which in turn was replaced by the Urn and willow tree (peak 1840–1859).

Seriation has been used in an archaeological context by the American archaeologist Frank Hole in his excavations in the Deh Luran Plain in Iran. The **Neolithic**

	Death's head	Cherub	Urn and willow
1860–69			████████████
1850–59			████████████
1840–49		██	████████
1830–39		██	████████
1820–29		██	██████
1810–19	██	████	██████
1800–09	██	████	████
1790–99		██████	██
1780–89	██	██████	
1770–79	████	██████	
1760–69	████	████	
1750–59	████	██	
1740–49	█████		
1730–39	████████		
1720–29	████████		
1710–19	████████	██	
1700–09	██████		

■ = 10% of the stones in a 10-year period

Seriation: changes in the popularity of central Connecticut tombstone designs.

ceramic assemblages he was studying were derived from stratigraphic excavations, so it was possible to compare the sequences obtained through **frequency seriation** with the true stratigraphic sequences discovered in their excavations. There were no serious contradictions, again proving the validity of the method.

KEY CONCEPTS: RELATIVE DATING METHODS

- *Stratigraphy:* in a succession of layers the bottom layer is the earliest and the top layer the latest

- *Association:* objects found in the same stratigraphic layer were buried at the same time

- *Typological Sequences:* artifacts with similar characteristics were produced at the same time. "Like goes with like"

- *Seriation:* assemblages of objects can be arranged in serial order to create a relative chronology

ENVIRONMENTAL SEQUENCES

So far in this chapter we have been discussing sequences that can be established either stratigraphically for individual sites, or typologically for artifacts. In addition, there is a major class of sequences, based on changes in the earth's climate, that has proved useful for relative dating on a local, regional, and even global scale. Some of these environmental sequences can also be dated by various absolute methods.

The Ice Age (or Pleistocene epoch, dating from 1.7 million years ago to 10,000 years ago), when world temperatures were usually much lower and ice covered large parts of the earth's surface, was not one long unbroken spell of cold. A complex sequence of cold periods (called *glacials*) were separated by warmer interludes (called *interglacials*). The interglacial period we now live in, known as the Holocene, covers the last 10,000 years. These climatic fluctuations are recorded in **deep-sea cores**, **ice cores**, and sediments containing pollen.

Deep-Sea Cores and Ice Cores.   The most coherent record of climatic changes on a worldwide scale is provided by deep-sea cores. These cores contain shells of microscopic marine organisms known as foraminifera, laid down on the ocean floor through the slow continuous process of sedimentation. Variations in the chemical structure of these shells are a good indicator of the sea temperature at the time the organisms were alive. Cold episodes in the deep-sea cores relate to glacial periods of ice advance, and the warm episodes to interglacial periods of ice retreat. Radiocarbon and uranium-series dating (see below) can also be applied to the foraminiferan shells to provide absolute dates for the sequence, which now stretches back 2.3 million years.

As with deep-sea cores, cores extracted from the polar ice of the Arctic and Antarctic have yielded impressive sequences revealing past climatic changes. The layers of compacted ice represent annual deposits for the last 2000–3000 years that can be counted – thus giving an absolute chronology for this part of the sequence. For earlier time periods – at greater depths – the annual stratification is no longer visible, and dating of the ice cores is much less certain. Good correlations have been made with climatic variations deduced from the study of the deep-sea cores.

Evidence of major volcanic eruptions can also be preserved in the ice cores, theoretically meaning that particular eruptions, such as the huge Thera eruption in the Aegean roughly 3500 years ago (associated by some scholars with the destruction of Minoan palaces on Crete), can be given a precise absolute date. In practice, though, it is hard to be certain that a volcanic event preserved in the ice actually relates to a particular historically documented eruption – it could relate to an unknown eruption that happened somewhere else in the world.

Pollen Dating. All flowering plants produce grains called pollen, and these are almost indestructible, surviving for many thousands (and even millions) of years in all types of conditions. Its preservation in bogs and lake sediments has allowed pollen experts (palynologists) to construct detailed sequences of past vegetation and climate. These sequences are an immense help in understanding ancient environments, but they have also been – and to some extent still are – important as a method of relative dating.

The best-known pollen sequences are those developed for the Holocene of northern Europe, where an elaborate succession of so-called *pollen zones* covers the last 10,000 years. By studying pollen samples from a particular site, that site can often be fitted into a broader pollen zone sequence and thus assigned a relative date. Isolated artifacts and finds such as bog bodies discovered in contexts where pollen is preserved can also be dated in the same way. However, it is important to remember that the pollen zones are not uniform across large areas. Regional pollen zone sequences must first be established, and then the sites and finds in the area can be linked to it. If tree-ring or radiocarbon dates are available for all or part of the sequence, we can work out an absolute chronology for the region.

Thanks to the durability of pollen grains, they can yield environmental evidence even as far back as 3 million years ago for sites in East Africa. Different interglacial periods in areas such as northern Europe have also been shown to have characteristic pollen sequences, which means that the pollen evidence at an individual site in the area can sometimes be matched to a particular interglacial – a useful dating mechanism since radiocarbon cannot be used for these early time periods.

KEY CONCEPTS:
ENVIRONMENTAL DATING METHODS

- *Deep-sea cores:* analysis of the chemical structure of microscopic marine organisms in datable layers of sediment can be used to reconstruct climate and provide a relative chronology

- *Ice cores:* similarly, layers of annual ice deposits can produce a chronology of world climate

- *Pollen dating:* pollen produced by past vegetation in a given area can reveal the climate of particular pollen zones and help to produce a relative chronology

The spans of time for which the main three absolute dating methods are applicable.

ABSOLUTE DATING

Although relative dating methods can be extremely useful, archaeologists ultimately want to know how old sequences, sites, and artifacts are in calendar years. To achieve this they need to use the methods of absolute dating described in the following sections. The three most commonly used and most important to the archaeologist are calendars and historical chronologies, tree-ring dating, and **radiocarbon dating**. DNA dating is also now beginning to be used to date population events.

CALENDARS AND HISTORICAL CHRONOLOGIES

Until the development of the first scientific dating techniques around the beginning of the twentieth century, dating in archaeology depended almost entirely on historical methods. That is to say, it relied on archaeological connections with chronologies and calendars that people in ancient times had themselves established. Such dating methods are still of immense value today.

In the ancient world, literate societies recorded their own history in written documents. In Egypt, the Near East, and ancient China, for example, history was recorded in terms of the successive kings, who were organized in groups of "dynasties." As we shall see, there were also very precise calendrical systems in Mesoamerica.

Archaeologists have to bear in mind three main points when working with early historical chronologies. First, the chronological system requires careful reconstruction, and any list of rulers or kings needs to be reasonably complete. Second, the list, although it may reliably record the number of years in each reign, has still to be linked with our own calendar. Third, the artifacts, **features**, or structures to be dated at a particular site have somehow to be related to the historical chronology, for example by their association with an inscription referring to the ruler of the time.

These points can be well illustrated by the Egyptian and Maya chronologies. Egyptian history is arranged in terms of 31 dynasties, themselves organized into the Old, Middle, and New Kingdoms. The modern view is a synthesis based on several documents including the so-called Turin Royal Canon. This synthesis gives an estimate of the number of years in each reign, right down to the conquest of Egypt by Alexander the Great in the year 332 BC (a date recorded by Greek historians). So the Egyptian dynasties can be dated by working backward from there, although the exact length of every reign is not known. This system can be confirmed and refined using astronomy: Egyptian historical records describe observations of certain astronomical events that can be independently dated using current astronomical knowledge and knowledge of where in Egypt the ancient observations were carried out. Egyptian dates are generally considered to be quite reliable after about 1500 BC, with a margin of error of perhaps one or two decades at most, but by the time we go back to the beginning of the dynastic period, around 3100 BC, the accumulated errors might amount to some 200 years or so.

Of the calendrical systems of Mesoamerica, the Maya calendar was the most elaborate and precise. It was used for recording exact dates of historical (and mythical) events in inscriptions on stone columns or **stelae** erected at Maya sites during the so-called Classic period (AD 300–900). The Maya had glyphs or signs for the days and the months, and a straightforward system of numerals, with a dot representing "one" and a bar "five." The Maya actually had two concurrent calendrical systems, the first of which, the Calendar Round, was used for everyday purposes. Any day in the Calendar Round was identified by the conjunction of two different cycles: a Sacred Round of 260 days, and a solar year of 365 days. Thus a specific day would only reoccur once every 52 years. The second system, the Long Count, recorded days past since a mythical zero or starting point – 13 August 3113 BC in terms of our own calendar – and was used to refer to historical (or future) dates. The understanding of the Maya calendar, and the more recent decipherment of the Maya glyphs, mean that a well-dated Maya history is now emerging in a way which seemed impossible a few decades ago.

Using a Historical Chronology

It is relatively easy for the archaeologist to use a historical chronology when abundant artifacts are found that can be related closely to it. Thus, at major Maya sites such as Tikal or Copan there are numerous stelae with calendrical inscriptions that can often be used to date the buildings with which they are associated. The artifacts associated with the buildings can in turn be dated: for instance, if a pottery typology has been worked out, the finding of known types of pottery in such historically dated contexts allows the pottery typology itself to be dated. Contexts and buildings on other sites lacking inscriptions can be dated approximately through the occurrence of similar pot types.

Sometimes artifacts themselves carry dates, or the names of rulers that can be dated. This is the case with many Maya ceramics that bear hieroglyphic inscriptions. For the Roman and medieval periods of Europe, coins normally carry the name of the issuing ruler, and inscriptions or records elsewhere usually allow the ruler to be dated. But it is crucial to remember that to date a coin or an artifact is not the same thing as to date the context in which it is found. The date of the coin indicates the year in which it was made. Its inclusion within a sealed archaeological deposit establishes simply a *terminus post quem* (Latin for "date after which"): in other words, the deposit can be no earlier than the date on the coin – but it could be later (perhaps much later) than that date.

A well-established historical chronology in one country may be used to date events in neighboring and more far-flung lands that lack their own historical records but are mentioned in the histories of the literate homeland. Similarly, archaeologists can use exports and imports of objects to extend chronological linkages by means of *cross-dating* with other regions. For instance, the presence of foreign pottery in well-dated ancient Egyptian contexts establishes a *terminus ante quem* ("date before which") for the manufacture of that pottery: it cannot be more recent than the Egyptian context. In addition, Egyptian objects, some with inscriptions allowing them to be accurately dated in Egyptian terms, occur at various sites outside Egypt, thereby helping to date the contexts in which they are found.

Dating by historical methods remains the most important procedure for the archaeologist in countries with a reliable calendar supported by a significant degree of literacy. Where there are serious uncertainties over the calendar, or over its correlation with the modern calendrical system, the correlations can often be checked using other absolute dating methods, to be described below.

Outside the historic and literate lands, however, cross-dating and broad typological comparisons have been almost entirely superseded by the various scientifically based dating methods described below. So that now, all the world's **cultures** can be assigned absolute dates.

ANNUAL CYCLES

Any absolute dating method depends on the existence of a regular, time-dependent process. The most obvious of these is the system by which we order our modern calendar: the rotation of the earth around the sun once each year. Because this yearly cycle produces regular annual fluctuations in climate, it has an impact on features of the environment which can in certain cases be measured to create a chronology. For absolute dating purposes the sequence needs to be a long one (with no gaps), linked somehow to the present day, and capable of being related to the structures or artifacts we actually want to date.

Evidence of these annual fluctuations in climate is widespread. For example, the changes in temperature in polar regions result in annual variations in the thickness of polar ice, which scientists can study from cores drilled through the ice (see section above, Environmental Sequences). Similarly, in lands bordering the polar regions, the melting of the ice sheets each year when temperatures rise leads to the formation of annual deposits of sediment in lake beds, called **varves**, which can be counted. Considerable deposits of varves were found in Scandinavia, representing thousands of years, stretching (when linked together) from the present back to the beginning of the retreat of the glacial ice sheets in Scandinavia some 13,000 years ago. The method allowed, for the first time, a fairly reliable estimate for the date of the end of the last Ice Age, and hence made a contribution to archaeological chronology not only in Scandinavia but in many other parts of the world as well.

But today, while varves remain of restricted use, another annual cycle, that of *tree-rings,* has come to rival radiocarbon as the main method of dating for the last few thousand years in many parts of Europe, North America, and Japan.

Tree-Ring Dating

The modern technique of **tree-ring dating** (**dendrochronology**) was developed by an American astronomer, A.E. Douglass, in the early decades of the last century – although many of the principles had been understood long before that. Working on well-preserved timbers in the arid American Southwest, by 1930 Douglass could assign absolute dates to many of the major sites there, such as Mesa Verde and Pueblo Bonito. But it was not until the end of the 1930s that the technique was introduced to Europe, and only in the 1960s that the use of statistical procedures and computers laid the foundations for the establishment of the long tree-ring chronologies now so fundamental to modern archaeology. Today dendrochronology has two distinct archaeological uses: (1) as a successful means of calibrating or correcting radiocarbon dates (see below); and (2) as an independent method of absolute dating in its own right.

Basis of Method.   Most trees produce a ring of new wood each year and these circles of growth can easily be seen in a cross-section of the trunk of a felled tree. These rings are not of uniform thickness. In an individual tree, they will vary for two reasons. First, the rings become narrower with the increasing age of the tree. Second, the amount a tree grows each year is affected by fluctuations in climate. In arid regions, rainfall above the average one year will produce a particularly thick annual ring. In more temperate regions, sunlight and temperature may be more critical than rainfall in affecting a tree's growth. Here, a sharp cold spell in spring may produce a narrow growth ring.

Dendrochronologists measure and plot these rings and produce a diagram indicating the thickness of successive rings in an individual tree. Trees of the same species growing in the same area will generally show the same pattern of rings so that the growth sequence can be matched between successively older timbers to build up a chronology for an area. (It is not necessary to fell trees in order to study the ring sequence: a usable sample can be extracted by boring without harming the tree.) By matching sequences of rings from living trees of different ages as well as

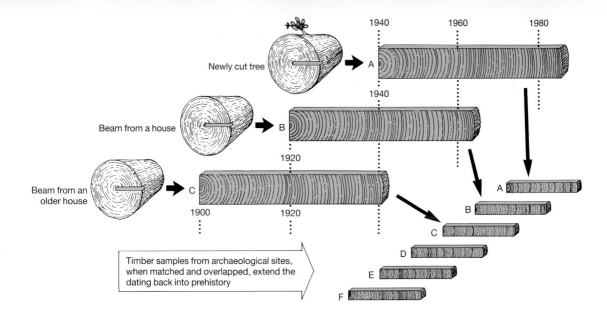

Tree-ring dating: annual growth rings can be counted, matched, and overlapped, to build up a master sequence for a particular region.

Timber samples from archaeological sites, when matched and overlapped, extend the dating back into prehistory

from old timber, dendrochronologists can produce a long, continuous sequence, such as that in the diagram above, extending back hundreds, even thousands, of years from the present. Thus, when an ancient timber of the same species (e.g. Douglas fir in the American Southwest or oak in Europe) is found, it should be possible to match its tree-ring sequence of, say, 100 years with the appropriate 100-year length of the master sequence or chronology. In this way, the felling date for that piece of timber can usually be dated to within a year.

Applications.   One of the most important uses of tree-ring dating has been the development of long tree-ring sequences, against which it is possible to check radiocarbon dates. The pioneering research was done in Arizona on a remarkable species, the Californian bristlecone pine which can live up to 4900 years. By matching samples from dead trees also, an unbroken sequence was built up back from the present as far as 6700 BC. The importance of this for the calibration of radiocarbon dates is discussed below. The research in the American Southwest has been complemented by studies in Europe of tree-rings of oak, often well preserved in waterlogged deposits. The oak sequence in Northern Ireland stretches back unbroken to *c.* 5300 BC, and the master sequence in western Germany to *c.* 8500 BC.

Direct tree-ring dating of preserved timber found in archaeological contexts has itself been important in several areas, but results are particularly impressive in the American Southwest, where the technique is longest established and wood is well preserved in the arid conditions. For instance, Betatakin, a cliff dwelling in Arizona, has been precision dated using dendrochronology, so that not only do we know that the settlement was founded in AD 1267, but we also can track the expansion of the site room by room, year by year until it reached a peak in the mid-1280s, before being abandoned shortly thereafter.

KEY CONCEPTS: TREE-RING DATING

- *Method:* based on the annual cycle of tree-ring growth

- *Date range:* 0–11,500 years ago

- *Applications:* direct dating of wood; calibration of radiocarbon dates

- *Limitations:* restricted to regions outside the tropics and to certain species of tree (although calibration is thought to work on a worldwide scale); care must be taken when interpreting results

Limiting Factors. Unlike radiocarbon, dendrochronology is not a worldwide dating method because of two basic limitations:

1 it applies only to trees in regions outside the tropics where pronounced differences between the seasons produce clearly defined annual rings;

2 for a direct tree-ring date it is restricted to wood from those species that (a) have yielded a master sequence back from the present and (b) people actually used in the past, and where (c) the sample affords a sufficiently long record to give a unique match.

In addition, there are important questions of interpretation to consider. A tree-ring date refers to the date of felling of the tree. This is determined by matching the tree-ring sample ending with the outermost rings (the sapwood) to a regional sequence. Where most or all of the sapwood is missing, the felling date cannot be identified. But even with an accurate felling date, the archaeologist has to make a judgment – based on context and formation processes – about how soon after felling the timber entered the archaeological deposit. Timbers may be older or younger than the structures into which they were finally incorporated, depending on whether they were reused from somewhere else, or used to make a repair in a long-established structure. The best solution is to take multiple samples, and to check the evidence carefully on-site. Despite these qualifications, dendrochronology looks set to become the major dating technique alongside radiocarbon for the last 8000 years in temperate and arid lands.

RADIOACTIVE CLOCKS

Many of the most important developments in absolute dating since World War II have come from the use of what might be called "radioactive clocks," based on that widespread and regular feature in the natural world, **radioactive decay**. The best known of these methods is radiocarbon, today the main dating tool for the last 50,000 years or so.

Radiocarbon Dating

Radiocarbon is the single most useful method of dating for the archaeologist. As we shall see, it has its limitations, both in terms of accuracy, and for the time range where it is useful. Archaeologists themselves are also the cause of major errors, thanks to poor sampling procedures and careless interpretation. Nevertheless, radiocarbon has transformed our understanding of the past, helping archaeologists to establish for the first time a reliable chronology of world cultures.

History and Basis of Method.   In 1949, the American chemist Willard Libby published the first radiocarbon dates. During World War II he had been studying cosmic radiation, the sub-atomic particles that constantly bombard the earth. These produce high-energy neutrons which in turn react with nitrogen atoms in the atmosphere to produce atoms of carbon-14 (^{14}C), or radiocarbon, which are unstable because they have eight neutrons in the nucleus instead of the usual six as for ordinary carbon (see box on the principles of radioactive decay below). This instability leads to radioactive decay of ^{14}C at a regular rate. Libby estimated that it took 5568 years for half the ^{14}C in any sample to decay – its **half-life** (see diagram opposite) – although modern research indicates that the more accurate figure is 5730 years.

THE PRINCIPLES OF RADIOACTIVE DECAY

Like most elements occurring in nature, carbon exists in more than one isotopic form. It has three isotopes: ^{12}C, ^{13}C, and ^{14}C – the numbers correspond to the atomic weights of these isotopes. In any sample of carbon 98.9 percent of atoms are of ^{12}C type and have six protons and six neutrons in the nucleus, and 1.1 percent are of the ^{13}C type with six protons and seven neutrons. Only one atom in a million millions of atoms of carbon will be that of the isotope ^{14}C with eight neutrons in the nucleus. This isotope of carbon is produced in the upper atmosphere by cosmic rays bombarding nitrogen (^{14}N) and it contains an excess of neutrons, making it unstable. It decays by the emission of weak beta radiation back to its precursor isotope of nitrogen – ^{14}N – with seven protons and seven neutrons in a nucleus. Like all types of radioactive decay the process takes place at a constant rate, independent of all environmental conditions.

The time taken for half of the atoms of a radioactive isotope to decay is called its half-life. In other words, after one half-life, there will be half of the atoms left; after two half-lives, one-quarter of the original quantity of isotope remains, and so on. In the case of ^{14}C, the half-life is now agreed to be 5730 years.

Half-lives of radioactive isotopes of other elements can range from thousands of millions of years to a minute fraction of a second. But in every case, there is a regular pattern to the decay.

Carbon-12 atom

Carbon-14 atom

● Neutron

● Proton

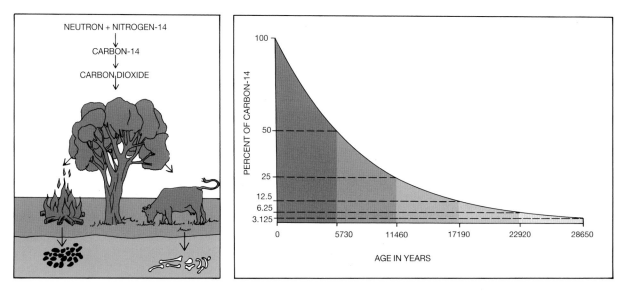

Libby realized that the decay of radiocarbon at a constant rate should be balanced by its constant production through cosmic radiation, and that therefore the proportion of ^{14}C in the atmosphere should remain the same throughout time. Furthermore, this steady atmospheric concentration of radiocarbon is passed on uniformly to all living things through carbon dioxide, as part of what is known as the "carbon cycle." Plants take up carbon dioxide during photosynthesis, they are eaten by herbivorous animals, which in turn are eaten by carnivores. When a plant or animal dies the uptake of ^{14}C ceases, and the steady concentration of ^{14}C begins to decline through radioactive decay. Thus, knowing the decay rate or half-life of ^{14}C, Libby recognized that the age of dead plant or animal tissue could be calculated by measuring the amount of radiocarbon left in a sample. Samples usually consist of organic materials found on archaeological sites, such as charcoal, wood, seeds, and other plant remains, and human or animal bone. Inorganic materials, like stone, are not part of the carbon cycle and so cannot be radiocarbon dated.

Libby's great practical achievement was to devise an accurate means of measurement. He discovered that each atom of ^{14}C decays by releasing beta particles, and he succeeded in counting these emissions using a Geiger counter, still the basis of the conventional method employed by many radiocarbon laboratories today. Advances were made in the late 1970s and early 1980s with the introduction of special gas counters capable of taking measurements from very small samples. In the conventional method some 5 g of pure carbon after purification were needed, which means an original sample of some 10–20 g of wood or charcoal, or 100–200 g of bone. The special gas-counting equipment required only a few hundred milligrams (mg) of charcoal.

Several laboratories now use the accelerator mass spectrometry (AMS) method, which requires smaller samples still. Disregarding their radioactivity, AMS counts

(Above left) Radiocarbon is produced in the atmosphere and absorbed by plants through carbon dioxide, and by animals through feeding off plants or other animals. Uptake of ^{14}C ceases when the plant or animal dies. (Above) After death, the amount of ^{14}C decays at a known rate (50 percent after 5730 years, etc.). Measurement of the amount left in a sample gives the date.

the atoms of ^{14}C directly. The minimum sample size is reduced to as little as 5–10 mg – thus enabling precious organic materials, such as the Turin Shroud (see below), to be sampled and directly dated, and making feasible the direct dating of pollen. Initially it was hoped that the datable timespan for radiocarbon using AMS could be pushed back from 50,000 to 80,000 years, although this is proving difficult to achieve, in part because of sample contamination.

Radiocarbon dates are usually quoted in years BP (before the present, currently taken to be AD 1950), but because the accurate measurement of the ^{14}C activity of a sample is affected by counting errors, background cosmic radiation, and other intrinsic factors, there is always an element of uncertainty to the measurements. Thus there is always a statistical error or "standard deviation" attached to a radiocarbon date, expressed as a plus/minus term. A radiocarbon date quoted as 3700 ±100 BP, for example, implies that there is a 68 percent probability, or two chances in three, that the correct estimate in radiocarbon years lies between 3800 and 3600 BP. Double the standard deviation, and there is a 95 percent chance (19 chances in 20) that the radiocarbon age of the sample lies between 3900 and 3500 BP. But there is a complication: these dates still do not, unfortunately, equate with true calendar years. To convert radiocarbon years into calendar years requires *calibration*.

Calibration of Radiocarbon Dates. One of the basic assumptions of the radiocarbon method has turned out to be not quite correct. Libby assumed that the concentration of ^{14}C in the atmosphere has been constant through time, but we now know that it has varied. The method that demonstrated the inaccuracy – tree-ring dating – has also provided the means of correcting or calibrating radiocarbon dates.

Radiocarbon dates obtained from tree-rings show that before about 1000 BC dates expressed in radiocarbon years are increasingly too young in relation to true calendar years. In other words, before 1000 BC trees (and all other living things) were exposed to greater concentrations of atmospheric ^{14}C than they are today. By obtaining radiocarbon dates systematically from the long tree-ring master sequences of bristlecone pine and oak (see above), scientists have been able to plot radiocarbon ages against tree-ring ages (in calendar years) to produce calibration curves, such as the one shown overleaf. Very broadly, these curves, show that radiocarbon ages diverge increasingly from true ages before 1000 BC, so that by 5000 BC in calendar years the radiocarbon age is 900 years too young. Thus an age estimate in radiocarbon years of 6050 BP might well in fact when calibrated be somewhere near 5000 BC. For dates beyond the scope of tree-ring dating, scientists have been able to use data from uranium-thorium dated corals and varve-counted marine sediments to produce a calibration curve going back some 24,000 years. The box opposite gives a more detailed explanation of the calibration process.

HOW TO CALIBRATE RADIOCARBON

Radiocarbon laboratories will generally supply calibrated dates of their samples, but archaeologists may need to calibrate raw radiocarbon dates themselves, usually from a calibration graph.

The section of tree-ring calibration curve shown in the diagram (below) illustrates the relationship between radiocarbon years (BP) and tree-ring samples dated in actual calendar years (Calibrated or "Cal" BC/AD).

The so-called wiggles in the curve can have a big impact on calibration: occasionally, sections of the curve run so flat that two samples with the same age in radiocarbon years might

in reality be 400 years apart in calendar years. This particularly affects the period 800–400 BC in calendar years.

In order to find the calibrated age range of a radiocarbon sample dated 2200 ±100 BP using this curve, the simplest method is to draw two horizontal lines (A1 and A2) from the appropriate dates on the radiocarbon years axis to the calibration curve, and drop lines (B1 and B2) from these intercept points to the calendar axis. The calibrated date is then quoted as the range enclosed between the vertical lines. In this instance the result would be an approximately 68

percent chance that the date of the sample falls between c. 395 Cal BC and 110 Cal BC. Doubling the standard deviation (to 200 years either side of 2200 BP in this case) results in a 95 percent chance that the date of the sample falls between c. 405 Cal BC and Cal AD 5.

Unfortunately, though, this method does not reflect the true complexity of the probability information stored in the radiocarbon result. A specialized form of statistical analysis, necessitating the use of a computer program, is required for a fully accurate calibration.

A calibrated age range of 405 Cal BC to Cal AD 5 is too broad to be useful for most archaeological purposes. There are two ways of narrowing the age range: high-precision dates and multiple dates. High-precision dates, obtainable so far from only a handful of the world's radiocarbon laboratories, can offer dates quoted with a realistic error of ±20 years, which, after calibration, generally allows the sample to be dated within a century or less (at the 95 percent probability level). Otherwise archaeologists use multiple dates of the same sample to produce mean dates with a smaller standard deviation.

Calibration programs and curves can be obtained directly from the *Radiocarbon* website at www.radiocarbon.org.

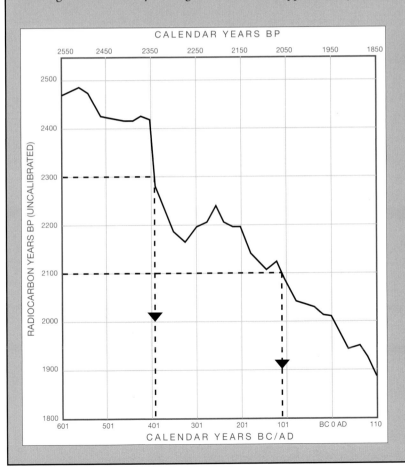

A section of calibration curve to show the simple intercept method to obtain calibrated dates.

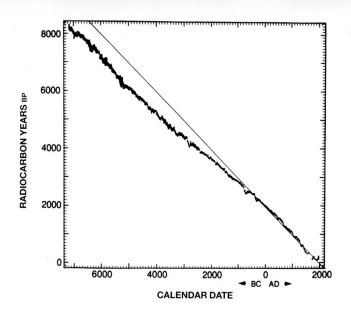

A calibrated radiocarbon timescale based on Irish oak. The straight line indicates the ideal 1:1 radiocarbon/ calendar age timescale.

Contamination and Interpretation of Radiocarbon Samples. Although radiocarbon dates have certain inescapable levels of error associated with them, inaccurate results are as likely to derive from poor sampling and incorrect interpretation by the archaeologist as from inadequate laboratory procedures. The major sources of error in the field are summed up below:

- *Contamination before sampling.* Problems of contamination of the sample within the ground can be serious. For instance, groundwater on waterlogged sites can dissolve organic materials and also deposit them, thus changing the amount of ^{14}C in a sample. These matters can usually be tackled in the laboratory.

- *Contamination during or after sampling.* Any modern organic material coming into contact with a sample can contaminate it, but some, such as roots and earth, cannot always be avoided. However, such sources of contamination can be eliminated in the laboratory.

- *Context of deposition.* Most errors in radiocarbon dating arise because the excavator has not fully understood the formation processes of the context in question. Unless it is appreciated how the organic material found its way to the position where it was found, and how and when (in terms of the site) it came to be buried, then precise interpretation is impossible.

- *Date of context.* Too often, it is assumed that a radiocarbon determination, e.g. on charcoal, will give a straightforward estimate for the date of the charcoal's burial context. However, if that charcoal derives from roof timbers that might themselves have been several centuries old when destroyed by fire, then some early construction is being dated, not the fire. For this reason, samples with a short life are often preferred, such as twigs of brushwood, or charred cereal grains that are not likely to be old at the time of burial.

KEY CONCEPTS: RADIOCARBON DATING

- *Method:* based on the regular decay of a radioactive isotope of carbon

- *Date range:* 400–50,000 years ago

- *Applications:* dating of any organic matter; new techniques allow very small sample sizes, meaning grain, seeds, and very precious objects can be dated

- *Calibration:* radiocarbon dates must be calibrated to arrive at a calendar date

- *Limitations:* samples must be carefully chosen; samples can easily be contaminated with more recent (or older) material; results can be difficult to interpret correctly and require statistical treatment

A strategy for sampling should be based on the wise saying that "one date is no date": several are needed. The best procedure is to work toward an internal relative sequence of dates – for instance, in the stratigraphic succession on a well-stratified site such as the Gatecliff Shelter, Monitor Valley, Nevada, shown overleaf. If the samples can be arranged in relative sequence in this way with the lowest unit having the earliest date and so on, then there is an internal check on the coherence of the laboratory determinations and on the quality of field sampling. Some of the dates from such a sequence may come out older than expected. This is quite reasonable as some of the material may have been "old" at the time of burial. But if they come out younger (i.e. more recent) than expected, then there is something wrong. Either some contamination has affected the samples, or the laboratory has made a serious error, or the stratigraphic interpretation is wrong.

The Impact of Radiocarbon Dating. Radiocarbon has undoubtedly offered the most generally useful way of answering the question "When?" in archaeology. The greatest advantage is that the method can be used anywhere, whatever the climate, as long as there is material of organic (i.e. living) origin. Thus the method works as well in South America or Polynesia as it does in Egypt or Mesopotamia. And it can take us back 50,000 years – although at the other end of the timescale it is too imprecise to be of much use for the 400 years of the most recent past. Radiocarbon has been incredibly important in establishing for the first time broad chronologies for the world's cultures that previously lacked timescales (such as calendars) of their own. Calibration of radiocarbon has increased, not diminished, this success.

Radiocarbon dating by the AMS technique is opening up new possibilities. Precious objects and works of art can now be dated because minute samples are all that is required. In 1988 AMS dating resolved the longstanding controversy over the age of the Turin Shroud, a piece of cloth with the image of a man's body on it

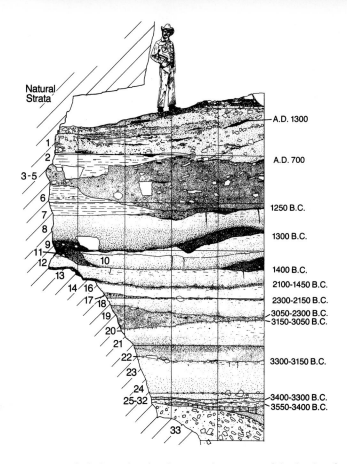

Natural Strata

1
2
3-5
6
7
8
9
11
12
10
13
14 16
17 18
19
20
21
22
23
24
25-32
33

A.D. 1300
A.D. 700
1250 B.C.
1300 B.C.
1400 B.C.
2100-1450 B.C.
2300-2150 B.C.
3050-2300 B.C.
3150-3050 B.C.
3300-3150 B.C.
3400-3300 B.C.
3550-3400 B.C.

Master profile for Gatecliff Shelter, Nevada, showing how dates derived from radiocarbon determinations are consistent with the stratigraphic succession.

that many genuinely believed to be the actual imprint of the body of Christ. Laboratories at Tucson, Oxford, and Zurich all placed it in the 14th century AD, not from the time of Christ at all, although this remains a matter of controversy.

Other Radiometric Methods

Radiocarbon is likely to maintain its position as the main dating tool back to 50,000 years ago for organic materials, but the half-life of radiocarbon is such that, for particularly old samples, there is hardly any radioactivity left to measure. So, for inorganic or very ancient materials, other methods have to be used. The most important of them are also radiometric – they depend upon the measurement of natural radioactivity. But they use elements whose radioactive isotopes have very much longer half-lives than the 5730 years of carbon-14. They have two drawbacks. In the first place, they depend upon elements less frequently found in archaeological contexts than is carbon. And secondly, the long half-lives generally mean that the datings are less precise.

Potassium-Argon Dating   The **potassium-argon** (K-Ar) method is used by geologists to date volcanic rocks hundreds or even thousands of millions of years old, but no more recent than around 100,000 years old.

KEY CONCEPTS

Potassium-Argon Dating

- Based on the decay of radioactive potassium-40 into argon-40

- Dates volcanic rocks, and the archaeological remains associated with them

Uranium Series Dating

- Based on the decay of radioactive isotopes of uranium

- Dates travertine (calcium carbonate), and associated archaeological remains

- Useful in areas where there is no volcanic activity

Fission-Track Dating

- Dates a variety of rocks and minerals which contain radioactive uranium-238

K-Ar dating is based on the steady but very slow decay of the radioactive isotope potassium-40 (^{40}K) to the inert gas argon-40 (^{40}AR) in volcanic rock. Knowing the decay rate of ^{40}K – its half life is around 1.3 billion years – a measure of the quantity of ^{40}Ar trapped within a 10g rock sample gives an estimate of the date of the rock's formation. The principal limitation of the technique is that it can only be used to date sites buried by volcanic rock.

The dates produced are effectively geological dates for the date of eruption leading to the formation of volcanic strata. Fortunately, some of the most important areas for the study of the Lower Paleolithic, notably the Rift Valley in East Africa, are areas of volcanic activity. The chronology of Olduvai Gorge, for example, which has provided important fossil remains of **Australopithecus**, *Homo habilis*, and *Homo erectus*, has been well established by K-Ar dating. At this and other similar sites, archaeological remains often lie on volcanic strata, which are suitable for K-Ar dating, and moreover they are often overlain by comparable volcanic rock, so that dates for these two geological strata provide a time range for the material we are trying to date.

Uranium-Series Dating This dating method is based on the radioactive decay of isotopes of uranium. It has proved particularly useful for the period 500,000 to 50,000 years ago, which again lies outside the time range of radiocarbon dating. In Europe, where there are relatively few volcanic rocks suitable for dating by the potassium-argon technique, **uranium series** (U-series) **dating** may be the method of first choice for early human sites – it has been used effectively, for example, on the skulls and other skeletal remains of very early *Homo sapiens* found at Qafzeh and Skhul caves in Israel.

The method dates the time of formation of travertine (calcium carbonate) which is often deposited on cave walls and floors, and hence can be used to date any material, such as an artifact or bone, embedded in a layer of travertine or in another type of sediment between two layers of it. The method is also applicable to teeth, since these absorb water soluble uranium when buried. High-precision measurement can give an error margin of less than 1000 years for a 100,000 year-old sample, and the method can also be cross-checked with **electron spin resonance** dates using the same materials (see below).

Fission-Track Dating **Fission-track dating** depends upon the spontaneous fission (or division) of radioactive uranium atoms (^{238}U), present in a wide range of rocks and minerals, which causes damage to the structures of the minerals involved. In materials where ^{238}U is present, such as volcanic and manufactured glasses, and minerals like zircon and apatite found within rock formations, the damage is recorded in pathways called fission tracks. The tracks can be counted in the laboratory under an optical microscope. Since we know the rate of fission of ^{238}U, this allows the date of formation of the rock or glass to be determined.

In this case, the radioactive clock is set at zero by the formation of the mineral or glass, either in nature (as with **obsidian**) or at the time of manufacture (as with manufactured glass). The method produces useful dates from suitable rocks that contain or are adjacent to those containing archaeological evidence, and has been used with success at early Paleolithic sites such as Olduvai Gorge, Tanzania, providing independent confirmation of potassium-argon and other results.

OTHER ABSOLUTE DATING METHODS

There are several more dating methods which can be used in special circumstances, but none is as important in practice to archaeologists as those already described. Some are of relevance to the solution of specific problems, such as the dating of Paleolithic rock art. Several of the most significant are mentioned below, so that the overview given in this chapter is reasonably complete. But the discussion here is deliberately kept brief, to give a flavour of a field which can easily become rather complicated, yet which is not directly relevant to much mainstream archaeology. The rather special case of DNA dating is of particular interest.

Thermoluminescence Dating **Thermoluminescence** (TL) dating can be used to date crystalline materials (minerals) buried in the ground which have been fired – usually pottery, but also baked clay, burnt stone, and in some circumstances

KEY CONCEPTS

Thermoluminescence Dating

- Dates minerals that have been sufficiently heated and then buried

- Can be applied to pottery, other baked clay, and burnt stone

- Methodological complications and limited accuracy

Optical Dating

- Similar to TL dating, but dates minerals that have been exposed to light and then buried

Electron Spin Resonance Dating

- Dates tooth enamel, bone and shell

Archaeomagnetism and Geomagnetic reversals

- Changes in the Earth's magnetic field over time can be tracked in the archaeological record

burnt soil. But unfortunately it is a method which is difficult to make precise, and so it is generally used when other methods, such as radiocarbon dating, are not available.

Like many other methods it depends upon radioactive decay, but in this case it is the amount of radioactivity received by the specimen since the start date which is of interest, not the radiation emitted by the specimen itself. When atoms located within the structure of a mineral are exposed to radiation from the decay of radioactive elements in the nearby environment, some of that energy is "trapped." If the amount of radiation remains constant over time, then this energy will accumulate at a uniform rate and the total amount of energy will depend upon the total time of exposure. When a sample is heated to 500°C or more, the trapped energy is released as thermoluminescence, and the "radioactive clock" is set back to zero.

This means that archaeological artifacts, such as pottery, will have had their clocks reset when they were originally fired, and that by reheating samples from these objects, we can measure the thermoluminescence released and hence date the material. The main complication of the method is that the level of background radiation that a sample might have been exposed to is not uniform – it must be measured for every sample by burying a small capsule containing a radiation-sensitive material, or by using a radiation counter, at the exact spot the sample was found. In general, the difficulties of making these measurements mean that TL dates rarely have a precision of better than ±10 percent of the age of the sample.

A good example of the archaeological application of TL is the dating of the terracotta head known as the Jemaa head, from the alluvium of a tin mine near the Jos Plateau of Nigeria. The head and similar examples belong to the Nok culture, but such sculptures could not be dated reliably at the site of Nok itself because of the lack of any plausible radiocarbon dates. A TL reading on the head gave an age of 1520 ±260 BC, allowing this and similar heads from the Nok region to be given a firm chronological position for the first time.

Optical Dating   This method is similar in principle to TL, but it is used to date minerals that have been exposed to light, rather than heat. Most minerals contain some trapped energy that will be released by several minutes' exposure to sunlight. Such exposure is in effect the start point. Once buried they begin to accumulate electrons once more as a result of radioactive radiation experienced in the soil. In the laboratory, optically stimulated luminescence (OSL) is produced by directing light of a visible wavelength onto the sample, and the resultant luminescence is measured. And once again the background radiation at the place of burial has to be measured, so optical dating suffers from many of the same complications as TL.

Electron Spin Resonance Dating   Electron spin resonance (ESR) is a technique similar to but less sensitive than TL, but it can be used for materials which decompose when heated and thus where TL is not applicable. Its most successful application so far has been for the dating of tooth enamel. Newly formed tooth enamel contains no trapped energy, but it begins to accumulate once the tooth is buried and exposed to natural background radiation. The precision of the method when used to date tooth enamel is in the order of 10–20 percent, but it is still very useful for the study of early humans and the cross-checking of other dating methods.

Archaeomagnetic Dating and Geomagnetic Reversals   **Archaeomagnetic** (or Paleomagnetic) **dating** has so far been of limited use in archaeology. It is based on the constant change, both in direction and intensity, of the earth's magnetic field. The direction of that magnetic field at a particular time is recorded in any baked clay structure (oven, kiln, hearth etc.) that has been heated to a temperature of 650 to 700°C. At that temperature the iron particles in the clay permanently take up the earth's magnetic direction and intensity at the time of firing. This principle is called *thermoremanent magnetism* (TRM). Charts can be built up of the variation through time which can be used to date baked clay structures of unknown age, whose TRM is measured and then matched to a particular point on the master sequence.

Another aspect of Archaeomagnetism, relevant for the dating of the Lower Paleolithic, is the phenomenon of complete reversals in the earth's magnetic field (magnetic north becomes magnetic south, and vice versa). The most recent major reversal occurred about 780,000 years ago, and a sequence of such reversals stretching back several millions of years has been built up with the aid of potassium-argon and other dating techniques. The finding of part of this sequence of reversals in the rock strata of African early hominid sites has proved a helpful check on the other dating methods that have been used at those sites.

DNA Dating   The methods now being used by molecular geneticists present rather a special case. They use DNA samples from living human populations to date population events, notably migrations. Using assumptions about genetic mutation rates they can date approximately the appearance of new genetic categories and so give a date to such important processes such as the 'out-of-Africa' dispersal of our species (around 60,000–55,000 years ago). It is the information within living humans that provides the data, not ancient excavated samples: our past within us!

WORLD CHRONOLOGY

As a result of the application of the various dating techniques discussed above, it is possible to summarize the world archaeological chronology, from the evolution of human ancestors millions of years ago in Africa, to the spread of our own species around the world, and the eventual development of agriculture and complex societies.

WORLD CHRONOLOGY: KEY EVENTS

- Earliest stone tools — 2.5 million years ago
- Acheulian hand-axes — 1.6 million years ago
- *Homo sapiens sapiens* — at least 100,000 years ago
- First Australians — 45,000 years ago
- First Americans — 14,000 years ago or more
- First farmers — at least 10,000 years ago in the Near East
  9,000 years ago in China
  9,000 years ago in the Americas
  8,500 years ago in Europe
- First state societies — 5,500 years ago in the Near East
  3,500 years ago in China
  3,500 years ago in the Americas

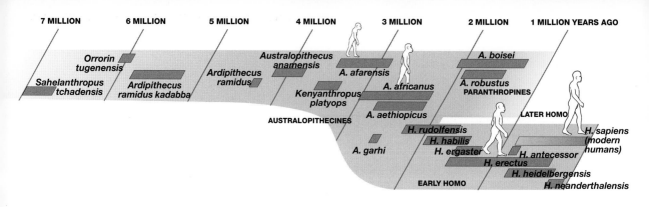

Paleoanthropologists hold strongly differing views on how the fossil remains for human evolution should be interpreted. This family tree presents the evidence as four adaptive radiations: the australopithecines, paranthropines, early *Homo*, and later *Homo* (including modern humans).

The human story as understood at present begins in East Africa, with the emergence there of the earliest hominids of the genus *Australopithecus*, such as *A. afarensis*, around 4 million years ago, and the possibly earlier *Ardipithecus*. By around 2 million years ago, there is clear fossil evidence for the first known representative of our own genus, *Homo habilis*, from such sites as Koobi Fora (Kenya) and Olduvai Gorge (Tanzania). The earliest stone tools (from Hadar, Ethiopia) date from about 2.5 million years ago, but it is not known which hominid made them because *Homo habilis* fossils of this age have not yet been found. It is possible that australopithecines also had a tool culture before or during *Homo habilis*'s time. The early toolkits, comprising flake and pebble tools, are called the **Oldowan industry**, after Olduvai Gorge where they are particularly well represented.

By more than 1.6 million years ago, the next stage in human evolution, *Homo erectus*, had emerged in East Africa. These hominids had larger brains than *Homo habilis*, their probable ancestor, and were makers of the characteristic teardrop-shaped stone tools flaked on both sides called Acheulian hand-axes. These artifacts are the dominant tool form of the Lower Paleolithic. By the time *Homo erectus* became extinct (400,000–200,000 years ago), the species had colonized the rest of Africa, southern, eastern, and western Asia, and central and western Europe.

The Middle Paleolithic period – from about 200,000 to 40,000 years ago – saw the emergence of *Homo sapiens*. Neanderthals, who are generally classed as a subspecies of *Homo sapiens* (*Homo sapiens neanderthalensis*), lived in Europe, and western and central Asia from about 130,000 to 30,000 years ago, when they died out. There is increasing evidence for fully modern people – that is our own subspecies, *Homo sapiens sapiens* – in Africa by at least 100,000 years ago. An archaic variety seems to have reached the eastern Mediterranean 100,000–90,000 years ago but probably became extinct. The ancestors of all modern humans beyond Africa seem to have participated in an "out-of-Africa" expansion around 60,000 years ago, reaching Europe and Asia by at least 40,000 years ago. Australia was colonized by humans at least 50,000 years ago (the date is currently being hotly debated, since it falls at the very limit of radiocarbon dating).

It is uncertain when humans first crossed from northeastern Asia into North America across the Bering Strait, and south to Central and South America. The earliest secure dates for early Americans are around 14,000 years ago, but there is controversial evidence that the continent was populated before then.

By 10,000 BC, most of the land areas of the world, except the deserts and Antarctica, were populated. The most conspicuous exception is the Pacific, where Western Polynesia does not seem to have been colonized until the 1st millennium BC, and Eastern Polynesia progressively from *c.* AD 300. By around AD 1000 the colonization of Oceania was complete. The spread of humans around the world is summarized in the map overleaf.

Nearly all the groups of humans so far mentioned may be regarded as **hunter-gatherer** societies, made up of relatively small groups of people.

One of the most significant occurrences in world history or **prehistory** at a global level is the development of food production, based on domesticated plant species and also (although in some areas to a lesser extent) of domesticated animal species. One of the most striking facts of world prehistory is that the transition from hunting and gathering to food production seems to have occurred independently in several areas, in each case after the end of the Ice Age, i.e. after *c.* 10,000 years ago.

In the Near East, we can recognize the origins of this transition even before this time, for the process may have been gradual, the consequence (as well as the cause) of restructuring of the social organization of human societies. At any rate, well-established farming, dependent on wheat and barley as well as sheep and goats (and later cattle), was under way there by about 8000 BC. Farming had spread to Europe by 6500 BC, and is documented in South Asia at Mehrgarh in Baluchistan at about the same time.

A separate development, based at first on the cultivation of millet, seems to have taken place in China, in the valley of the Huang Ho by 5000 BC or even earlier. Rice cultivation began at about the same time in the Yangzi Valley in China and spread to Southeast Asia. The position in Africa south of the Sahara is more complicated due to the diversity of environments, but millet and sorghum wheat were cultivated by the 3rd millennium BC. The Western Pacific (Melanesian) complex of root and tree crops had certainly developed by that time: indeed, there are indications of field drainage for root crops very much earlier.

In the Americas, a different range of crops was available. Cultivation of beans, squash, peppers, and some grasses may have begun by 7000 or even 8000 BC in Peru, and was certainly under way there and in Mesoamerica by the 7th millennium BC. Other South American species, including manioc and potato, were soon

First colonization of the world by modern humans, with very approximate dates – in years BP – and ice sheets (darker shading) and low sea levels (white areas outside present coastline) of *c.* 18,000 BP. Many scholars believe the Americas were settled as early as 30,000–15,000 BP.

added, but the plant with the greatest impact on American agriculture was maize, believed to have been brought into cultivation in Mexico by 5600 years ago, though possibly earlier in northwest Argentina.

These agricultural innovations were rapidly adopted in some areas (e.g. in Europe), but in others, such as North America, their impact was less immediate. Certainly, by the time of Christ, hunter-gatherer economies were very much in the minority.

The urban revolution, the next major transformation that we recognize widely, is not simply a change in settlement type: it reflects profound social changes. Foremost among these is the development of **state** societies displaying more clearly differentiated institutions of government than do **chiefdoms**. Many state societies had writing. We see the first state societies in the Near East by about 3500 BC, in Egypt only a little later, and in the Indus Valley by 2500 BC. In the Near East, the period of the early Mesopotamian city-states was marked by the rise of famous sites such as Ur, Uruk, and later Babylon, and was followed in the 1st millennium BC by an age of great empires, notably those of Assyria and Achaemenid Persia. In Egypt, it is possible to trace the continuous development of cultural and political traditions over more than 2000 years, through the pyramid age of the Old Kingdom and the imperial power of New Kingdom Egypt.

On the western edge of the Near East, further civilizations developed: Minoans and Mycenaeans in Greece and the Aegean during the 2nd millennium BC, Etruscans and Romans in the 1st millennium BC. At the opposite end of Asia, state societies with urban centers appear in China before 1500 BC, marking the beginnings of the Shang civilization. At about the same time, Mesoamerica saw the rise of the Olmec, the first in a long sequence of Central American civilizations including Maya, Zapotec, Toltec, and Aztec. On the Pacific coast of South America, the Chavín (from 900 BC), Moche, and Chimú civilizations laid the foundations for the rise of the vast and powerful Inca empire that flourished in the 15th century AD.

The further pattern is the more familiar one of literate history, with the rise of the Classical world of Greece and Rome as well as of China, and then of the world of Islam, the Renaissance of Europe and the development of the colonial powers. From the 18th century to the present there followed the independence of the former colonies, first in the Americas, then in Asia and in Africa. We are talking now not simply of state societies but of nation states and, especially in colonial times, of empires.

SUMMARY

• The answer to the question "When?" in archaeology has two main components. Relative dating methods allow us to determine that something is *relatively* older or younger than something else. Absolute methods make it possible to give a date in years. Archaeological dating is at its most reliable when the two methods are used together, e.g. when the relative order assigned to layers in an excavation can be confirmed by absolute dates for each layer. Wherever possible, results from one absolute method should be cross-checked by those from another.

• In areas where ancient calendars and historical chronologies are available, such as Mesoamerica, these remain one of the most important methods of dating. Elsewhere, the two methods most useful to the archaeologist are radiocarbon dating and tree-ring dating. Although many other absolute dating techniques exist, these tend to be reserved either for very specific applications or for sites that are beyond the range of radiocarbon back in the Paleolithic period.

• Ultimately the precision of dating attainable for each period helps determine the kinds of questions we ask about the past – for the Paleolithic, questions are about long-term change; for later periods, the questions are more usually concerned with the shorter-term variations in worldwide human development.

FURTHER READING

The following provide a good introduction to the principal dating techniques used by archaeologists:

Aitken, M.J. 1990. **Science-based Dating in Archaeology.** LONGMAN: LONDON & NEW YORK.

Biers, W.R. 1993. **Art, Artefacts and Chronology in Classical Archaeology.** ROUTLEDGE: LONDON.

Bowman, S.G.E. 1990. **Radiocarbon Dating.** BRITISH MUSEUM PUBLICATIONS: LONDON; UNIVERSITY OF TEXAS PRESS: AUSTIN.

Brothwell, D.R. & Pollard, A.M. (eds.). 2001. **Handbook of Archaeological Sciences.** WILEY: CHICHESTER & NEW YORK.

Taylor, R.E. & Aitken, M.J. (eds.). 1997. **Chronometric Dating in Archaeology.** PLENUM: NEW YORK.

Wintle, A.G. 1996. **Archaeologically relevant dating techniques for the next century.** JOURNAL OF ARCHAEOLOGICAL SCIENCE 23, 123–38.

5 How Were Societies Organized?

social archaeology

Some of the most interesting questions we can ask about early societies are social. They are about people and about relations between people, about the exercise of power, and about the nature and scale of organization. But the answers are not directly visible in the archaeological record: we have to ask the right questions of the data, and devise the means of answering them.

In this respect **archaeology** is very different from cultural or social **anthropology**, where the observer can actually visit the living society and rapidly form conclusions about its social and power structures before moving on to other more complex matters, such as the details of the kinship system or the minutiae of ritual behavior. The archaeologist has to work hard to gain even basic details of these kinds, but the prize is a rich one: an understanding of the social organization not just of societies in the present or very recent past (like cultural anthropology) but of societies at many different points in time, with all the scope that that offers for studying change. Only the archaeologist can obtain that perspective, and hence seek some understanding of the processes of long-term change.

Different kinds of society need different kinds of question and the techniques of investigation will need to vary radically with the nature of the evidence. We cannot tackle a **Paleolithic hunter-gatherer** camp in the same way as the capital city of an early **state**. Thus, the questions we put, and the methods for answering them, must be tailored to the sort of community we are dealing with. So it is all the more necessary to be clear at the outset about the general nature of that community, which is why the most basic social questions are always the first ones to ask.

We must first address the size or *scale* of the society. The archaeologist will often be excavating a single site. But was that an independent political unit, like a Maya or Greek city-state, or a simpler unit, like the base camp of a hunter-gatherer group? Or was it, on the other hand, a small cog in a very big wheel, a subordinate settlement in some far-flung empire, like that of the Incas of Peru? Any site we consider will have its own hinterland, or catchment area, for the feeding of its population. But one of our interests is to go beyond that local area, and to understand how that site interacts with others. From the standpoint of the individual site – which is often a convenient perspective to adopt – that raises questions of *dominance*. Was the site politically independent, autonomous? Or, if it was part of a larger social system, did it take a dominant part (like the capital city of a kingdom) or a subordinate one?

If the scale of the society is a natural first question, the next is certainly its internal organization. What kind of society was it? Were the people forming it on a more-or-less equal social footing? Or were there instead prominent differences in status, rank, and prestige within the society – perhaps different social classes? And what of the professions: were there people who specialized in particular crafts? And if so, were they controlled within a centralized system, as in some of the palace economies of the Near East and Egypt? Or was this a freer economy, with a flourishing free exchange, where merchants could operate at will in their own interest?

These questions, however, may all be seen as "top-down" questions, looking at the society from above and investigating its organization. But increasingly an alternative perspective is being followed, looking first at the individual, and at the way the identity of the individual in the society in question is defined – a "bottom-up" perspective. Archaeologists are coming to realize that the way such important social aspects as gender, status, and even age are constituted in a society are not "givens," but are specific to each different society. These insights are leading to new fields: the archaeology of the individual and the archaeology of identity.

ESTABLISHING THE NATURE AND SCALE OF THE SOCIETY

The first step in social archaeology is so obvious that it is often overlooked. It is to ask, what was the scale of the largest social unit, and what kind of society, in a very broad sense, was it? The largest social unit could be anything from a small and completely independent hunter-gatherer **band** to a great empire. In the case of a complex society it can comprise many lesser units.

In terms of research in the field, the question is often best answered from a study of settlement: both in terms of the scale and nature of *individual sites* and in relationships between them, through the analysis of *settlement pattern*. But we should not forget that *written records*, where a society is literate and uses writing, *oral tradition*, and *ethnoarchaeology* – the study from an archaeological point of view of present-day societies – can be equally valuable in assessing the nature and scale of the society under review.

First, however, we need a frame of reference, a hypothetical classification of societies against which to test our ideas.

Classification of Societies

The American anthropologist Elman Service developed a four-fold classification of societies that many archaeologists have found useful, though his terminology has since been amended. Particular kinds of site and settlement pattern are associated with each of the societies. Some archaeologists question the value of broad classifications such as "**chiefdom**", but at a preliminary stage of analysis they are useful, especially if they are not taken too seriously. The classification is summarized in the box opposite.

Mobile hunter-gatherer groups. These are small-scale societies of hunters and gatherers (sometimes called "bands"), generally of fewer than 100 people, who move

KEY CONCEPTS: THE CLASSIFICATION OF SOCIETIES

	MOBILE HUNTER-GATHERER GROUPS	SEGMENTARY SOCIETY	CHIEFDOM	STATE
	San hunters, South Africa	Man plowing, Valcamonica, Italy	Horseman, Gundestrup caldron	Terracotta army, tomb of first emperor of China
TOTAL NUMBERS	Less than 100	Up to few 1000	5000–20,000+	Generally 20,000+
SOCIAL ORGANIZATION	Egalitarian Informal leadership	Segmentary society Pan-tribal associations Raids by small groups	Kinship-based ranking under hereditary leader High-ranking warriors	Class-based hierarchy under king or emperor Armies
ECONOMIC ORGANIZATION	Mobile hunter-gatherers	Settled farmers Pastoralist herders	Central accumulation and redistribution Some craft specialization	Centralized bureaucracy Tribute-based Taxation Laws
SETTLEMENT PATTERN	Temporary camps	Permanent villages	Fortified centers Ritual centers	Urban: cities, towns Frontier defenses Roads
RELIGIOUS ORGANIZATION	Shamans	Religious elders Calendrical rituals	Hereditary chief with religious duties	Priestly class Pantheistic or monotheistic religion
ARCHITECTURE	Temporary shelters Paleolithic skin tents, Siberia	Permanent huts Burial mounds Shrines Neolithic shrine, Çatalhöyük, Turkey	Large-scale monuments Stonehenge, England - final form	Palaces, temples, and other public buildings Pyramids at Giza Castillo, Chichén Itzá, Mexico
ARCHAEOLOGICAL EXAMPLES	All Paleolithic societies, including Paleo-Indians	All early farmers (Neolithic/Archaic)	Many early metalworking and Formative societies	All ancient civilizations, e.g. in Mesoamerica, Peru, Near East, India and China; Greece and Rome
MODERN EXAMPLES	Inuit San, southern Africa Australian Aborigines	Pueblos, Southwest USA New Guinea Highlanders Nuer and Dinka, E. Africa	Northwest Coast Indians, USA 18th-century Polynesian chiefdoms in Tonga, Tahiti, Hawaii	All modern states

seasonally to exploit wild food resources. Most surviving hunter-gatherer groups today are of this kind, such as the San of southern Africa. Band members are generally kinsfolk, related by descent or marriage, and bands do not have formal leaders, so there are no marked economic differences or disparities in status among their members.

Because bands are mobile groups, their sites consist mainly of seasonally occupied camps, and other smaller and more specialized sites. These include kill or butchery sites – locations where large mammals are killed and sometimes butchered – and work sites, where tools are made or other specific activities carried out. Camps may show evidence of insubstantial dwellings or temporary shelters, along with the debris of residential occupation.

During the Paleolithic period (before 12,000 years ago) most archaeological sites seem to conform to one or other of these categories – camp sites, kill sites, work sites – and archaeologists usually operate on the assumption that most Paleolithic societies were organized into bands.

Segmentary societies.   These are generally larger than mobile hunter-gatherer groups, but their population rarely numbers more than a few thousand, and their diet or subsistence is based largely on cultivated plants and domesticated animals. They are sometimes referred to as **tribes**. Typically, they are settled farmers, but they may be nomad pastoralists with a mobile economy based on the intensive exploitation of livestock. **Segmentary societies** generally consist of many individual communities integrated into the larger society through kinship ties. Although some have officials and even a "capital" or seat of government, such officials lack the economic base necessary for effective use of power.

The typical settlement pattern for segmentary societies is one of settled agricultural homesteads or villages. Characteristically, no one settlement dominates any of the others in the region. Instead, the archaeologist finds evidence for isolated, permanently occupied houses (a *dispersed* settlement pattern) or for permanent villages (a *nucleated* pattern). Such villages may be made up of a collection of free-standing houses, like those of the first farmers of the Danube valley in Europe, *c.* 4500 BC. Or they may be clusters of buildings grouped together – so-called *agglomerate* structures, for example, the pueblos of the American Southwest.

Chiefdoms.   These societies are characterized by ranking – differences in social status between people. Different **lineages** (a lineage is a group claiming descent from a common ancestor) are graded on a scale of prestige, and the senior lineage, and hence the society as a whole, is governed by a chief. Prestige and rank are determined by closeness of relationship to the chief. There is no true stratification into classes, and the role of the chief is crucial. Chiefdoms vary greatly in size, but the range is generally between about 5000 and 20,000 persons.

Often, there is local specialization in craft production, and surpluses of these and of foodstuffs are periodically paid as obligations to the chief. He uses these to maintain his close personal followers, and may use them for redistribution to his subjects.

The chiefdom generally has a center of power, often with temples, residences of the chief and his retainers, and craft specialists. It is a permanent ritual and ceremonial center that acts as a central focus for the entire group. However, this is not a permanent urban center (such as a city) with an established bureaucracy, as we find in state societies. But chiefdoms do give indications that some sites were more important than others (or in other words, that there was a site hierarchy). An example is Moundville in Alabama, USA, which flourished *c.* AD 1000–1500 (see box on pp. 144–145).

The personal ranking characteristic of chiefdom societies is also visible in the very rich grave-goods that often accompany the burials of deceased chiefs.

Early States.   These share many of the features of chiefdoms, but the ruler (perhaps a king or sometimes a queen) has explicit authority to establish laws and also to enforce them by the use of a standing army. Society no longer depends totally upon kin relationships: it is now stratified into different classes. Agricultural workers or serfs and the poorer urban dwellers form the lowest classes, with the craft specialists above, and the priests and kinsfolk of the ruler higher still. The functions of the ruler are often separated from those of the priest: palace is distinguished from temple. The territory is "owned" by the ruling lineage and populated by tenants who have an obligation to pay taxes. Taxes and other revenues are collected by officials based in the central capital, and then distributed to government, army, and craft specialists. Many early states developed complex redistributive systems to support these essential services.

Early state societies generally show a characteristic urban settlement pattern in which *cities* play a prominent part. The city is typically a large population center (often of more than 5000 inhabitants) with major public buildings, including temples and work places for the administrative bureaucracy. Often, there is a pronounced settlement hierarchy, with the capital city as the major center, and with subsidiary or regional centers as well as local villages.

This rather simple social typology should not be used unthinkingly. For instance, there is some difference between the rather vague idea of the "tribe" and the more modern concept of the "segmentary society." The term "tribe," implying a larger grouping of smaller units, carries with it the assumption that these communities share a common ethnic identity and self-awareness, which is now known not generally to be the case. The term "segmentary society" refers to a relatively small and autonomous group, usually of agriculturalists, who regulate their own affairs: in some cases, they may join together with other comparable segmentary societies to form a larger ethnic unit or "tribe"; in other cases, they do not. For the remainder of this chapter, we shall therefore refer to *segmentary societies* in preference to the term "tribe." And what in Service's typology were called "bands" are now more generally referred to as "mobile hunter-gatherer groups."

Certainly, it would be wrong to overemphasize the importance of the four types of society given above, or to spend too long trying to decide whether a specific group should be classed in one category rather than another. It would also be wrong to assume that somehow societies inevitably evolve from hunter-gatherer groups to segmentary societies, or from chiefdoms to states. One of the challenges of archaeology is to attempt to explain why some societies become more complex and others do not.

Nevertheless, Service's categories provide a good framework to help organize our thoughts. They should not, however, deflect us from focusing on what we are really looking for: changes over time in the different institutions of a society – whether in the social sphere, the organization of the food quest, technology, contact and exchange, or spiritual life. Archaeology has the unique advantage of being able to study processes of change over thousands of years, and it is these processes we are seeking to isolate. Fortunately there are sufficiently marked differences between simple and more complex societies for us to find ways of doing this.

As we saw above in the description of Service's four types of society, complex societies show in particular an increased specialization in, or separation between, different aspects of their **culture**. In complex societies people no longer combine, say, the tasks of obtaining food, making tools, or performing religious rites but become specialists at one or other of these tasks, either as full-time farmers, craftspeople, or priests. As technology develops, for example, groups of individuals may acquire particular expertise in pottery-making or metallurgy, and will become full-time *craft specialists*, occupying distinct areas of a town or city and thus leaving distinct traces for the archaeologist to discover. Likewise, as farming develops and population grows, more food will be obtained from a given piece of land (food production will *intensify*) through the introduction of the plow or irrigation. As this specialization and intensification take place, so too does the tendency for some people to become wealthier and wield more authority than others – differences in social status and *ranking* develop.

It is the methods for looking at these processes of increasing specialization, intensification, and social ranking that help us identify the presence of more complex societies in the archaeological record. For simpler groups like hunter-gatherers, other methods are needed if we are to identify them archaeologically, as will become apparent.

METHODS OF SOCIAL ANALYSIS

Different methods are suitable for investigating the social interactions and social structures of different kinds of societies. The principal source of data about early societies comes from settlement analysis and **excavation**. The study of burials with their associated **artifacts** is often a very good way of assessing the dress, possessions and status of deceased individuals in a society. For some societies, the study of the monuments which they have built can also be very informative.

The data available from a hunter-gatherer camp are naturally very different from those from a city. For one thing, state societies are often literate societies, and written records may be available. For societies for which no written testimony is available, archaeologists have often relied upon ethnographic analogy, drawing upon what anthropologists have observed in more recent non-urban societies so as to suggest interpretations for what is found in the archaeological record. Ethnoarchaeology, as this field is known, seeks to use the experience derived from living societies to suggest interpretive and explanatory approaches to archaeological data.

KEY CONCEPTS: METHODS OF SOCIAL ANALYSIS

- *Settlement Analysis:* the main method of investigating past social organization. Data are collected by survey and excavation, but the specific methods used can vary greatly depending on the society in question

- *Burial Analysis:* rank and social status are best revealed by the analysis of grave-goods within individual burials

- *Monuments and Public Works:* the scale of monuments and public works, as well as their distribution, can be a good indicator of social organization

- *Written Records:* an excellent source of information about the organization of early state societies

- *Ethnoarchaeology:* the study of living societies in order to help interpret the past, with a specific emphasis on the use and significance of artifacts, buildings and structures, and how these material things might become incorporated into the archaeological record

Settlement analysis and site hierarchy

One of the principal ways of answering the basic question "what is the scale of the society" is through an understanding of *settlement pattern*, and this can only come from survey. Whatever the period in question, we should be interested in finding the major center or centers of settlement along with any smaller **sites**. We can use many of the survey, sampling, and remote sensing techniques described in Chapter 3 to do this, but the exact nature of the work will depend on the society in question – it is much harder to find the scanty traces that are left by mobile hunter-gatherers than it is to find an ancient city, so more intensive survey is needed.

Any survey will result in a map and a catalog of the sites discovered, together with details of each site including size, chronological range (as may be determined from surface remains such as pottery), architectural features, and possibly an approximate estimate of population. The aim is then to reach some classification of the sites on the basis of their relative importance – a *site hierarchy*. Possible categories for the different types of site encountered might include, for instance, Regional Center, Local Center, Nucleated Village, Dispersed Village, and Hamlet.

Various techniques can be used to establish the site hierarchy of a region, but the simplest is based solely on site size. Sites are arranged in rank order by size and then displayed as a histogram, which will usually show that the small sites are the most frequent. Such histograms allow comparisons to be made between the site hierarchies of different regions, different periods, and different types of society. In band societies, for example, there will usually be only a narrow range of variation in site size and all the sites will be relatively small. State societies, on the other hand, will have both hamlets and farmsteads and large towns and cities. The degree to which a single site is dominant within a settlement system will also be evident from this type of analysis, and the organization of the settlement system will often be a direct reflection of the organization of the society which created it. In a general way, the more hierarchical the settlement pattern, the more hierarchical the society.

Work by Gregory Johnson on the Early Dynastic (*c.* 2800 BC) settlement sites in a region of Mesopotamia showed this very clearly, as can be seen in the graph opposite. The sites ranged in size from 25 ha (60 acres) to just over one tenth of a hectare (0.25 acres), and could be divided into five categories based on their size: Johnson called these large towns, towns, large villages, small villages, and hamlets. The existence of a settlement hierarchy of this kind has been used by some archaeologists as an indicator of a state society.

However, the excavation of settlement remains is the major source of information about social relations within a society. This applies for any level of complexity,

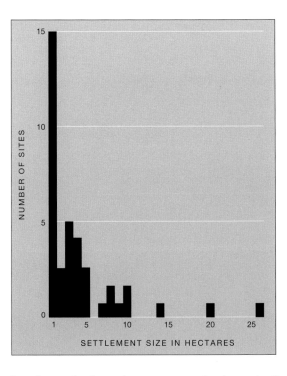

Site hierarchy for Early Dynastic settlements in a region of Mesopotamia.

but the methods used can vary greatly, the main distinction being between mobile and sedentary societies.

Mobile Hunter-Gatherer Societies. In mobile hunter-gatherer societies organization is exclusively at a local level, with no permanent administrative centers. So having identified various sites, the first approach is to concentrate on the sites themselves, with the aim being to understand the nature of the activities that took place there, and of the social group that used them.

Among mobile communities of hunter-gatherers archaeologists draw a distinction between *cave sites* and *open sites*. Occupation deposits in cave sites tend to be deep, usually indicating intermittent human activity over thousands or tens of thousands of years, and meticulous excavation and recording are required to interpret the stratigraphy of the site accurately. Open sites may have been occupied for shorter periods of time, but the deposits, without the protection provided by a cave, may have suffered greater erosion.

If it proves possible to distinguish single short phases of human occupation at a hunter-gatherer site, we can then look at the distribution of artifacts and bone fragments within and around **features** and structures (hut foundations, remains of hearths) to see whether any coherent patterns can be observed. However, it is not always clear whether the distribution is the result of human activity on the spot (or *in situ*) or whether the materials have been transported by flowing water and redeposited. In some cases, too, especially with bone debris, distribution may be the result of the action of predatory animals, not of humans.

BONES

STONES

CONJOINING BONES

CONJOINING STONES

0   30 ft

0   10 m

Glynn Isaac's research at the Early Paleolithic site of Koobi Fora, Kenya, East Africa. (Top row) Location of bones and stone artifacts. (Second row) Lines joining bones and stones that could be fitted back together, perhaps indicating activity areas.

The study of such questions requires sophisticated sampling strategies and very thorough analysis. The work of Glynn Isaac's team at the Early Paleolithic site of Koobi Fora on the eastern shore of Lake Turkana, Kenya, gives an indication of the recovery and analytical techniques involved. The excavation procedure was highly controlled, with exact recording of the coordinates of every piece of bone or stone recovered, and careful analysis of the degree of post-depositional disturbance. Isaac's team was able to fit some fragments of bone and stone back together again. They interpreted the network of joins (see diagram above) as showing areas where hominids broke open bones to extract marrow, and where stone tools were knapped – so called activity areas.

For a wider perspective, we need to consider the entire territory in which the group or band operated, and the relationship between sites. Ethnoarchaeology (see below) has helped to establish a framework of analysis, so that we may think in terms of an annual home range (i.e. the whole territory covered by the group in the course of a year) and specific types of site within it, such as a home base camp (for a particular season), transitory camps, hunting blinds, butchery or kill sites, storage caches, and so on. These issues are basic to hunter-gatherer archaeology, and a regional perspective is essential to understand the annual life cycle of the

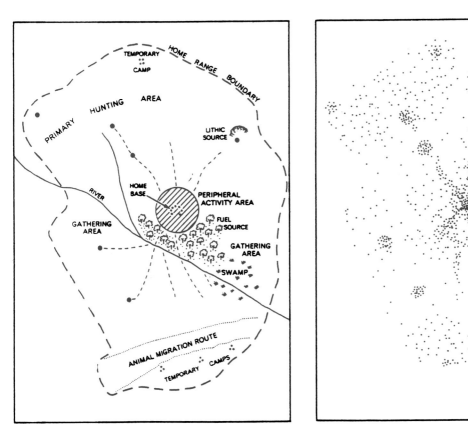

group and its behavior. This means that, in addition to conventional sites (with a high concentration of artifacts), we need to look for sparse scatters of artifacts, consisting of perhaps just one or two objects in every 10-m survey square. One must also study the whole regional environment and the likely human use of it by hunter-gatherers.

A good example is provided by the work of the British anthropologist Robert Foley in the Amboseli region of southern Kenya. He collected and recorded some 8531 stone tools from 257 sample locations within a study area covering 600 sq. km (232 sq. miles). From this evidence he was able to calculate the rate of discard of stone tools within different environmental and vegetation zones, and interpret the distribution patterns in terms of the strategies and movements of hunter-gatherer groups. In a later study, he developed a general model of stone tool distribution based on a number of studies of hunter-gatherer bands in different parts of the world. One conclusion was that a single band of some 25 people might be expected to discard as many as 163,000 artifacts within their annual territory in the course of a single year. These artifacts would be scattered across the territory, but with significant concentrations at home base camps and temporary camps. According to Foley's study, however, only a very small proportion of the artifacts discarded would

Robert Foley's model (left) of activities within the annual home range of a hunter-gatherer band, and the artifact scatters (right) resulting from such activities.

be found by archaeologists working at a single site, and it is vitally important that individual site assemblages are interpreted as parts of a broader pattern.

Sedentary Societies.   Investigation of the social organization of sedentary communities, which include segmentary societies, chiefdoms, and states, is best approached with an investigation of settlement (although, as we shall see below, cemeteries and public monuments evident in these societies also form useful areas of study).

Although much can be learned from survey, for effective analysis of the community as a whole some structures need to be excavated completely and the remainder sampled intensively enough to obtain an idea of the variety of different structures. The careful excavation of individual houses and of complete villages is a standard procedure when dealing with smaller sedentary communities. This opens the way to the study of households, and of community structure, as well as to well-founded estimates of population.

A good example is offered by Kent Flannery's excavation of Early Formative houses at Tierras Largas in Oaxaca, Mexico. He was able to establish the first map showing the layout of a Formative village in Oaxaca. Evidence for differences in social status emerged. Residences, deduced to be of relatively high status, had not only a house platform built of higher-quality adobe and stone, but a greater quantity of animal bone, imported **obsidian**, and imported marine shell than the area of wattle-and-daub houses deduced to be of lower status. Significantly, locally available (and therefore less prestigious) chert formed a higher proportion of the tools in the lower-status area.

Most of the techniques of analysis appropriate to less developed societies remain valid for the study of centralized chiefdoms and states, which incorporate within themselves most of the social forms and patterns of interaction seen in the simpler societies. Additional techniques are needed because of the centralization of society, the hierarchy of sites, and the organizational and communicational devices that characterize chiefdom and state societies. A good example is provided by the work at the Mississippian site of Moundville, described in the box overleaf.

One of the first steps when looking at a complex society is to identify one or more primary centers, and this is done by considering the size of a site, either in absolute terms, or in terms of the distances between major centers, so as to determine which are dominant and which subordinate. With this information a map can be created identifying the principal independent centers and the approximate extent of the territories surrounding them.

The reliance on size alone, however, can be misleading, and it is necessary to seek other indications of which are the primary centers. The best way is to try to find out how the society in question viewed itself and its territories. This might

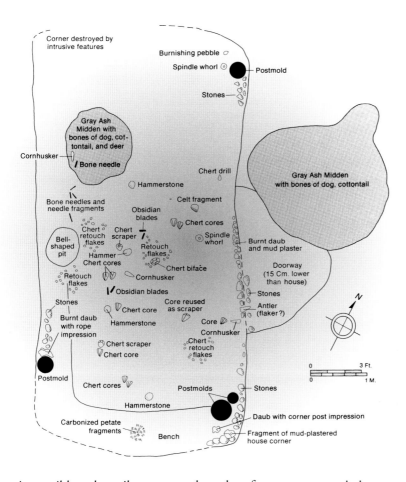

Corner destroyed by
intrusive features

Burnishing pebble

Spindle whorl — Postmold

Stones

Gray Ash
Midden with
bones of dog, cot-
tontail, and deer

Cornhusker

Bone needle

Chert drill

Gray Ash Midden
with bones of dog, cottontail

Hammerstone

Celt fragment

Bone needles and
needle fragments

Obsidian
blades

Chert cores

Chert
retouch
flakes

Chert
scraper

Spindle
whorl

Burnt daub
and mud plaster

Bell-
shaped
pit

Hammer
Chert cores

Retouch
flakes

Chert biface

Doorway
(15 Cm. lower
than house)

Retouch
flakes

Cornhusker

Obsidian blades

Stones

Stones

Chert core

Core reused
as scraper

Antler
(flaker ?)

Burnt daub
with rope
impression

Hammerstone

Core

N

Cornhusker

Chert scraper

Chert core

Chert
retouch
flakes

Postmold

Chert cores

Postmolds

Stones

0   3 Ft.

Hammerstone

0   1 M.

Carbonized petate
fragments

Daub with corner post impression

Bench

Fragment of mud-plastered
house corner

Plan of a house at Tierras
Largas, *c.* 900 BC, with certain
artifacts plotted in position.

seem an impossible task until one remembers that, for most state societies at any rate, written records exist. These may name various sites, identifying their place within the hierarchy. The archaeologist's task is then to find those named sites, usually by the discovery of an actual inscription including the name of the relevant site – one might for example hope to find such an inscription in any substantial town of the Roman empire. In recent years, the decipherment of Maya hieroglyphs has opened up a whole new source of evidence of this sort.

Usually, however, site hierarchy must be deduced by more directly archaeological means, without relying on the written word. A "highest-order" center, such as the capital city of an independent state, can best be identified from direct indications of central organization, on a scale not exceeded elsewhere, and comparable with that of other highest-order centers of equivalent states.

One indication is the existence of an archive (even without understanding anything of what it says) or of other symbolic indications of centralized organization. For instance, many controlled economies used seals to make impressions in clay as indications of ownership, source, or destination. The finding of a quantity of such materials can indicate organizational activity. Indeed, the whole practice of literacy

SOCIAL ANALYSIS AT MOUNDVILLE

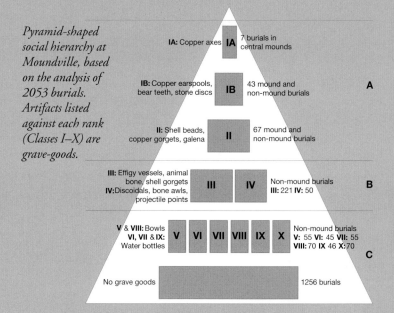

During its heyday in the 14th and 15th centuries AD, Moundville was one of the greatest ceremonial centers of the Mississippian culture in North America. The site takes its name from an impressive group of 20 mounds constructed within a palisaded area, 150 ha (370 acres) in extent, on the banks of the Black Warrior river in west-central Alabama. Moundville was first dug into as long ago as 1840, but major excavations did not take place until the 20th century. Recently, Christopher Peebles and his colleagues have combined systematic survey with limited excavation and reanalysis of earlier work to produce a convincing social study of the site.

Peebles and his team first needed a reliable chronology. This was

Changing settlement patterns in the Moundville region. In Phase I (AD 1050–1250) Moundville was simply a site with a single mound, like other similar sites in the area. By Phase II, however, it had grown larger, establishing itself as the major regional center. After its heyday in Phase III, Moundville disappeared as a significant site in Phase IV (after 1550), when the region no longer had a dominant center.

achieved through an analysis of the pottery. The resultant relative chronology was then cross-checked with excavated ceramics from radiocarbon dated contexts to produce an absolute chronology.

This chronology enabled the team to study the development of the site through several phases. Preliminary survey of neighboring sites also established the regional settlement pattern for each phase, summarized in the maps below.

Over 3000 burials have been excavated at Moundville, and Peebles used statistical techniques to group 2053 of them according to social rank. Peebles observed that the small number of people of highest rank (Segment A: classes IA, IB and II in the pyramid diagram below) were buried in or near the mounds with artifacts exclusive to them, such as copper axes and earspools. Lower-ranking individuals of Segment B (Classes III and IV) had non-mound

Pyramid-shaped social hierarchy at Moundville, based on the analysis of 2053 burials. Artifacts listed against each rank (Classes I–X) are grave-goods.

IA: Copper axes — **IA** — 7 burials in central mounds

IB: Copper earspools, bear teeth, stone discs — **IB** — 43 mound and non-mound burials — **A**

II: Shell beads, copper gorgets, galena — **II** — 67 mound and non-mound burials

III: Effigy vessels, animal bone, shell gorgets
IV: Discoidals, bone awls, projectile points — **III** **IV** — Non-mound burials III: 221 IV: 50 — **B**

V & VIII: Bowls
VI, VII & IX: Water bottles — **V VI VII VIII IX X** — Non-mound burials V: 55 VI: 45 VII: 55 VIII: 70 IX 46 X: 70 — **C**

No grave goods — 1256 burials

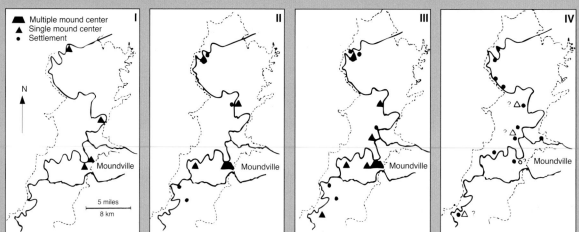

Multiple mound center
▲ Single mound center
• Settlement

I

II

III

IV

N

5 miles
8 km

Moundville

burials with some grave-goods but no copper artifacts, while those of Segment C, buried on the periphery, had few or no grave-goods.

Peebles found interesting differences according to age and sex. The 7 individuals in Class IA, the top of the social pyramid, were all adults, probably males. Those of Class IB were adult males and children, while Class II comprised individuals of all ages and both sexes. It seems clear that adult males had the highest status. The presence of children in Class IB suggests that their high status was inherited at birth.

Peebles's study suggests a regional organization with a well-marked hierarchy of sites, controlled by a highly ranked community at Moundville itself – what Peebles terms a chiefdom society.

and of symbolic expression is so central to organization that such indications are valuable evidence.

A further indication of central status is the presence of buildings of standardized form known to be associated with central functions of high order. Examples of such buildings include palaces, such as those found in Minoan Crete; buildings of ritual function (since in most early societies the control of administration and control of religious practice were closely linked), for example a Maya temple complex; fortifications; and mints for producing coinage.

In a hierarchically organized society, it always makes sense to study closely the functions of the center, considering such possible factors as kinship, bureaucratic organization, redistribution and storage of goods, organization of ritual, craft specialization, and external trade. All of these offer insights into how the society worked.

Burial analysis: The Study of Ranking from Individual Burials

In archaeology, the individual is seen all too rarely. One of the most informative insights into the individual and his or her social status is offered by the discovery of human physical remains – the skeleton or the ashes – accompanied by artifacts deposited in the grave. Examination of the skeletal remains by a physical anthropologist will often reveal the sex and age at death of each individual, and possibly any dietary deficiency or other pathological condition (see Chapter 8). Communal or collective burials (burials of more than one individual) may be difficult to interpret, because it will not always be clear which grave-goods go with which deceased person. It is, therefore, from single burials that we can hope to learn most.

In segmentary societies, and others with relatively limited differentiation in terms of rank, a close analysis of grave-goods can reveal much about disparities in social status. However, it is important to remember that what is buried with a deceased person is not simply the exact equivalent either of status or of material goods owned or used during life. Burials are made by living individuals, and are used by them to express and influence their relationships with others still alive as much as to symbolize or serve the dead. But there is nevertheless often a relationship between the role and rank of the deceased during life and the manner in which the remains are disposed of and accompanied by artifacts.

The analysis will seek to determine differences between male and female burials, and to assess whether these differences carry with them distinctions in terms of wealth or higher status. The other common factor involved with rank or status is age, and age differences may be systematically reflected in the treatment of the deceased. In relatively egalitarian societies, high status won through the individual's own achievements (e.g. in hunting) in his or her own lifetime is something commonly encountered, and often reflected in funerary practice. But the archaeologist must ask, from the evidence available, whether such a burial really reflects status achieved by the individual or instead hereditary status through birth. To distinguish between the two is not easy. One useful criterion is to investigate whether children are in some cases given rich burial goods and other indications of preferential attention. If so, there may have been a system of hereditary ranking, because at so early an age the child is unlikely to have reached such a status through personal distinction.

Once the graves in the cemetery have been dated, the first step in most cases is simply to produce a frequency distribution (a histogram) of the number of different artifact types in each grave. For further analysis, however, it is more interesting to seek some better indication of wealth and status so that greater weight can be given to valuable objects, and less weight to commonplace ones. This at once raises the problem of the recognition of value (for we cannot assume that past societies had the same ideas of value as we do). One answer might be to assume that valuable objects were those that took a long time to make, or were made of materials brought from a distance or difficult to obtain. We must also remember that ranking is not expressed solely in the grave-goods, but in the entire manner of burial.

A good example of the analysis of an entire cemetery is offered by the excavations of Charles Higham and Rachanie Thosarat at the site of Khok Phanom Di, a large mound inland from the Gulf of Siam in central Thailand. The settlement had been occupied for about 500 years from *c.* 2000 BC, and left a cemetery containing 154 human burials with bone and shell ornaments intact. The graves occurred in clusters with spaces between them. A very detailed burial sequence was worked out which provided insights into the community's kinship system over about 20 generations. The ability to trace families down the generations like this is extremely rare in **prehistory**. In the later phases there was a predominance of women, some of them buried with considerable wealth, such as the so-called "Princess." Also there was a clear link between the wealth of children and the adults with whom they were buried – poor children accompanied poor adults. The analysis of a complete

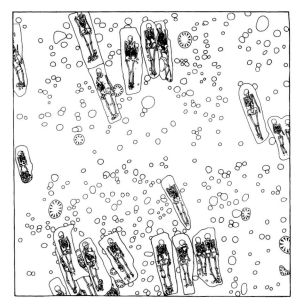

cemetery in this way can yield many insights which are not available even from the very careful examination of a single grave.

Monuments and Public Works

Some societies invest a great deal of labor and considerable resources in the construction of monuments and public works. Such monuments were generally built with the intention of being conspicuous and in some cases – like the pyramids of Egypt – they remain conspicuous today. Many early state societies had at their center a major ceremonial site, and the monuments at such sites are informative not only about the religious beliefs of the society in question but also about aspects of their social organisation.

The great plazas at the ceremonial centers of Mesoamerica are a good example. Monte Albán in Oaxaca, Mexico, became the principal center of the Zapotec state around 200 BC. Its wonderfully situated central plaza, shown overleaf, dominated the surrounding countryside. From this time on Monte Albán was the home of some 10,000 to 20,000 people, and the primary center of Oaxaca. Its monuments celebrate and reflect the power of the state and the city's central authority.

In some segmentary societies the surviving monuments, often burial monuments, were much more conspicuous than the often not very substantial settlements. In some cases the settlements are rarely recovered, sometimes obliterated by erosion, while clear traces of the monuments still remain. This is the case for the **Neolithic** period in the Wessex area of southern England where earthen burial mounds, called "long barrows" are the most evident trace of the early farmers who lived there from *c.* 4000 BC.

Khok Phanom Di. (Above left) The "Princess," who was accompanied by a set of shell jewelry, with over 120,000 beads, a headdress, and a bracelet, as well as fine pottery vessels. (Above) The dead were buried individually, in neat, clustered rows.

View south across the central plaza at Monte Albán, with the restored ruins of several temples visible. The site was founded on a mountain top in 500 BC.

Each mound in this part of Neolithic Wessex was the territorial focus for a small group of farmers. This was a segmentary society, where no one group was dominant.

Whitesheet Hill

5 miles
8 km

There are reasons for thinking that each mound was the focal point in the landscape for a single community. If we draw lines between each mound, as shown in the diagram below we can see how the landscape might have been divided territorially into units of approximately equal size, each serving as the homeland of the farming community associated with a single burial monument.

The spatial analysis of monuments undertaken in this way can be supplemented by a consideration of the labor input needed to construct them. It is estimated that each Wessex long barrow required 10,000 work hours to construct. A class of larger monuments contemporary with the long barrows, known as "causewayed camps" and formed essentially of a circular ditch, may have each taken 100,000 work hours to construct. The long barrow/causewayed camp phase was succeeded around 2500 BC by a phase in which still larger bank-and-ditch monuments, termed "henges" were built. The great henges have approximately the same distribution as the earlier causewayed camps, but to construct each required an estimated 1,000,000 work hours. Towards the end of this phase, around 2100 BC, the great stone structure at Stonehenge was built, requiring some 30,000,000 hours of work. So great a construction may suggest some centralizing organization at this time for the whole Wessex area.

Although the calculations are very approximate they do show how some notion of the changing social organization can be formed through the study of the monuments, even at a time when the traces of domestic settlement are very scanty indeed.

The structures built at this early time can be very impressive. Stonehenge is certainly one of the largest, but it is not the oldest. Indeed over much of northwestern Europe there are stone monuments of the Neolithic period, mainly collective

APPROX. WORK HOURS REQUIRED FOR CONSTRUCTION

	Late Neolithic
	STONEHENGE 30,000,000
	HENGE 1,000,000
	Early Neolithic
	CAUSEWAYED CAMP 100,000
	LONG BARROW 10,000

KEY

■ Stonehenge

▲ Henge

◉ Causewayed camp

■ Long barrow

tombs, which are often termed "megalithic" (from the Greek megas (great) and lithos (stone)).

Some of these go back as far as 4000 BC, a millennium before the pyramids of Egypt. In the Orkney Islands, beyond the northern tip of Scotland, the local sandstone could readily be worked, already before the use of metal tools, and the remaining monuments, some of them well preserved, are sophisticated works of stone architecture.

For instance, in the chambered tomb at Quanterness in the Orkney Islands, off the north coast of Scotland, dating to *c.* 3300 BC, remains of a large number of individuals were found, perhaps as many as 390. Males and females were about equally represented, and the age distribution could represent the pattern of deaths in the population at large; that is to say, that the age at death of the people buried in the tomb (46 percent below 20 years, 47 percent aged 20–30 years, and only 7 percent over the age of 30 years) could in proportional terms be the same as that of the whole population. The excavators concluded that this was a tomb equally available to most sectors of the community, and representative of a segmentary society rather than a hierarchical one, which the sophistication of its architecture might at first have suggested.

Written Records

For literate societies – those that use writing, for instance all the great civilizations in Mesoamerica, China, Egypt, and the Near East – historical records can answer many of the social questions set out at the beginning of this chapter. One of the main goals of the archaeologist dealing with these societies is therefore to find appropriate texts. Many of the early excavations of the great sites of the Near East, for example, concentrated on the recovery of archives of clay writing tablets. Major finds of this kind are still made today – for example, at the ancient city of Ebla (Tell Mardikh) in Syria in the 1970s, where an archive of 5000 clay tablets written in an early, probably provincial, dialect of Akkadian (Babylonian) was discovered.

In each early literate society, writing had its own functions and purposes. For instance, the clay tablets of Mycenaean Greece, dating from *c.* 1200 BC, are almost

Analysis of the scale of the Wessex monuments in terms of labor hours needed for their construction suggests the emergence of a hierarchy in the later phase that may mirror a development in social relations and the emergence of a ranked society. Stonehenge, built at this time, is the greatest of the Wessex monuments. In the earlier Neolithic the scale of monuments is commensurate with an egalitarian, segmentary society.

Some of the 5000 clay tablets discovered in the royal palace at Ebla (Tell Mardikh in modern Syria), dating from the late 3rd millennium BC. The tablets formed part of the state archives, recording over 140 years of Ebla's history. Originally they were stored on wooden shelving, which collapsed when the palace was sacked.

without exception records of commercial transactions (goods coming in or going out) at the Mycenaean palaces. This gives us an impression of many aspects of the Mycenaean economy, and a glimpse into craft organization (through the names for the different kinds of craftspeople), as well as introducing the names of the offices of state. But here, as in other cases, accidents of preservation may be important. It could be that the Mycenaeans wrote on clay only for their commercial records, and used other, perishable materials for literary or historical texts now lost to us. It is certainly true that for the Classical Greek and Roman civilizations, it is mainly official decrees inscribed on marble that have survived. Fragile rolls of papyrus – the predecessor of modern paper – with literary texts on them, have usually only remained intact in the dry air of Egypt, or, for example, buried in the volcanic ash covering Pompeii. Coinage is also an important written source. The findspots of coins give interesting economic evidence about trade. But the inscriptions themselves are informative about the issuing authority – whether city-state (as in ancient Greece) or sole ruler (as in Imperial Rome, or the kings of medieval Europe).

The decipherment of an ancient language transforms our knowledge of the society that used it. In recent years one of the most significant advances has been the decipherment of Maya inscriptions, the inscribed symbols (glyphs) often found on stone stelae at the largest centers. It had been widely assumed that Maya inscriptions were exclusively of a calendrical nature, or that they dealt with purely religious matters, notably the deeds of deities. But the inscriptions can now in many cases be interpreted as relating to real historical events, mainly the deeds of the Maya kings.

We can also now begin to deduce the likely territories belonging to individual Maya centers. Maya history has thus taken on a new dimension.

A more detailed example of the value of written sources for reconstructing social archaeology is Mesopotamia, where a huge number of records of Sumer and Babylon (*c.* 3000–1600 BC), mainly in the form of clay tablets, have been preserved. The uses of writing in Mesopotamia may be summarized as follows:

Recording information for future use	- Administrative purposes
	- Codification of law
	- Formulation of a sacred tradition
	- Annals
	- Scholarly purposes
Communicating current information	- Letters
	- Royal edicts
	- Public announcements
	- Texts for training scribes
Communicating with the gods	- Sacred texts, amulets, etc.

Perhaps most evocative of all are the law codes, of which the most impressive example is the law code of Hammurabi of Babylon, written in the Akkadian language (and in cuneiform script) around 1750 BC. The ruler is seen at the top of the stone, standing before Shamash, the god of justice. The laws were promulgated, as Hammurabi states, "so that the strong may not oppress the weak, and to protect the

The famous law code of the Babylonian king Hammurabi, *c.* 1750 BC.

rights of the orphan and widow." These laws cover many aspects of life – agriculture, business transactions, family law, inheritance, terms of employment for different craftspeople, and penalties for crimes such as adultery and homicide.

Impressive and informative as it is, Hammurabi's law code is not straightforward to interpret, and emphasizes the need for the archaeologist to reconstruct the full social context that led to the drafting of a text. As the British scholar Nicholas Postgate has pointed out, the code is by no means complete, and seems to cover only those areas of the law that had proved troublesome. Moreover, Hammurabi had recently conquered several rival city states, and the law code was therefore probably designed to help integrate the new territories within his empire.

Ethnoarchaeology

A fundamental method of approach for the social archaeologist is ethnoarchaeology. It involves the study of both the present-day use and significance of artifacts, buildings, and structures within living societies, and the way these material things become incorporated into the archaeological record – what happens to them when they are thrown away or (in the case of buildings and structures) torn down or abandoned. It is therefore an *indirect* approach to the understanding of any past society.

There is nothing new in the idea of looking at living societies to help interpret the past. In the 19th and early 20th centuries European archaeologists often turned for inspiration to researches done by ethnographers among societies in Africa or Australia. But the so-called "ethnographic parallels" that resulted often simply and crudely likened past societies to present ones, stifling new thought rather than promoting it. In the United States archaeologists were confronted from the beginning with the living reality of complex Native American societies, which taught them to think rather more deeply about how ethnography might be used to aid archaeological interpretation. Nevertheless, fully-fledged ethnoarchaeology is a development really of only the last 35 years. The key difference is that now it is archaeologists themselves, rather than ethnographers or anthropologists, who carry out the research among living societies.

A good example is the work of Lewis Binford among the Nunamiut Eskimo, a hunter-gatherer group of Alaska. In the 1960s Binford was attempting to interpret archaeological sites of the Middle Paleolithic of France (the Mousterian period, 180,000–40,000 years ago). He realized that only by studying how *modern* hunter-gatherers used and discarded bones and tools, or moved from site to site, could he begin to understand the mechanisms that had created the Mousterian archaeological record – itself almost certainly the product of a mobile hunter-gatherer economy. Between 1969 and 1973 he lived intermittently among the

Nunamiut and observed their behavior. For instance, he studied the way bone debris was produced and discarded by men at a seasonal hunting camp (the Mask site, Anaktuvuk Pass, Alaska). He saw that, when sitting round a hearth and processing bone for marrow, there was a "drop zone" where small fragments of bone fell as they were broken. The larger pieces, which were thrown away by the men, formed a "toss zone," both in front and behind them.

The Nunamiut might not provide an exact "ethnographic parallel" for Mousterian societies, but Binford recognized that there are certain actions or *functions* likely to be common to all hunter-gatherers because – as in the case of the processing of

Ethnoarchaeology: the work of Lewis Binford. (Below left) The "drop zone" and "toss zones" model derived from observations of the Nunamiut. (Left) At the site of Pincevent, France, the excavator Leroi-Gourhan interpreted three hearths as being evidence for a complex skin tent (plan and reconstruction shown). (Below) Binford applied his "outside hearth model" to the three Pincevent hearths, and deduced from the distribution of bones that his model fitted the evidence better than that of Leroi-Gourhan: i.e. that the hearths lay outside, and not within a tent.

FORWARD TOSS AREA

HEARTH

DROP ZONE

BACKWARD TOSS AREA

"MEN'S" OUTSIDE HEARTH MODEL

FORWARD TOSS ZONE

BACKWARD TOSS ZONE

BONE DISTRIBUTION RELATIVE TO "MEN'S" OUTSIDE HEARTH MODEL
PINCEVENT No. 1

bone – the actions are dictated by the most convenient procedure when seated round a camp fire. The discarded fragments of bone then leave a characteristic pattern round the hearth for the archaeologist to find and interpret – indeed, Binford went on to use his model to reinterpret data from a Paleolithic camp site. From such analysis, it also proved possible to infer roughly how many people were in the group, and over what period of time the camp site was used. These are questions very relevant to our understanding of the social organization (including the size) of hunter-gatherer groups.

Ethnoarchaeology is not restricted to observations at the local scale. The British archaeologist Ian Hodder, in his study of the female ear decorations used by different tribes in the Lake Baringo area of Kenya, undertook a regional study to investigate the extent to which material culture (in this case personal decoration) was being used to express differences between the tribes. Partly as a result of such work, archaeologists no longer assume that it is an easy task to take archaeological assemblages and group them into regional "cultures," and then to assume that each "culture" so formed represents a social unit. Such a procedure might, in fact, work quite well for the ear decorations Hodder studied, because the people in question chose to use this feature to assert their tribal distinctiveness. But, as Hodder showed, if we were to take other features of the material culture, such as pots or tools, the same pattern would not necessarily be followed. His example documents the important lesson that material culture cannot be used by the archaeologist in a simple or unthinking manner in the reconstruction of supposed ethnic groups.

THE ARCHAEOLOGY OF THE INDIVIDUAL AND OF IDENTITY

The discussion so far in this chapter has as its starting point the concept of the society and its organization. This is a deliberate feature of the structure of this book: before questions are asked about the variety of human experience it is necessary first to form some view about the scale of a society and its complexity. But at the same time this might be criticized as a "top-down" approach, beginning with questions of organization and of hierarchy, of power and of centralization, and only then turning to the individual who actually lives in society, to that person's role, gender, and status and to what it was really *like* to live there at that time and in that social context.

It would be equally valid to start with the individual and with social relationships, including kinship relations, and to work outward from there: what one might term a "bottom-up" approach. This involves the consideration of issues such as social inequality, **ethnicity**, and gender.

One important aspect of the individual to remember is that most sides of our "humanness" and many of the concepts that we enshrine as "human," including

KEY CONCEPTS: FINDING THE INDIVIDUAL

- Many aspects of individual human behavior are not a cross-cultural "given" but are learned, and differ widely across both ancient and modern cultures

- The existence of ethnic groups is difficult to recognize from the archaeological record: an affiliation to a particular style of material culture, for example, does not necessarily equate to ethnicity

- It is important to recognize gender in the archaeological record (particularly the roles of women which have traditionally been overlooked). There is also a distinction between sex and gender: sex is biologically determined whereas gender roles in different societies vary greatly

our schemes of perception, thought, gender, and sense of morals, our ways of moving our bodies around and communicating (such as standing, sitting, looking, speaking, and walking), and even the way we respond to our senses (such as our sense of smell and taste), are not natural "givens" but are in fact culturally specific: they are developed and adopted by humans within a society and vary through time and space. If we are to really know what it was like to live in a past society, we must be careful not to make assumptions based on our own experience of what it is to be "human."

Social Inequality

The theme of the archaeology of social inequality has perhaps not been very comprehensively addressed yet, but in the field of historical archaeology there have been systematic studies of the material culture of some underprivileged groups, including some interesting studies of town areas known from documentary accounts to be considered poor.

The infamous Five Points slum area of lower Manhattan, New York, described by early 19th-century writers including Charles Dickens, has been investigated through rescue excavations at the site of a new federal courthouse at Foley Square, providing some graphic insights. For instance, the excavated area included the site of a cellar brothel at 12 Baxter Street, historically documented (in the 1843 indictment of its keeper) as a "disorderly house – a nest for prostitutes and others of ill fame and name, where great numbers of characters are in the nightly practice of revelling until late and improper hours of the night." The excavations revealed further insights based upon the material culture:

> The quality of the household goods found in the privy behind 12 Baxter far
> exceeded that of goods found anywhere else on the block. The prostitutes

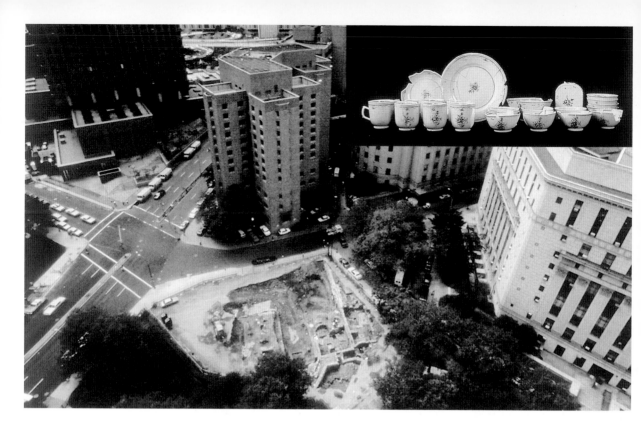

A view of the rescue excavation of the 19th-century slum area of Five Points in lower Manhattan, New York. The cellar of a brothel was investigated and yielded much information concerning the daily lives of inhabitants. While of a low social rank, the prostitutes at least enjoyed the use of a set of Chinese porcelain (inset) for afternoon tea.

lived well, at least when they were at work. One attraction was the opportunity to live in a style that seamstresses, laundresses, and maids could not afford. Afternoon tea at the brothel was served on a set of Chinese porcelain that included matching teacups and coffee cups, saucers and plates, a slop bowl and a tea caddie. Meals consisted of steak, veal, ham, soft-shell clams and many kinds of fish. There was a greater variety of artifacts from the brothel than from other excavated areas of the courthouse block.... Other personal items suggested the occupational hazards of prostitution. Two glass urinals, designed especially for women, were probably used when venereal disease confined a prostitute to bed.

Not far from Foley Square another excavation, that of the African Burial Ground, formerly known as the Negros Burial Ground, which was recorded on a plan of 1755, has proved highly informative and has had wide repercussions.

The rescue excavation of skeletons there in 1991 provoked outrage in the African-American community of today, which felt it had not been adequately consulted, and ultimately led to the establishment of a Museum of African and African-American History in New York City. There were no grave markers, and other than wood, coffin nails, and shroud pins, few artifacts were found. Studies of the skeletons have combined DNA analysis with cranial metrics, morphology, and

A Yoruba priestess and a Khamite priest perform a libation ceremony for the ancestors over the grave of a person buried in the African Burial Ground in lower Manhattan, New York.

historical data, to discover where the people came from. The large size of the sample will allow study of nutrition and pathology. The remains of 419 individuals disinterred during the excavations were ceremonially reburied in October 2003, after being taken in a procession up Broadway.

Certainly the controversy and the excavation have proved a stimulus toward the development of African-American archaeology, already well-defined through the investigation of plantation sites.

Ethnicity and Conflict

Ethnicity (i.e. the existence of ethnic groups, including tribal groups) is difficult to recognize from the archaeological record. For example, the idea that such features as pottery decoration are automatically a sign of ethnic affiliation has been questioned. This is a field where ethnoarchaeology is only now beginning to make some progress.

The theme of ethnicity is a difficult one to approach archaeologically, unless with the help of written records, since ethnicity is based largely upon self-awareness. There is often a correlation between ethnic groups and language groups, which can offer further avenues for study. Questions of group self-identity, which is often much the same as ethnicity, often underlie conflict and warfare.

The role of *warfare* in early societies is one topic that merits further investigation. It has long been agreed that warfare is a recurrent feature of early state societies, but for prehistoric times it has been more common to think in terms of peace-loving "noble savages." There is, however, an increasing amount of evidence to suggest that warfare in prehistory was not so much the exception as the norm. A good example is provided by the Neolithic ditched enclosures (*c.* 5000 to 2000 BC) of Talheim,

Skeletons found in a pit at Talheim, Germany, dating to *c.* 5000 BC, indicative of mass killing.

Germany. Fieldwork suggested that they were not simply of symbolic significance, as many archaeologists had thought, but genuine fortifications. One pit contained the bodies of eighteen adults and sixteen children, all killed by blows from at least six different axes, contradicting the notion of a peaceful early farming society.

War need not be undertaken with the objective of permanently occupying the lands of the vanquished in a process of territorial expansion. The American archaeologist David Freidel made this point in his study of Maya warfare, based on the wall paintings at the site of Bonampak and also from deductions from early written sources. According to Freidel's analysis, the function of Maya warfare was not to conquer new territory, and thus enlarge the frontiers of the state in question, but instead to give Maya rulers the opportunity of capturing kings and princes from neighboring states, many of whom were then later offered as sacrifices to the gods. Warfare thus allowed the Maya rulers to reaffirm their royal status: it had a central role in upholding the system of government, but that role was not one of territorial expansion.

Investigating Gender

An important aspect of the study of social archaeology is the investigation of gender. Initially this was felt to overlap with feminist archaeology, which often had the explicit objective of exposing and correcting the male bias (androcentrism) of archaeology. There is no doubt that in the modern world the role of women professionals, including archaeologists, has often been a difficult one. For instance, Dorothy

Garrod, the first woman professor of archaeology in Britain, was appointed in 1937, at a time when female undergraduates in her university (Cambridge) were not allowed to take a degree at the end of their course, as male undergraduates did, but only a diploma. There was – and still is – an imbalance to be rectified in the academic world, and that was one of the early objectives of feminist archaeology. A second was to illuminate the roles of women in the past more clearly, where often they had been overlooked, and to rectify the male bias in so much archaeological writing.

But the study of gender is much more than simply the study of women. An important central idea soon became the distinction between sex and gender. It was argued that sex – female or male – may be regarded as biologically determined and can be established archaeologically from skeletal remains. But gender – at its simplest woman or man – is a social construct, involving the sex-related roles of individuals in society. Gender roles in different societies vary greatly both from place to place and through time. Systems of kinship, of marriage, inheritance, and the division of labor are all related to biological sex but not determined by it. These perspectives permitted a good deal of profitable work in this second phase of gender studies in archaeology, but they have now in their turn been criticized by a new "third wave" feminism, as emphasizing supposedly "inherent" differences between women and men, and emphasizing women's links to the natural world through reproduction.

The work of Marija Gimbutas on the prehistory of southeast Europe, for example, is now criticized by more recent workers in the field of gender archaeology. In her pioneering work she argued that the predominantly female figurines seen in the Neolithic and Copper Age of southeast Europe and in Anatolia demonstrate the important status of women at that time. She had a vision of an Old Europe influenced by feminine values which was to disappear with the succeeding Bronze Age with the dominance of a warlike male hierarchy, supposedly introduced by Indo-European warrior nomads from the east.

Marija Gimbutas became something of a cult figure in her own right, and her support for the concept of a great "Mother Goddess" representing a fertility principle has been embraced by modern "ecofeminist" and New Age enthusiasts. The current excavations by Ian Hodder at the early Neolithic site of Çatalhöyük in Turkey, where female figurines of baked clay have been found, are now visited regularly by devotees of the "Goddess" whose views are treated respectfully by the excavators, even though they do not share them. Hodder has argued instead that the figurines may represent the subordination of women as objects of ownership and male desires. Comparable figurines from the Aegean can often be shown to lack definite features diagnostic of sex or gender, and studies of rather similar

Different images symbolizing female power? (Top) A Neolithic vase from Romania. (Above) A Zapotec figurine from Oaxaca, Mexico.

baked clay figurines from Oaxaca, Mexico, have suggested that they were made by women for use in rituals relating to ancestors rather than deities. The notion that they represented a "Mother Goddess" lacks supporting evidence.

The third phase in the development of gender archaeology, in tune with the "third wave" of feminists of the 1990s, takes a different view of gender in two senses. First, in the narrower sense, and, as Lynn Meskell puts it, "led by women of color, lesbian feminists, queer theorists and postcolonial feminists," it recognizes that the field of gender and gender difference is more complex than a simple polarity between male and female, and that other kinds of difference have to be recognized. Indeed the very recognition of a simple structural opposition between male and female is itself, even in our own society, an over-simplification. In many societies children are not regarded as socially male or female until they reach the age of puberty – in the modern Greek language, for instance, while men and women are grammatically male and female in gender, the words for children generally belong to the third, neuter gender.

This leads on to the second point, that gender is part of a broader social framework, part of the social process – in Margaret Conkey's words "a way in which social categories, roles, ideologies and practices are defined and played out." While gender is, in any society, a system of classification, it is part of a larger system of social differences, including age, wealth, **religion**, ethnicity and so forth. Moreover these are not static constructs but fluid and flexible, constructed and re-constructed in the practice of daily life.

The complexities in analyzing burial data with respect to gender are indicated by the study by Bettina Arnold of the so-called "Princess of Vix" burial from east-central France. The grave contained skeletal remains which analysis indicated were female, but the grave-goods consisted of various prestige items normally thought to be indicative of males. This exceptionally rich 5th-century BC burial was initially interpreted as a transvestite priest because it was considered inconceivable that a woman could be honored in such a way. Arnold's careful reanalysis of the grave-goods supported the interpretation of the burial as an elite female. This may lead to a fresh assessment of the potentially powerful, occasionally paramount role that women played in Iron Age Europe. But this work may yet lead on to a wider consideration of gender distinctions in the Iron Age in a context which may reassess whether in individuals of very high status the traditional bipolar concept of gender is appropriate.

SUMMARY

- This chapter has shown that a formidable battery of techniques is now available to archaeologists who wish to investigate the social organization of early societies. Only the main themes have been touched on, but these will have made it clear that the potential for understanding the more complex and highly organized societies represented by states and chiefdoms is especially great. Written records, when they exist (only in state societies) can be an important resource.

- We can investigate ranked societies through their site hierarchies and, in the case of state societies, through their urban centers. It should in this way be possible to identify the ruling center using archaeological methods alone, and the extent of the area over which it held jurisdiction.

- For ranked or stratified societies (chiefdoms and states), the study of the buildings and other evidence of administration at the center gives valuable information about the social, political, and economic organization of society, as well as a picture of the life of the ruling elite. We can identify and analyze their palaces and tombs, and studies of lower-order administrative centers give further information about the social and political structure. The study of the differences in the treatment accorded to different individuals at death, in both the size and wealth of grave offerings, can reveal the complete range of status distinctions in a society.

- Similar approaches may be applied to segmentary societies: the study of individual settlements, the evidence for social ranking revealed by burials, and the existence of cooperative communal mechanisms for the construction of major monuments.

- On a smaller scale (and particularly important for the Paleolithic period), the camps of mobile hunter-gatherer societies and the seasonal movement between different sites may also be studied using the methods outlined in this chapter, especially when the insights provided by ethnoarchaeological research on living societies are used in conjunction with direct study of the archaeological record.

- In recent studies a "bottom-up" perspective in social archaeologies has become important: the archaeology of individuals and of identity. Gender studies in particular are now adding new insight into the structure of society.

FURTHER READING

The following works illustrate some of the ways in which social organization can be reconstructed:

Binford, L.R. 2002. **In Pursuit of the Past**. UNIVERSITY OF CALIFORNIA PRESS: BERKELEY & LONDON.

Hodder, I. 1982. **Symbols in Action**. CAMBRIDGE UNIVERSITY PRESS: CAMBRIDGE & NEW YORK.

Journal of Social Archaeology (since 2001).

Meskell, L. 1999. **Archaeologies of Social Life: Age, Sex, Class etc. in Ancient Egypt**. BLACKWELL: OXFORD.

Pyburn, K.A. (ed.). 2004. **Ungendering Civilization**. ROUTLEDGE: LONDON & NEW YORK.

6 What Was the Environment? What Did They Eat?

environment, subsistence, and diet

Environment and diet constitute two of the most fundamental and crucial factors of human life which the archaeologist needs to assess. The *environment* governs human life: latitude and altitude, landforms and climate determine the vegetation, which in turn determines animal life, and both of these determine diet. And all these things taken together determine how and where humans have lived – or at least they did until very recently.

The reconstruction of the environment first requires an answer to very general questions of global climate change. What was the global climate like when the human activities under study took place? Does a **context** belong to a glacial or interglacial phase? These broad questions can be answered by relating the date of a context to evidence of long-term climatic fluctuations obtained from sea and ice cores, as well as from tree-rings.

More specific questions about past environments will follow, and these are particularly relevant for all postglacial contexts, after about 10,000 years ago. There are two main sources of evidence: plant and animal remains. Analysis of these will not only reveal the range of flora and fauna that people would have encountered at a particular time and place, but since many plants and animals are quite sensitive to climate change, we can also find out what the regional and local environment would have been like.

Unfortunately, owing to the poor preservation of many forms of organic evidence, and to the distorted samples we recover, we can never be certain about our conclusions. We simply have to aim for the best approximation available. No single method will give a full and accurate picture – all are distorted in one way or another – and so as many methods as data and funds will allow need to be applied to build up a composite image.

Once we know what the environment might have been like, as well as the kinds of plants and animals present, we can try to find out how people exploited those conditions and resources and what they might have been eating. *Subsistence*, the quest for food, is one of the most basic of all necessities and there is a variety of evidence for it to be found in the archaeological record. Plant and animal remains and the residues found on **artifacts** such as pots or stone tools can give indirect clues to what peoples' *diet* might have consisted of, but the only direct evidence we have is from the study of actual human remains: stomach contents, fecal material, teeth, and bones.

INVESTIGATING ENVIRONMENTS ON A GLOBAL SCALE

The first step in assessing previous environmental conditions is to look at them globally. Local changes make little sense unless seen against this broader climatic background. Tree-rings are a good source of information for the last 10,000 years or so, but since water covers almost three-quarters of the earth, we should begin by examining evidence about past climates that can be obtained from this area, including data within glaciers and ice caps. We will then go on to look at what can be learned about past environments at a more local level from plant and animal remains.

Evidence from Oceans and Ice

The sediments of the ocean floor accumulate very slowly, just a few centimeters every thousand years, but they can contain evidence of thousands or even millions of years of climate history. In some areas ocean sediments consist primarily of an ooze made up of microfossils such as the shells of foraminifera – tiny one-celled marine organisms that live in the surface water of the oceans and sink to the bottom when they die. As in an archaeological **stratigraphy**, we can trace changes in environmental conditions through time by studying cores extracted from the sea bed and fluctuations in the species represented and the physical form of single species through the sequence. *Oxygen isotope analysis* of foraminifera can also reveal changes in the environment (see box opposite).

Thousands of deep-sea cores have now been extracted and studied, but cores can also be obtained from stratified ice sheets (some containing hundreds of thousands of annual growth layers), and here the oxygen isotopic composition also gives some guide to climatic oscillations. Results from cores in Greenland and the Antarctic, and Andean and Tibetan glaciers are consistent with, and add detail to, those from deep-sea cores. It is also possible to analyze bubbles of ancient methane gas trapped in the ice (resulting from plant decomposition, which is sensitive to temperature and moisture variations).

Ancient Winds. Isotopes can be used not merely for temperature studies but also for data on precipitation. And since it is the temperature differences between the equatorial and polar regions that largely determine the storminess of our weather, isotope studies can even tell us something about winds in different periods.

As air moves from low latitudes to colder regions, the water it loses as rain or snow is enriched in the stable isotope oxygen 18, while the remaining vapour becomes correspondingly richer in the other stable isotope of oxygen, oxygen 16. Thus from the ratio between the two isotopes in precipitation at a particular place, we can calculate the temperature difference between that place and the equatorial region.

Using this technique, the changing ratios found over the last 100,000 years in ice cores from Greenland and the Antarctic have been studied. The results show that during glacial periods the temperature difference between equatorial and polar

RECONSTRUCTING CLIMATES FROM SEA CORES

The stratigraphy of sediment on the ocean floor is obtained from cores taken out of the sea bed, usually about 10–30 m (33–98 ft) in length.

Dates for the different layers in the core are obtained by radiocarbon, paleomagnetism, or the uranium-series method (Chapter 4). Changing environmental conditions in the past are then deduced by two kinds of tests on microscopic fossils of tiny one-celled organisms called foraminifera found in the sediment. First, scientists study the simple presence, absence, and fluctuations of different foraminiferan species. Second, they analyze, by mass spectrometer, fluctuations in the ratio of the stable oxygen isotopes 18 and 16 in the calcium carbonate of the foraminiferan shells. Variations discernible by these two tests reflect not simply changes in temperature, but also oscillations in the continental glaciers. For example, as the glaciers grew, water was drawn up into them, reducing sea levels and increasing the density and salinity of the oceans, and thus causing changes in the depths at which certain foraminiferan species lived. At the same time the proportion of oxygen 18 in seawater increased. When the glaciers melted during periods of warmer climate, the proportion of oxygen 18 decreased.

Microscopic fossils of the foraminiferan species Globorotalia truncatulinoides, *which coils to the left during cold periods and to the right during warm ones.*

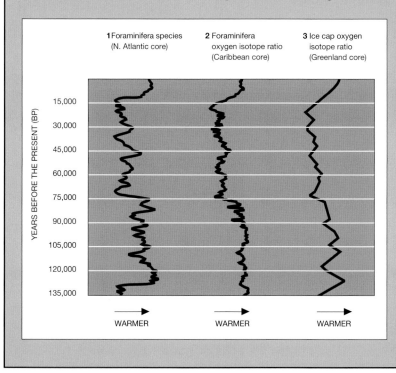

1 Foraminifera species (N. Atlantic core)

2 Foraminifera oxygen isotope ratio (Caribbean core)

3 Ice cap oxygen isotope ratio (Greenland core)

YEARS BEFORE THE PRESENT (BP)

15,000
30,000
45,000
60,000
75,000
90,000
105,000
120,000
135,000

WARMER   WARMER   WARMER

Three climate records compared. Left to right: proportions of different shell species in a deep-sea core; ratio of oxygen 18 to oxygen 16 in shells from a deep-sea core; and oxygen ratios from an ice core. The resemblance of the three records is good evidence that long-term climatic variation has been worldwide.

regions increased by 20–25 percent, and thus wind circulation must have been far more violent. Confirmation has come from a deep-sea core off the coast of West Africa, analysis of which led to estimates of wind strength over the last 700,000 years. Apparently wind "vigor" was greater by a factor of two during each glacial episode than at the present; and wind speeds were 50 percent greater during glacial than interglacial phases. In future, analysis of the minute plant debris in these cores may also add to the history of wind patterns.

Why should archaeologists be interested in ancient winds? The answer is that winds can have a great impact on human activity. For example, it is thought that increased storminess may have caused the Vikings to abandon their North Atlantic sea route at the onset of a cold period. Similarly, some of the great Polynesian migrations in the southwestern Pacific during the 12th and 13th centuries AD seem to have coincided with the onset of a short period of slightly warmer weather, when violent storms would have been rare. These migrations were brought to an end a few centuries later by the Little Ice Age, which may have caused a sharp increase in the frequency of storms. Had the Polynesians been able to continue, they might conceivably have gone on from New Zealand to reach Tasmania and Australia.

Tree-Rings and Climate

Tree-rings have a growth that varies with the climate, being strong in the spring and then declining to nothing in the winter; the more moisture available, the wider the annual ring. As we saw in Chapter 4, these variations in ring width have formed the basis of a major dating technique. However, study of a particular set of rings can also reveal important environmental data, for example whether growth was slow (implying dense local forest cover) or fast (implying light forest). Tree growth is complex, and many other factors may affect it, but temperature and soil moisture do tend to be dominant.

Annual and decade-to-decade variations show up far more clearly in tree-rings than in ice cores, and tree-rings can also record sudden and dramatic shocks to the climate. For example, data from Virginia indicate that the alarming mortality and near abandonment of Jamestown Colony, the first permanent white settlement in America, occurred during an extraordinary drought, the driest 7-year episode in 770 years (AD 1606–12).

KEY CONCEPTS: RECONSTRUCTING THE ENVIRONMENT ON A GLOBAL SCALE

- *Evidence from sea and ice cores:* analysis of isotopic ratios within dateable layers of ocean sediment and ice can give an accurate idea of climate. Studies from all over the world are all in broad agreement about what global climate was like over the past few million years

- *Evidence from tree-rings:* Similar analysis of tree-rings gives a finer-scale idea of what the environment was like in different areas up to about 10,000 years ago

The study of tree-rings and climate (dendroclimatology) has also progressed by using X-ray measurements of cell-size and density as an indication of environmental productivity. More recently, ancient temperatures have been derived from tree-rings by means of the carbon isotope ratios preserved in their cellulose. Isotopic evidence preserved in the cellulose of timbers of the tamarisk tree, contained in the ramp which the Romans used to overcome the besieged Jewish citadel of Masada in AD 73, have revealed to Israeli archaeologists that the climate at that time was wetter and more amenable to agriculture than it is today.

The role of tree-rings makes it clear that it is organic remains above all that provide the richest source of evidence for environmental reconstruction. We now take a look at the surviving traces of plants and animals and what these can tell us about ancient environments.

RECONSTRUCTING THE PLANT ENVIRONMENT

The prime goal in archaeological plant studies is to try to reconstruct what the vegetation was like in the past at any particular time or place. But we should not forget that plants lie at the base of the food chain. The plant communities of a given area and period will therefore provide clues to local animal and human life, and will also reflect soil conditions and climate. Some types of vegetation react relatively quickly to changes in climate (though less quickly than insects, for instance), and the shifts of plant communities in both latitude and altitude are the most direct link between climatic change and the terrestrial human environment, for example in the Ice Age.

Plant studies in **archaeology** have always been overshadowed by faunal analysis, simply because bones are more conspicuous than plant remains in **excavation**. Bones may sometimes survive better, but usually plant remains are present in greater numbers than bones. Thanks to the discovery that some of the constituent parts of a plant are much more resistant to decomposition than was believed, and that a huge amount of data survives which can tell us something about long-dead vegetation, plant studies have become very important. As with so many of the specializations on which archaeology can call, these analyses require a great deal of time and funds.

Some of the most informative techniques for making an overall assessment of plant communities in a particular period involve analysis not of the biggest remains but of the tiniest, microbotanical remains, especially pollen.

Microbotanical Remains

Pollen Analysis. **Palynology**, or the study of pollen grains (see box overleaf), was developed by a Norwegian geologist, Lennart von Post, at the beginning of the 20th century. It has proved invaluable to archaeology, since it can be applied to a

POLLEN ANALYSIS

All hayfever sufferers will be aware of the pollen "rain" that can afflict them in the spring and summer. Pollen grains – the tiny male reproductive bodies of flowering plants – have an almost indestructible outer shell (exine) that can survive in certain sediments for tens of thousands of years. In pollen analysis the exines are extracted from the soil, studied under the microscope, and identified according to the distinctive exine shape and surface ornamentation of different families and genera of plants. Once quantified, these identifications are plotted as curves on a pollen diagram. Fluctuations in the curve for each plant category may then be studied for signs of climatic fluctuation, or forest clearance and crop-planting by humans.

Preservation

The most favorable sediments for preservation of pollen are acidic and poorly aerated peat bogs and lake beds, where biological decay is impeded and grains undergo rapid burial. Cave sediments are also usually suitable because of their humidity and constant temperature. Other contexts, such as sandy sediments or open sites exposed to weathering, preserve pollen poorly.

In wet sites, or unexcavated areas, samples are extracted in long cores, but in dry sites a series of separate samples can be removed from the sections. On an archaeological excavation, small samples are usually extracted at regular stratified intervals. Great care must be taken to avoid contamination from the tools used or from the atmosphere. Pollen can also be found in mud bricks, vessels, tombs, mummy wrappings, the guts of preserved bodies, fossil feces, and many other contexts.

Examination and Counting

The sealed tubes containing the samples are examined in the

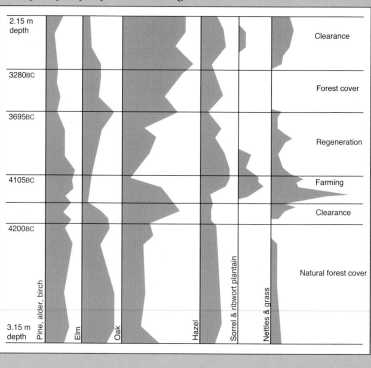

A selection of pollen grains, as seen under the microscope.

Alnus (alder)

Betula (birch)

Corylus (hazel)

Hedera helix (ivy)

Quercus (oak)

Salix (willow)

Tilia (lime)

Ulmus (elm)

Pollen data from Northern Ireland reveal the impact of the first farmers in the region.

2.15 m depth							Clearance
3280BC							Forest cover
3695BC							Regeneration
4105BC							Farming
							Clearance
4200BC							Natural forest cover
3.15 m depth	Pine, alder, birch	Elm	Oak	Hazel	Sorrel & ribwort plantain	Nettles & grass	

laboratory, where a small portion of each sample is studied under the microscope in an attempt to identify a few hundred grains in that sample. Each family and almost every genus of plant produce pollen grains distinctive in shape and surface ornamentation, but it is difficult to go further and pinpoint the species. This imposes certain limits on environmental reconstruction, since different species within the same genus can have markedly different requirements in terms of soil, climate, etc.

After identification, the quantity of pollen for each plant-type is calculated for each layer – usually as a percentage of the total number of grains in that layer – and then plotted as a curve. The curves can be seen as a reflection of climatic fluctuations through the sequence, using the present-day tolerances of these plants as a guide.

The curves can also show the human impact on past vegetation.

The diagram shown here is based on a pollen core from Northern Ireland, and reveals the impact of the first farmers in the region. Forest clearance is indicated *c.* 4150 BC with a fall in tree pollen (especially elm and oak) and a marked increase in open-country and field species such as grass and sorrel. The subsequent regeneration of forest cover, followed by a second period of clearance, shows the non-intensive nature of early farming in the area.

wide range of **sites** and provides information on chronology as well as environment and forest clearance.

While palynology cannot produce an exact picture of past environments, it does give some idea of fluctuations in vegetation through time, whatever their causes may be (whether climatic or human) which can be compared with results from other methods. Pollen studies can also supply much-needed information for environments as ancient as those of the Hadar sediments and the Omo valley in Ethiopia around 3 million years ago. It is usually assumed that these regions were always as dry as they are now, but pollen analysis has shown that they were much wetter and greener between 3.5 and 2.5 million years ago, with even some tropical plants present. The Hadar, which is now semi-desert with scattered trees and shrubs, was rich, open grassland, with dense woodland by lakes and along rivers. The change to drier conditions, around 2.5 million years ago, can be seen in the reduction of tree pollen in favor of more grasses.

Phytoliths. A better-known and fast-developing branch of microbotanical studies concerns **phytoliths**, which were first recognized as components in archaeological contexts as long ago as 1908, but have only been studied systematically in the last few decades. These are minute particles of silica (plant opal) derived from the cells of plants, and they survive after the rest of the organism has decomposed or been burned. They are common in hearths and ash layers, but are also found inside pottery, plaster, and even on stone tools and the teeth of animals: grass phytoliths have been found adhering to herbivorous animal teeth from Bronze Age, Iron Age, and medieval sites in Europe.

These crystals are useful because, like pollen grains, they are produced in large numbers, they survive well in ancient sediments, and they have myriad distinctive shapes and sizes that vary according to type. They inform us primarily about the use people made of particular plants, but their simple presence adds to the picture of the environment built up from other sources.

Phytoliths are minute particles of silica in plant cells which survive after the rest of the plant has decomposed. Some are specific to certain parts of the plant (e.g. stem or leaf).

In particular, a combination of phytolith and pollen analysis can be a powerful tool for environmental reconstruction, since the two methods have complementary strengths and weaknesses. The American scholar Dolores Piperno has studied cores from the Gatun Basin, Panama, whose pollen content had already revealed a sequence of vegetation change from 11,300 years ago to the present. She found that the phytoliths in the cores confirmed the pollen sequence, with the exception that evidence for agriculture and forest clearance (i.e. the appearance of maize, and an increase in grass at the expense of trees) appeared around 4850 years ago in the phytoliths, about 1000 years earlier than in the pollen. This early evidence is probably attributable to small clearings which do not show up in pollen diagrams because grains from the surrounding forest overwhelm the samples.

Diatom Analysis. Another method of environmental reconstruction using plant microfossils is **diatom analysis**. Diatoms are single-cell algae that have cell walls of silica instead of cellulose, and these silica cell walls survive after the algae die. They accumulate in great numbers at the bottom of any body of water in which the algae live; a few are found in peat, but most come from lake and shore sediments.

Diatoms have been recorded, identified, and classified for over 200 years. The process of identifying and counting them is much like that used in palynology, as is the collection of samples in the field. Their well-defined shapes and ornamentations permit identification to a high level, and their assemblages directly reflect the types of algae present and their diatom productivity, and, indirectly, the water's salinity, alkalinity, and nutrient content. From the environmental requirements of different species (in terms of habitat, salinity, and nutrients), one can determine what their immediate environment was at different periods.

A variety of diatoms, the microscopic single-cell algae, whose silica cell walls survive in many sediments after death. Study of the changing species in a deposit can help scientists reconstruct fluctuations in past environments.

Since diatom assemblages can indicate whether water was fresh, brackish, or salt, they have been used to identify, for example, the period when lakes became isolated from the sea in areas of **tectonic** uplift, to locate the positions of past shore-lines, and to reveal water pollution. For instance, the diatom sequence in sediments at the site of the former Lake Wevershoof, Medemblick (the Netherlands) suggests that in around AD 800 seawater entered and overcame what had been a freshwater lake, causing a hiatus in human occupation of the immediate area.

All these microbotanical techniques mentioned – studies of pollen, phytoliths, and diatoms – can only be carried out by specialists. For archaeologists, however, a far more direct contact with environmental evidence comes from the larger plant remains that they can actually see and conserve in the course of excavation.

Macrobotanical Remains

A variety of bigger types of plant remains are potentially retrievable, and provide important information about which plants grew near sites, which were used or con-sumed by people, and so on. Here we shall focus on the valuable clues that macrobotanical remains can provide to local environmental conditions.

Retrieval of vegetation from sediments has been made easier by the develop-ment of screening (sieving) and **flotation** techniques able to separate organic material from soil. In flotation, samples of soil from an excavation are poured into an overflowing tank, the lighter organic material floating to the top and spilling over the lip to be caught in sieves of different grades. This material is then dried and identified.

Sediments are by no means the only source of plant remains, which have also been found in the stomachs of frozen mammoths and preserved bog bodies; in fos-silized feces; on teeth; on stone tools; and in residues inside vessels. The remains themselves are varied:

Seeds and Fruits. Ancient seeds and fruits can usually be identified to species, despite changes in their shape caused by charring or waterlogging. In some cases, the remains have disintegrated but have left their imprint behind – grain impres-sions are fairly common on pottery, leaf impressions are also known, and imprints exist on materials ranging from plaster to leather and corroded bronze. Identifica-tion, of course, depends on type and quality of the traces. Not all such finds necessarily mean that a plant grew locally: grape pips, for example, may come from imported fruit, while impressions on potsherds may mislead since pottery can travel far from its place of manufacture.

Plant Residues. Chemical analysis of plant residues in vessels will be dealt with below in the context of human diet, but the results can give some idea of what species were available. Pottery vessels themselves may incorporate plant fibers (not to mention shell, feathers, or blood) as a tempering material, and microscopic analysis can sometimes identify these remains – for example, study of early pots from South Carolina and Georgia in the United States revealed the presence of shredded stems of Spanish Moss, a member of the pineapple family.

Remains of Wood. Study of *charcoal* (burnt wood) is making a growing contribution to archaeological reconstruction of environments and of human use of timber. A very durable material, charcoal is commonly found by the archaeologist during excavation. Fragments can be examined by the specialist under the microscope, and identified (thanks to the anatomy of the wood) normally at the genus level, and sometimes to species. Charcoal and charred seeds have also proved the most reliable material from which to take samples for **radiocarbon dating** (Chapter 4).

Many charcoal samples are the remains of firewood, but others may come from wooden structures, furniture, and implements burnt at some point in a site's history. Samples therefore inevitably tend to reflect human selection of wood rather than the full range of species growing around the site. Nevertheless, the totals for each species provide some idea of one part of the vegetation at a given time.

Occasionally, charcoal analysis can be combined with other evidence to reveal something not only of local environment but also of human adaptation to it. At Boomplaas Cave, in southern Cape Province (South Africa), excavation has uncovered traces of human occupation stretching back 70,000 years. There is a clear difference between Ice Age and post-Ice Age charcoals: at times of extreme cold when conditions were also drier, between 22,000 and *c.* 14,000 years ago, the species diversity both in the charcoals and the pollen was low, whereas at times of higher rainfall and/or temperature the species diversity increased. A similar pattern of species diversity is seen also in the small mammals.

The vegetation around Boomplaas Cave at the time of maximum cold and drought was composed mainly of shrubs and grass with few plant resources that could be used by people; the larger mammal fauna was dominated by grazers that included "giant" species of buffalo, horse, and hartebeest, which became extinct by about 10,000 years ago.

The Boomplaas charcoal directly reflects the gradual change in climate and vegetation which led to the disappearance of the large grazers, and to a corresponding shift in subsistence practices by the cave's occupants. The charcoal analysis also highlights more subtle changes that reflect a shift in the season of maximum rainfall. The woody vegetation in the Cango Valley today is dominated by the thorn tree, *Acacia karroo*, characteristic of large areas in southern Africa where it is relatively dry and rain falls mostly in summer. Thorn tree charcoal is absent in the Ice

Scanning electron microscope photograph of charcoal from the thorn tree *Acacia karroo* found at Boomplaas Cave.

Age samples at Boomplaas but it appears from about 5000 years ago and by 2000 years ago is the dominant species, indicating a shift to hot, relatively moist summers. As the number of species that enjoy summer rainfall increased, the inhabitants of the cave were able to make more use of a new range of fruits, the seeds of which can be found preserved at the site.

KEY CONCEPTS: RECONSTRUCTING THE PLANT ENVIRONMENT

Microbotanical remains:

• Pollen – most useful for the study of minor fluctuations in climate over the last 12,000 years, although pollen can be preserved for millions of years in some contexts

• Phytoliths – survive very well in most archaeological sediments and can add to the picture of the environment built up from other sources

• Diatoms – found in lake and shore sediments and thus useful for the analysis of past marine environments

Macrobotanical remains:

• Seeds and fruits – can usually be identified to species, but interpretation can be difficult since they can be brought in to a site from elsewhere

• Plant residues – can give some idea of what species were available

• Wood – charcoal survives well in the archaeological record, and can be identified to species, but what is found tends to reflect human selection of wood rather than the full range of species growing around a site

By no means all wood subjected to this kind of analysis is charred. Increasing quantities of *waterlogged wood* are recovered from wet sites in many parts of the world. And in some conditions, such as extreme cold or dryness, *desiccated wood* may survive without either burning or waterlogging.

Other Sources of Evidence.   A great deal of information on vegetation in the less remote periods studied by archaeologists can be obtained from art, from texts (e.g. the writings of Pliny the Elder, Roman farming texts, accounts and illustrations by early explorers such as Captain Cook), and even from photographs.

No single category of evidence can provide us with a total picture of local or regional vegetation, of small-scale trends or long-term changes: each produces a partial version of past realities. Input is needed from every source available, and, as will be seen below, these must be combined with results from the other forms of data studied in this chapter in order to reconstruct the best approximation of a past environment.

In this section we have seen how we can use a variety of archaeological data to try to reconstruct the plant environment at any particular place or time in the past. But what evidence of animal life is there and what can this tell us about past environments?

RECONSTRUCTING THE ANIMAL ENVIRONMENT

Animal remains were the first evidence used by 19th-century archaeologists to characterize the climate of the prehistoric periods that they encountered in their excavations. It was realized that different species were absent, present, or particularly abundant in certain layers, and hence also in certain periods, and the assumption was that this reflected changing climatic conditions.

Today, in order to use faunal remains as a guide to environment, we need to look more critically at the evidence than did those 19th-century pioneers. For instance, we need to understand the complex relationship that exists between modern animals and their environment. We also need to investigate how the animal remains we are studying arrived at a site – either naturally, or through the activities of carnivores or people, and thus how representative they may be of the variety of animals in their period.

Microfauna

Small animals (microfauna) tend to be better indicators of climate and environmental change than are large species, because they are much more sensitive to small variations in climate and adapt to them relatively quickly. In addition, since microfauna tend to accumulate naturally on a site, they reflect the immediate environment more accurately than the larger animals whose remains are often accumulated through human or animal predation. As with pollen, small animals, and especially insects, are also usually found in far greater numbers than larger ones, which improves the statistical significance of their analysis.

The remains of a wide variety of insectivores, rodents, and bats are found on archaeological sites, but it is necessary to ensure as far as possible that the bones were deposited at the same time as the layer in question, and that burrowing has not occurred. Certain small species can be indicative of fairly specific environmental conditions, but it should be remembered that, even if the remains are not intrusive, they will not always indicate the immediate environment – if they come from owl pellets, for example, they may have been caught up to a few kilometers from the site (the contents of bird pellets can nevertheless be of great value in assessing local environments).

Bones of birds and fish are particularly fragile, but are well worth studying. They can for example be used to determine the seasons in which particular sites were occupied. Birds are sensitive to climatic change, and the alternation of "cold" and "warm" species in the last Ice Age has been of great help in assessing environment. One problem is that it is sometimes difficult to decide whether a bird is present naturally or has been brought in by a human or animal predator.

The calcium carbonate shells of land molluscs (such as snails) are preserved in many types of sediment. They reflect local conditions, and can be responsive to changes in microclimate, particularly to changes in temperature and rainfall. But we need to take into account that many species have a very broad tolerance, and their reaction to change is relatively slow, so that they "hang on" in adverse areas, and disperse slowly into newly acceptable areas. The changing percentages of marine mollusc species through time can reveal something of the nature of the coastal micro-environment – such as whether it was sandy or rocky – through study of the modern preferences of the species represented. The climatic change suggested by these alterations in the presence or abundance of different species can be matched with the results of oxygen isotope analysis of the shells.

A wide range of insects may also be found, in the form of adults, larvae, and (in the case of flies) puparia. The study of insects (**paleoentomology**) was rather neglected in archaeology until about 30 years ago, since when a great deal of pioneering work has been done. Insect exoskeletons can be quite resistant to decomposition, and some assemblages comprise thousands of individuals. Since we know the distribution and environmental requirements of their modern descendants, it is often possible to use insect remains as accurate indicators of the likely climatic conditions (and to some extent of the vegetation) prevailing in

Grasshopper engraved on a bone fragment from the late Ice Age (Magdalenian) site of Enlène, Ariège, France. Insects respond rapidly to climatic change, and are sensitive indicators of the timing and scale of environmental variations.

particular periods and local areas. Some species have very precise requirements in terms of where they like to breed and the kinds of food their larvae need. However, rather than use single "indicator species" to reconstruct a micro-environment, it is safer to consider a number of species (the ancient climate lying within the area of overlap of their tolerance ranges).

Macrofauna

Remains of large animals found on archaeological sites mainly help us build up a picture of past human diet (see below). As environmental indicators they have proved less reliable than was once assumed, primarily because they are not so sensitive to environmental changes as small animals, but also because their remains will very likely have been deposited in an archaeological context through human or animal action. Bones from animals killed by people or by carnivores have been selected, and so cannot accurately reflect the full range of fauna present in the environment. The ideal is therefore to find accumulations of animal remains brought about by natural accident or catastrophe – animals caught in a flash flood perhaps, or buried by volcanic eruption, or which became frozen in permafrost. But such discoveries are rare – very different from the usual accumulations of animal bones encountered by archaeologists.

Assuming a suitable bone assemblage has been found and identified to species, what can the results tell us about the ancient environment?

The anatomy and especially the teeth of large animals tell us something about their diet and hence, in the case of herbivores, of the type of vegetation they prefer. However, most information about range and habitat comes from studies of modern species, on the assumption that behavior has not changed substantially since the period in question. These studies also show that large animals will tolerate – that is, have the potential to withstand or exploit – a much wider range of temperatures and environments than was once thought. So the presence of a species such as a woolly rhinoceros in an Ice Age deposit should be regarded merely as proof of the ability of that species to tolerate low temperatures, rather than as evidence of a cold climate.

KEY CONCEPTS: RECONSTRUCTING THE ANIMAL ENVIRONMENT

- Microfauna are better indicators of climate and environmental change than macrofauna because they are much more sensitive to small variations in climate and adapt to them relatively quickly

- Microfauna tend to accumulate naturally on a site and reflect the immediate environment more accurately than the larger animals whose remains are often accumulated through human or animal predation

Large mammals are also not generally good indicators of *vegetation*, since herbivores can thrive in a wide range of environments and eat a variety of plants. Thus, individual species cannot usually be regarded as characteristic of one particular habitat, but there are exceptions. For example, reindeer reached northern Spain in the last Ice Age, as is shown not only by discoveries of their bones but also by cave art. Such major shifts clearly reflect environmental change. In the rock art of the Sahara, too, one can see clear evidence for the presence of species such as giraffe and elephant that could not survive in the area today, and thus for dramatic environmental modification.

As will be seen below, fauna can also be used to determine in which seasons of the year a site was occupied. In coastal sites, marine resources and herbivore remains may come and go through the archaeological sequence as changes in sea level extended or drowned the coastal plain, thus changing the sites' proximity to the shore and the availability of grazing.

We always have to bear in mind that faunal fluctuations can have causes other than climate or people; additional factors may include competition, epidemics, or fluctuations in numbers of predators. Moreover, small-scale local variations in climate and weather can have enormous effects on the numbers and distribution of wild animals, so that despite its high powers of resistance a species may decline from extreme abundance to virtual extinction within a few years.

SUBSISTENCE AND DIET

Having discussed methods for reconstructing the environment, we now turn to how we find out about what people extracted from it, in other words, how they subsisted. When reconstructing early subsistence, it is useful to make a distinction between *meals*, direct evidence of various kinds as to what people were eating at a particular time, and *diet*, which implies the pattern of consumption over a long period of time.

So far as meals are concerned, the sources of information are varied. Written records, when they survive, indicate some of the things people were eating, and so do representations in art. Even modern ethnoarchaeology helps indicate what they *might* have been eating by broadening our understanding of their range of options. And the actual remains of the foodstuffs eaten can be highly informative.

For the much more difficult question of diet, there are several helpful techniques of investigation. Some methods focus on human bones. Isotopic analyses of the skeletal remains of a human population can indicate, for example, the balance of marine and terrestrial foods in the diet, and even show differences in nutrition between the more and less advantaged members of the same society.

Most of our information about early subsistence, however, comes directly from the remains of what was eaten. Zooarchaeology (or **archaeozoology**), the study of past human use of animals, is now big business in archaeology. There can be few excavations anywhere that do not have a specialist to study the animal bones found. The Paleo-Indian rockshelter of Meadowcroft, Pennsylvania, for example, yielded about a million animal bones (and almost 1.5 million plant specimens). On medieval and recent sites, the quantities of material recovered can be even more formidable. **Paleo-ethnobotany** (or archaeobotany), the study of past human use of plants, is likewise a growing discipline, with a number of techniques for determining the plant species recovered. In both areas, a detailed understanding of the conditions of preservation on a site is a first prerequisite to ensure that the most efficient extraction technique is adopted. In both areas, too, the focus of interest has developed to include not just the species eaten, but the way these were managed. The process of domestication for both plants and animals is now a major research topic.

Interpretation of food remains can be problematic and requires quite sophisticated procedures. We can initially reconstruct the range of food available in the surrounding environment (see above), but the only incontrovertible proof that a particular plant or animal species was actually consumed is the presence of its traces in stomach contents or in desiccated ancient fecal matter. If such evidence is not available, the archaeologist must try to determine whether a foodstuff was actually eaten from the context or condition of the finds. For instance, if bones are cut or burned they may have been butchered and cooked.

Plants that were staples in the diet may be under-represented thanks to the generally poor preservation of vegetable remains; fish bones likewise may not survive well. The archaeologist therefore has to consider how far a site's food remains are representative of total diet. Here we need to assess a site's function, and whether it was inhabited once or frequently, for short or long periods, irregularly or seasonally (season of occupation can sometimes be deduced from plant and animal evidence as well). A long-term settlement is likely to provide more representative food remains than a specialized camp or kill site. Ideally, however, archaeologists should sample remains from a variety of contexts or sites before making judgments about diet.

We will now look at some of the main forms of evidence for human subsistence, as well as some of the different types of interpretations that can be made.

WHAT CAN PLANT FOODS TELL US ABOUT DIET?

We can learn something of diet from the study of microbotanical remains, particularly through the study of phytoliths, which can, for example, help in differentiating between wild and domestic species of plant. But the vast majority of plant evidence that reaches the archaeologist is in the form of macrobotanical remains, and these are much more useful when trying to reconstruct diet.

Macrobotanical Remains

Macrobotanical remains may be desiccated (only in absolutely dry environments such as deserts or high mountains), waterlogged (only in environments that have been permanently wet since the date of deposition), or preserved by charring. In exceptional circumstances, volcanic eruption can preserve botanical remains, such as Cerén in El Salvador where a wide variety have been found carbonized, or as impressions, in numerous vessels. Plant remains preserved in several different ways can sometimes be encountered within the same site, but in most parts of the world charring is the principal or only cause of preservation on habitation sites.

Occasionally, a single sample on a site will yield very large amounts of material. Over 27 kg (60 lb) of charred barley, wheat, and other plants came from one storage pit on a Bronze Age farm at Black Patch, southern England, for example. This can sometimes give clues to the relative importance of different cereals and legumes and weed flora, but the sample nevertheless simply reflects a moment in time. What the archaeologist really needs is a larger number of samples (each of preferably more than 100 grains) from a single period on the site, and, if possible, from a range of types of deposit, in order to obtain reliable information about what species were exploited, their importance, and their uses during the period of time in question.

When we have obtained enough samples we need to quantify the plant remains: for example by weight or by number of remains. Some archaeologists simply arrange samples in order of abundance. But this can be misleading, as was shown by the British archaeobotanist Jane Renfrew in her study of the material from the **Neolithic** settlement of Sitagroi, Greece. She noted that the most abundant plant may have been preserved by chance (such as an accident in the course of baking). Similarly, species that produce large quantities of seeds or grains may appear more

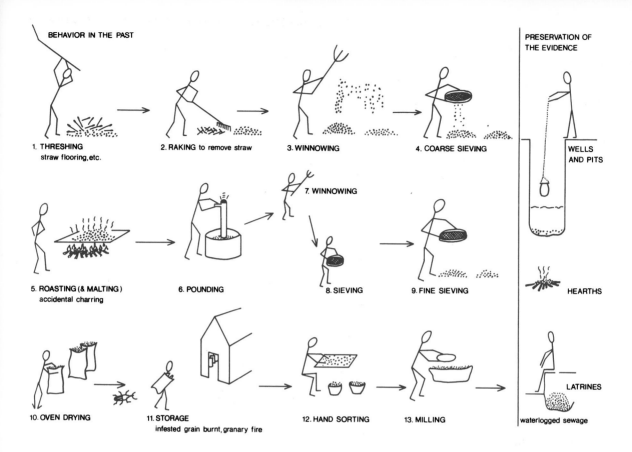

1. THRESHING
straw flooring, etc.

2. RAKING to remove straw

3. WINNOWING

4. COARSE SIEVING

WELLS AND PITS

5. ROASTING (& MALTING)
accidental charring

6. POUNDING

7. WINNOWING

8. SIEVING

9. FINE SIEVING

HEARTHS

10. OVEN DRYING

11. STORAGE
infested grain burnt, granary fire

12. HAND SORTING

13. MILLING

LATRINES

waterlogged sewage

Cereal crop processing: waste products from many of these stages may survive as charred or waterlogged remains.

important in the archaeological record than they actually were: at Sitagroi 19,000 seeds of knotgrass barely filled a thimble.

Interpreting the Context and the Remains. It is crucial for the archaeologist or specialist to try to understand the archaeological context of a plant sample, as this can reveal more about exactly how the plant was being used. In the past attention used to be focused primarily on the botanical history of the plants themselves, their morphology, place of origin, and **evolution**. Now, however, archaeologists also want to know more about the human use of plants in hunting and gathering economies, and in agriculture – which plants were important in the diet, and how they were gathered or grown, processed, stored, and cooked. This means understanding the different stages of traditional plant processing; recognizing the effect different processes have on the remains; and identifying the different contexts in the archaeological record. In many cases it is the plant remains that reveal the function of the location where they are found, and thus the nature of the context, rather than vice versa.

In a farming economy, for instance, there are many different stages of plant processing, summed up in the illustration above: cereals have to be threshed, winnowed, and cleaned before consumption, in order to separate the grain from the chaff, straw, and weeds; but seed corn also has to be stored for the next year's crop; and food grain might also be stored unthreshed in order to get the harvested crop out of the rain, and would then be threshed only when needed. From ethnoarchaeological and experimental observations it is known that certain of these activities leave characteristic residues with which archaeological samples can be compared, whether they are from ovens, living floors, latrines, or storage pits.

Chemical Residues in Plant Remains. Various chemicals survive in plant remains themselves which provide an alternative basis for their identification. These compounds include proteins, fatty lipids, and even DNA. The analysis of lipids has so far proved the most useful method for distinguishing different cereal and legume species, but always in combination with other non-chemical identification techniques. DNA offers the prospect of eventually resolving identification at an even more detailed level and of perhaps tracing family trees of the plants and patterns of trade in plant products.

Plant Impressions. Impressions of plant remains are quite common in fired clay, and do at least prove that the species in question was present at the spot where the clay was worked. Such impressions, however, do not necessarily prove that the plant was important in the economy or diet, since they constitute a very skewed sample and only seeds or grains of medium size tend to leave imprints. One has to be particularly careful with impressions on potsherds, because pottery can be discarded far from its point of manufacture, and in any case many pots were deliberately decorated with grain impressions, thus perhaps overemphasizing the importance of a species.

Analysis of Plant Residues on Artifacts

As we shall see in Chapter 7, microwear analysis of a tool edge can identify broadly whether the tool was used to cut meat, wood, or some other material. Discovery of phytoliths can show what type of grasses were cut by a tool. Microscopic study can also reveal and identify plant fibers. Another method is chemical analysis of residues on tool edges: certain chemical reagents can provide a means of proving whether plant residues are present on tools or in vessels – thus, potassium iodide turns blue if starch grains are present, and yellow-brown for other plant materials. Starch grains can also be detected by microscope and, for example, have been extracted with a needle from crevices in the surfaces of prehistoric milling stones from Aguadulce Shelter in the humid tropics of Panama. The species of the grains can be identified, and show that tubers such as manioc and arrowroot – which do not usually leave recoverable fossilized remains – were being cultivated here *c.* 5000 BC, the earliest recorded occurrence of manioc in the Americas.

Chemical investigation of fats preserved in vessels is also making progress, because it has been found that fatty acids, amino acids (the constituents of protein), and similar substances are very stable and preserve well. Samples are extracted from residues, purified, concentrated in a centrifuge, dried, and then analyzed by means of a spectrometer, and by a technique known as chromatography, which separates the major constituent components of the fats. Interpretation of the results is made by comparison with a reference collection of "chromatograms" (read-outs) from different substances.

For example, the German chemist Rolf Rottländer has identified mustard, olive oil, seed oils, butter, and other substances on potsherds, including specimens from Neolithic lake dwellings. In work on sherds from the German Iron Age hillfort of the Heuneburg, he has been able to prove that some amphorae – storage vessels usually associated with liquids – did indeed contain olive oil and wine, whereas in the case of a Roman amphora the charcoal-like black residue proved to be not liquid but wheat flour. This important technique not only provides dietary evidence, but also helps to define the function of the vessels with which the fats are associated. Ever more refined techniques are currently being developed for identifying food species from protein, lipid, and DNA biochemical analysis of small fragments of plant material.

The Domestication of Wild Plant Species

One of the major areas of debate in modern archaeology concerns the question of human management of plants, and particularly whether some species that we find were *wild* or *domesticated*, since this sheds light on one of the most crucial aspects of human history: the transition from a mobile (**hunter-gatherer**) to a settled (agricultural) way of life. It can often be difficult, impossible, or irrelevant to try to distinguish between wild and domesticated varieties since many types of cultivation do not change the form of the plant, and even in cases where such change occurs we do not know how long it took to appear. Experimental evidence suggests that the transition from wild to domestic could have been complete within only 20 to 200 years – without conscious intervention on the farmers' part. Any line drawn between wild and domestic plants does not necessarily correspond to a distinction between gathering and agriculture.

There are nevertheless cases where a clear distinction can be made between wild and fully domestic forms. Macrobotanical remains are of most use here. For example, the American archaeologist Bruce Smith found that 50,000 charred seeds of *Chenopodium* (goosefoot), nearly 2000 years old from Russell Cave, Alabama, exhibited a set of interrelated characteristics reflecting domestication. He was thus able to add this starchy-seed species to the brief list of cultivated plants – including

Wild and domestic cereals. Left to right: wild and domestic einkorn, domestic maize, extinct wild maize. The wild einkorn is sheds its grain easily. But the tougher domestic form does so only when threshed: a real advantage for the early farmer, since if grains fall off before threshing, they are lost.

bottle gourd, squash, marsh elder, sunflower, and tobacco – available in the garden plots of the Eastern Woodlands before the introduction of maize in about AD 200.

There has been some debate in recent years about whether wild and domestic legumes can be differentiated by their structure, but archaeobotanical work by the British scholar Ann Butler suggests that there is no foolproof way to do this, even in a scanning electron microscope. Cereals, on the other hand, where well preserved, are more straightforward, and domestication can be identified by clues such as the loss of anatomical features like the brittle rachis that facilitate the dispersal of seed by natural agents. In other words, once people began to cultivate cereals, they gradually developed varieties that retained their seeds until they could be harvested.

Plant Evidence from Literate Societies

Archaeologists studying the beginnings of plant cultivation, or plant use among hunter-gatherers, have to rely on the kind of scientific evidence outlined above, coupled with the judicious use of ethnoarchaeological research and modern experiments. For the student of diet among literate societies, however, particularly the great civilizations, there is a wealth of evidence for domestication of plants, as well as for farming practices, cookery, and many other aspects of diet to be found written in documents and in art.

The Greek writer Herodotus, for example, gives us plenty of information about eating habits in the 5th century BC, notably in Egypt, a civilization for which there is extensive evidence about food and diet. Much of the evidence for the pharaonic period comes from paintings and foodstuffs in tombs, so it has a certain upper-class bias, but there is also information to be found about the diet of humbler folk from plant remains in workers' villages such as that at Tell el-Amarna, and from hieroglyphic texts. In the later Ptolemaic period there are records of corn allowances for workers, such as the 3rd-century BC accounts concerning grain allotted to workers on a Faiyum agricultural estate. Models are also instructive about food preparation: the tomb of Meketre, a nobleman of the 12th dynasty (2000–1790 BC), contained

Harvesting and processing a cereal crop: scenes depicted on the walls of a New Kingdom tomb at Thebes in Egypt.

a set of wooden models, including women kneading flour into loaves, and others brewing beer. Three newly deciphered Babylonian clay tablets from Iraq, 3750 years old, present cuneiform texts containing 35 recipes for a wide variety of rich meat stews, and thus constitute the world's oldest cookbook.

In the New World, we owe much of our knowledge of Aztec food crops, fishing practices, and natural history to the invaluable writings of the 16th-century Franciscan scholar Bernardino de Sahagún, based on his own observations and on the testimony of his Indian informants.

It should be remembered, however, that written evidence and art tend to give a very short-term view of subsistence. Only archaeology can look at human diet with a long-term perspective.

KEY CONCEPTS: WHAT CAN PLANT FOODS TELL US ABOUT DIET?

- *Macrobotanical Remains:* these can give us a good idea of what plants were present at a site, but there are problems of quantification and interpretation. It's important to understand how a plant might have been processed and used

- *Plant Residues on Artifacts:* chemical traces of plants can be found on some artifacts (often pots and tools) and these can be tested and compared against a reference collection in order to identify a species

- *Domestication of Wild Plant Species:* various techniques can help to answer the crucial question of whether plant remains found in the archaeological record are from wild or domesticated species

INVESTIGATING DIET, SEASONALITY, AND DOMESTICATION FROM ANIMAL REMAINS

Although plant foods may always have constituted the greater part of the diet – except in special circumstances or high latitudes like the Arctic – meat may well have been considered more important, either as food or as a reflection of the prowess of the hunter or the status of the herder. Animal remains are usually better preserved on archaeological sites too so that, unlike plant remains, they have been studied since the very beginnings of archaeology.

The first question the archaeologist must face when interpreting animal remains is to decide whether they are present through human actions rather than through natural causes or other predators (as in the case of carnivore debris, owl pellets, burrowing animals, etc.). Animals may also have been exploited at a site for non-dietary purposes (skins for clothing, bone and antler for tools).

As with plant remains, therefore, one must be particularly careful to examine the context and content of faunal samples. This is usually straightforward in sites of recent periods, but in the **Paleolithic**, especially the Lower Paleolithic, the question is crucial.

Proving Human Exploitation of Animals in the Paleolithic.　In the past, association of animal bones and stone tools was often taken as proof that humans were responsible for the presence of the faunal remains, or at least exploited them. We now know, however, that this is not always a fair assumption, and since in any case many used bones are not associated with tools, archaeologists have sought more definite proof from the marks of stone tools on the bones themselves. A great deal of work is currently aimed at proving the existence of such marks, and finding ways of differentiating them from other traces such as scratches and punctures made by animal teeth, etching by plant roots, abrasion by sedimentary particles or post-depositional weathering, and damage by excavation tools. This is also part of the search for reliable evidence in the current major debate in Paleolithic studies as to whether early humans were genuine hunters, or merely scavenged meat from carcasses of animals killed by other predators.

Much attention has been directed to bones from the famous Lower Paleolithic sites of Olduvai Gorge and Koobi Fora, in East Africa, that are over 1.5 million years old. Archaeologists used a scanning electron microscope to examine suspected toolmarks on the bones, comparing their results with marks produced by known processes on modern bones. The diagnostic feature of a toolmark produced by a slicing action, for example, was a v-shaped groove with a series of longitudinal parallel lines at the bottom; marks made by carnivores were much more rounded

Carnivore marks or toolmarks? Bone surfaces analyzed in the scanning electron microscope. (Above) Round-bottomed groove made on a modern bone by a hyena. (Above right) V-shaped groove made on a modern bone by a sharp stone flake. (Right) Fossil bone from Olduvai Gorge that may show two slicing marks (s) made by a stone flake, and carnivore tooth marks (t) made later.

(see illustration above). They found that many bones had both toolmarks and carnivore scratches, suggesting some competition for the carcass. In some cases, the carnivore marks were clearly superimposed on the toolmarks, but in most cases the carnivores seem to have got there first!

However, recent work suggests that very similar marks can be produced by other causes, such as when bones are damaged by trampling. Thus microscopic features alone are not sufficient evidence to prove human intervention. The context of the find and the position of the marks need to be studied too.

More work still needs to be done before we can be sure of proving early human activity in this way, and also of identifying episodes where our early ancestors were hunters rather than scavengers. However, there are other types of evidence that can provide proof of human processing of bones. These include artificial concentrations of bones in particular places, such as the use of mammoth bones for the construction of huts in the Paleolithic of central and eastern Europe. Burning of bones is another clear indication of human processing.

Having demonstrated so far as possible that animal remains were indeed produced by human action, the archaeologist then can move on to try to answer the interesting questions such as what did people eat, in which seasons did they eat particular foods, how did they hunt and butcher the animals, and were the animals domesticated?

The most abundant and informative residues of animals are the macroremains – bones, teeth, antlers, shells, etc. Numerous techniques are now available to help extract information from data of this type.

In analyzing an assemblage of bones, we have first to identify them and then quantify them, both in terms of numbers of animals and of meat weight. The amount of meat represented by a bone will depend on the sex and age of the animal, the season of death, and geographical variation in body size and in nutrition. But if factors of age, sex, and season of death need to be allowed for, how are they established?

Strategies of Use: Deducing Age, Sex, and Seasonality from Large Fauna

Sexing is easy in cases where only the male has antlers (most deer), or large canines (pig), or where a penis bone is present (e.g. dog), or where the female has a different pelvic structure. Measurements of certain bones, such as the foot bones of some animals, can sometimes provide two distinct clusters of results, interpreted as male (large) and female (small).

The *age* of an animal can be assessed from features such as the degree of closure of sutures in the skull, or, to a certain extent, from the stage of development of limb bones. Age is then estimated by comparison with information on these features in modern populations. However, estimates of the age at which mammals were killed are usually based on the eruption and wear patterns of the teeth.

The season of death is also a crucial factor. There are many ways of studying *seasonality* from animal remains – for example, the identification of species only available at certain times of year, or which shed their antlers in specific seasons. If it is known at what time of year the young of a species were born, then remains of fetuses, or bones of the newly born, can pinpoint a season of occupation.

The Question of Animal Domestication

An entirely different set of methods is required to assess the status of the animals – i.e. whether they were wild or domesticated. Like the study of plant domestication described above, this is a crucial question about one of the most important developments in human history: the transition from a mobile to a settled, agricultural way of life. In some cases the answer can be obvious, such as where non-indigenous animals have been introduced on to islands by humans – for example, the appearance of cattle, sheep, goat, dog, and cat on Cyprus.

A meal as a funerary offering: the rich and elaborate food remains found in the 2nd-dynasty tomb of a noblewoman at Saqqara, Egypt. These include a triangular loaf of bread; nabk berries (similar in appearance to cherries); cut ribs of beef; a cooked quail; two cooked kidneys; stewed fruit, probably figs; cakes; pigeon stew; a cooked fish. Impressive as such remains are, they are unlikely to be representative of the everyday diet of the ancient Egyptians.

One criterion of animal domestication is human interference with the natural breeding habits of certain species, which has led to changes in the physical characteristics of those species from the wild state. But there are other definitions, and specialists disagree about which physical changes in animals are diagnostic of domestication. Too much emphasis on the wild/domestic dichotomy may also mask a whole spectrum of human-animal relationships, such as herd management without selective breeding. Nevertheless, domestication, by any definition, clearly occurred separately in many parts of the world, and archaeologists therefore need to differentiate fully wild from fully domestic animals, and to investigate the process of domestication.

Amongst a number of other possible lines of evidence, certain tools may indicate the presence of domesticated animals – for example, plows, yokes, and horse trappings. Deformities and disease can also provide convincing evidence for domestication. When used for traction, horses, cattle, and camels all sometimes suffer osteoarthritis or strain-deformities on their lower limbs. Work is also progressing on tracing the history of domestication through DNA.

Remains of Individual Meals

One of the most direct kinds of evidence of what people ate at a particular moment in the past comes from occasional finds of actual meals. At Pompeii, for example, meals of fish, eggs, bread, and nuts were found intact on tables, as well as food in shops. Food is often preserved in funerary contexts, as in the desiccated corncobs and other items in Peruvian graves, or at Saqqara, Egypt, where the 2nd-dynasty tomb of a noblewoman contained a huge variety of foodstuffs, constituting a rich and elaborate meal – cereals, fish, fowl, beef, fruit, cakes, honey, cheese, and wine – which, to judge by the tomb paintings, was not unusual. The Han period in China

KEY CONCEPTS: INFORMATION FROM ANIMAL RESOURCES

- Animal remains are often well-preserved on archaeological sites

- It's important to establish whether animal remains are present on a site through human agency or through other causes

- We can sex and age animal bones, study their seasonality, and deduce whether the animals were wild or domesticated, all of which helps us to understand how humans were exploiting the animal environment

(206 BC–AD 220) has tombs stocked with food: that of the wife of the Marquis of Dai has a unique collection of provisions, herbal medicines, and prepared dishes in containers of lacquer, ceramic, and bamboo, with labels attached, and even inventory slips giving the composition of the dishes! However, it is unlikely that such magnificent remains are representative of everyday diet. Even the meals found so wonderfully preserved in the buried city of Pompeii are merely a tiny sample from a single day. The only way in which we can really study what people ate habitually is to examine actual human remains.

ASSESSING DIET FROM HUMAN REMAINS

The only incontrovertible evidence that something was actually consumed by humans is its presence in either stomachs or feces. Both kinds of evidence give us invaluable information about individual meals and short-term diet.

The study of human teeth also helps us to reconstruct diet, but the real breakthrough in recent years in understanding long-term diet has come from the analysis of bone collagen. What human bones can reveal about general health will be examined in Chapter 8.

Individual Meals

Stomach Contents.   Stomachs survive only rarely in archaeological contexts, except in bog bodies. Some mummies also provide dietary evidence: the overweight wife of the Marquis of Dai from 2nd-century BC China, mentioned above, seems to have died of a heart attack caused by acute pain from her gallstones an hour or so after enjoying a generous helping of watermelon (138 melon seeds were discovered in her stomach and intestines).

When stomachs survive in bog bodies, the dietary evidence they provide can be of the greatest interest. Pioneering studies of the stomach contents of Danish Iron Age bogmen showed that Grauballe Man, for instance, had consumed over 60 species of wild seeds, together with one or two cereals and a little meat (as shown by some small bone splinters), while Tollund Man had eaten only plants. But we should keep in mind that these results, while fascinating, do not necessarily indicate everyday diet, since these victims were possibly executed or sacrificed, and thus their last meal may have been out of the ordinary.

Fecal Material. Experiments have been done to assess the survival properties of different foodstuffs relevant to the study of ancient diet, and it has been found that many organic remains can survive surprisingly well after their journey through the human digestive tract. Feces themselves survive only rarely, in very dry sites such as caves in the western United States and Mexico, or very wet sites (these feces are often wrongly called "**coprolites**," which means fossilized/petrified excrement). But, where they are preserved, they have proved to be a highly important source of information about what individuals ate in the past.

Macroremains can be extremely varied in human excrement, in fact this variety is an indication of human origin. Bone fragments, plant fibers, bits of charcoal, seeds, and the remains of fish, birds, and even insects are known. Shell fragments – from molluscs, eggs, and nuts – can also be identified. Hair can be assigned to certain classes of animals by means of its scale pattern, visible under the microscope, and thus help us to know which animals were eaten.

Exceptional conditions in Lovelock Cave, Nevada, have preserved 5000 feces dating from 2500 to 150 years ago, and Robert Heizer's study of their contents yielded remarkable evidence about diet, which seems to have comprised seeds, fish, and birds. Feather fragments were identified from waterfowl such as the heron and grebe; fish and reptile scales, which pass through the alimentary canal unaltered, also led to identification of several species. Fish remains were abundant in some of the feces; one, for example, from 1000 years ago, contained 5.8 g (0.2 oz) of fish bone which, it was calculated, came from 101 small chubs, representing a total live weight of 208 g (7.3 oz) – the fish component of a meal for a single person.

Excrement and fecal residues represent single meals, and therefore provide short-term data on diet, unless they are found in great quantities, as at Lovelock Cave, and even there the feces represent only a couple of meals a year. For human diet over whole lifetimes, we need to turn to the human skeleton itself.

Human Teeth as Evidence for Diet

Teeth survive in extremely good condition, made as they are of the two hardest tissues in the body, and microscopic examination of the abrasions on certain dental surfaces can provide evidence for the sort of food that their owners enjoyed. Abrasive particles in food leave striations on the enamel whose orientation and length are directly related to the meat or vegetation in the diet and its process of cooking. Modern meat-eating Greenland Eskimos, for instance, have almost exclusively vertical striations on their lateral tooth surfaces, while largely vegetarian Melanesians have both vertical and horizontal striations, with a shorter average length.

When these results are compared with data from fossil teeth hundreds of thousands of years old, it has been found that there is an increase in horizontal and a decrease in vertical striations, and a decrease in average striation length over time. In other words, less and less effort was needed to chew food, and meat may have decreased in importance as the diet became more mixed: early people crushed and broke down their food with their teeth, but less chewing was required as cooking techniques developed and improved.

Tooth decay as well as wear will sometimes provide us with dietary information. Remains of the California Indians display very marked tooth decay, attributed to their habit of leaching the tannin out of acorns, their staple food, through a bed of sand which caused excessive tooth abrasion. Decay and loss of teeth can also set in thanks to starchy and sugary foods. Dental caries became abundant on the coast of Georgia (USA) in the 12th century AD, particularly among the female population. It was in this period that the transition occurred from hunting, fishing, and gathering to maize agriculture. Anthropologist Clark Larsen believes that the rise in tooth decay over this period, revealed by a study of hundreds of skeletons, was caused by the carbohydrates in maize. Since the women of the group were more subject to the caries than were the men, it is probable that they were growing, harvesting, preparing, and cooking the corn, while the men ate more protein and less carbohydrate.

Isotopic Methods: Diet over a Lifetime

Recently, a revolution has taken place in dietary studies through the realization that **isotopic analysis** of human tooth enamel and bone collagen can reveal a great deal about long-term food intake. The method relies on reading the chemical signatures left in the body by different foods – we are what we eat.

Plants can be divided into three groups based on their differing ratios of two carbon isotopes: temperate, tropical, and marine plants. As animals eat plants, these different chemical signatures are passed along the food chain and are eventually fixed in human and animal bone tissue. They can show whether diet was based on land or marine plants. Only archaeological evidence, however, can provide more detail about precisely which species of plants or animals contributed to the diet.

Recently, for example, isotopic analysis of tooth enamel from four *Australopithecus africanus* individuals from Makapansgat, South Africa, revealed that they

KEY CONCEPTS: ASSESSING DIET FROM HUMAN REMAINS

- *Individual Meals:* we can find direct evidence of what humans in the past ate from the examination of preserved stomach contents and fecal material

- *Teeth:* evidence of wear on human teeth, which survive well in many archaeological sediments, can tell us about the relative importance of meat and plants in past diets

- *Isotopic Evidence:* can be used as evidence for long-term human diet, but needs to be combined with other evidence for a finer picture

ate not only fruits and leaves, as had been thought, but also large quantities of grasses or sedges, or the animals which ate those plants, or both. In other words, they regularly exploited fairly open environments (woodlands or grasslands) for food; and since their tooth wear lacks the characteristic scratches of grass-eaters, it is possible that they were indeed already consuming meat, by hunting small animals or scavenging larger ones.

SUMMARY

- Humankind has developed from being an inconsequential species at the mercy of the environment and the food resources it provided to one with a huge influence over its surroundings. The environment is of crucial importance to archaeology. During every period of the past it has played a vital role in determining where and how people could live, and on what. Archaeologists now have a battery of techniques, largely based on the analysis of plant and animal remains, to help reconstruct such past environments.

- Where food is concerned, the evidence available varies from botanical and animal remains, large and microscopic, to tools and vessels, plant and animal residues, and art and texts. We can discover what was eaten, in which seasons, and sometimes how it was prepared. We need to assess whether the evidence arrived in the archaeological record naturally or through human actions, and whether the resources were wild or under human control. Occasionally we encounter the remains of individual meals left as funerary offerings or the contents of stomachs or feces. Finally, the human body itself contains a record of diet in its toothwear and in the chemical signatures left in bones by different foods.

- Many of the techniques must be carried out by the specialist, particularly the biochemist, but archaeologists should know how to interpret the results, because the rewards are enormous for our knowledge of what the environment was like, what people ate, how they exploited their resources, and in what proportions.

FURTHER READING

General introductions to environmental archaeology and the subject of diet can be found in the following:

Brothwell, D. & P. 1997. **Food in Antiquity: A Survey of the Diet of Early Peoples.** JOHNS HOPKINS UNIV. PRESS: BALTIMORE, MD.

Dimbleby, G. 1978. **Plants and Archaeology**. PALADIN: LONDON.

Dincauze, D.F. 2000. **Environmental Archaeology**. CAMBRIDGE UNIVERSITY PRESS: CAMBRIDGE.

Gilbert, R.I. & Mielke, J.H. (eds.). 1985. **The Analysis of Prehistoric Diets.** ACADEMIC PRESS: NEW YORK & LONDON.

Klein, R.G. & Cruz-Uribe, K. 1984. **The Analysis of Animal Bones from Archaeological Sites**. UNIVERSITY OF CHICAGO PRESS: CHICAGO.

O'Connor, T. 2000. **The Archaeology of Animal Bones.** SUTTON: STROUD.

Reitz, E.J. & Wing, E.S. 1999. **Zooarchaeology.** CAMBRIDGE UNIVERSITY PRESS: CAMBRIDGE.

Roberts, N. 1998. **The Holocene: An Environmental History** (2nd ed.). BLACKWELL: OXFORD.

Smith, B.D. 1998. **The Emergence of Agriculture.** (2nd ed.). SCIENTIFIC AMERICAN LIBRARY: NEW YORK.

7 How Were Artifacts Made, Used, and Distributed?

technology, trade, and exchange

It is the physical remains of humanly made **artifacts** down the ages that form the bulk of the archaeological record. We have seen how archaeologists can find and date artifacts, but in this chapter we will start by addressing two questions of fundamental importance: how were artifacts made, and what were they used for? There are several approaches to these two questions – the purely archaeological, the scientific analysis of objects, the ethnographic, and the experimental.

When assessing ancient technologies, the archaeologist always needs to bear in mind that the sample preserved may well be biased. During the long **Paleolithic** period, for instance, implements of wood and bone must surely have rivaled those of stone in importance – as they do in hunting and gathering societies today – but stone tools dominate the archaeological record.

Once made, artifacts usually move around as they are acquired or passed on between individuals or groups – a phenomenon which can tell us a great deal about the frequency and extent of contacts between different groups, as well as about transportation, economics, and so forth. By analyzing where the materials used to make an artifact came from, as well as the distribution of artifacts as found by archaeologists, we can reconstruct something of these trading relationships: who was exchanging goods with who, and by what method?

When an archaeologist investigates an object, it must first be decided whether it was actually made or used by people in the past. For most periods the answer will be obvious (although we have to beware of fakes and forgeries), but for the Paleolithic, and especially the Lower Paleolithic, judgement can be more difficult. Where the very earliest tools are concerned, on which we would expect the traces of human work to be minimal, the question is not easy to resolve, since the crudest human working may be indistinguishable from the damage caused by nature.

We will make a convenient distinction in the next section on ancient technology between two classes of raw material used in creating objects –between those that are largely unaltered, such as flint, and those that are synthetic, the product of human activities, such as pottery or metal. Of course even supposedly unaltered materials have often been treated by heat or by chemical reactions in order to assist the manufacturing process. But synthetic materials have undergone an actual change in state, usually through heat treatment. The human use of fire – **pyrotechnology** – is a crucial factor here.

UNALTERED MATERIALS
Stone

From the first recognizable tools, dating back about 2.5 million years, up to the adoption of pottery-making, dated to 14,000 BC in Japan, the archaeological

Stone quarry on Easter Island: one of the giant statues lies flat on its back, unfinished but at an advanced stage of manufacture – yielding clues as to how it was made.

record is dominated by stone. How were stone artifacts, from the smallest stone tools to the greatest stone monuments, extracted, manufactured, and used?

Much of the stone for early tools was probably picked up from streambeds or other parts of the landscape; but the sources most visible archaeologically are the mines and quarries. The best-known *mines* are the **Neolithic** and later flint mines in various parts of northern Europe, such as Grimes Graves in England where multiple 15-m (50-ft) deep shafts were sunk into the chalk to reach the best quality flint layers; rough estimates suggest that the **site** could have produced 28 million flint axes. *Quarries* were a common source of larger stones for building or monuments. The job of the archaeologist is sometimes made easier by the discovery of unfinished or abandoned stones within or near to ancient quarry sites. One of the most impressive examples is the statue-quarry on Easter Island, where many statues lie in various stages of manufacture.

A combination of archaeological investigation and modern experimentation can give us valuable insights into how stones were worked. Here we will concentrate on stone tool manufacture, although much archaeological and experimental work is also done on larger stones and how they were moved, dressed, and fitted.

Stone Tool Manufacture and Function. Most stone tools are made by removing material from a pebble or "**core**" until the desired shape of the core has been attained. The first flakes struck off (primary flakes) bear traces of the outer surface (cortex). Trimming flakes are then struck off to achieve the final shape, and certain edges may then be "retouched" by further removal of tiny secondary flakes. Although the core is the main implement thus produced, the flakes themselves may well be used as knives, scrapers etc. The toolmaker's work will have varied in accordance with the type and amount of raw material available.

The history of stone tool technology (illustrated opposite) shows a sporadically increasing degree of refinement. The first recognizable tools are simple choppers and

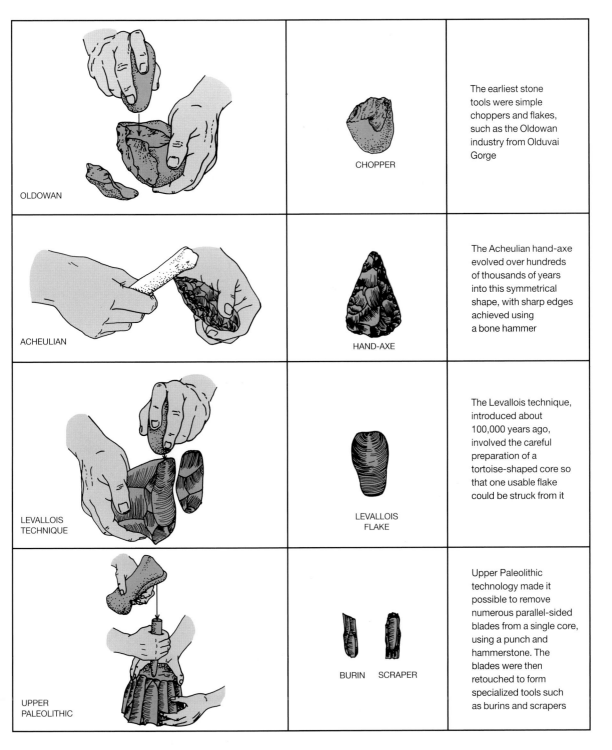

OLDOWAN	**CHOPPER**	The earliest stone tools were simple choppers and flakes, such as the Oldowan industry from Olduvai Gorge
ACHEULIAN	**HAND-AXE**	The Acheulian hand-axe evolved over hundreds of thousands of years into this symmetrical shape, with sharp edges achieved using a bone hammer
LEVALLOIS TECHNIQUE	**LEVALLOIS FLAKE**	The Levallois technique, introduced about 100,000 years ago, involved the careful preparation of a tortoise-shaped core so that one usable flake could be struck from it
UPPER PALEOLITHIC	**BURIN SCRAPER**	Upper Paleolithic technology made it possible to remove numerous parallel-sided blades from a single core, using a punch and hammerstone. The blades were then retouched to form specialized tools such as burins and scrapers

flakes made by knocking pieces off pebbles to obtain sharp edges. The best-known examples are the so-called Oldowan tools from Olduvai Gorge, Tanzania, the earliest of which date back some 2.5 million years. After hundreds of thousands of years, people progressed to flaking both surfaces of the tool, eventually producing the

The evolution of stone tools, from the earliest, Oldowan technology to the refined methods of the Upper Paleolithic.

symmetrical Acheulian **hand-axe** shape. The next improvement, dating to around 100,000 years ago, came with the introduction of the "Levallois technique" – named after a site in a Paris suburb where it was first identified – where the core was knapped in such a way that large flakes of predetermined size and shape could be removed.

Around 35,000 years ago, with the Upper Paleolithic period, blade technology became dominant in some parts of the world. Long, parallel-sided blades were systematically removed with a punch and hammerstone from a cylindrical core. This was a great advance, not only because it produced large numbers of blanks that could be further trimmed and retouched into a wide range of specialized tools (scrapers, burins, borers), but also because it was far less wasteful of the raw material, obtaining a much greater total length of working edges than ever before from a given amount of stone. This trend toward greater economy reached its peak around 10,000 years ago, with the rise to dominance of microliths, tiny stone tools many of which were probably used as barbs on composite implements.

To find out how a stone tool was made we must try to reconstruct the sequence of manufacturing steps, and there are two principal approaches to doing this: replication and **refitting**. Stone tool replication is a type of **experimental archaeology** that involves making exact copies of different types of stone tool – using only the technology available to the original makers – in order to assess the processes entailed, and the amount of time and effort required. Many years of patient practice are required to become proficient at tool replication.

One specific problem that expert knapper Donald Crabtree was able to solve through trial and error was how the Paleo-Indians of North America had made their fluted stone tools known as Folsom points, dating to some 11,000–10,000 years ago. In particular, how had they removed the "flute" or channel flake? This had remained a mystery and experiments with a variety of techniques met with disappointing results, until the decisive clue was found in a 17th-century text by a Spanish priest who had seen Aztecs make long knife-blades from **obsidian**. The method, as experiments proved, involves pressing the flake out, downward, by means of a T-shaped crutch placed against the chest; the crutch's tip is forced down against a precise point on the core which is clamped firm.

Replication cannot usually prove conclusively which techniques were used in the past, but it does narrow the possibilities and often points to the most likely method, as in the Folsom example above. *Refitting*, on the other hand, involves working with the original tools and demonstrates clearly the precise chain of actions of the knapper. This entails attempting to put tools and flakes back together again, like a 3-D jigsaw puzzle. The work is tedious and time-consuming, but when successful can allow us to follow the stages of the knapper's craft.

How were Paleo-Indian Folsom points made? Experiments by Donald Crabtree showed that the flakes were pressed from the core using a T-shaped crutch (top). Flintknappers have produced almost perfect replica points (above).

But how can we discover the function of a stone tool? Ethnographic observation of the use of similar tools in living societies often gives valuable clues, as do the minute traces of organic residues that can sometimes be found on tool surfaces; and experimentation can determine which uses are feasible or most probable. However, a single tool can be used for many different purposes – an Acheulian hand axe could be used for hacking wood from a tree, for butchering, smashing, scraping, and cutting – and conversely the same task can be done by many different tools. The only direct *proof* of function is to study the minute traces, or microwear patterns, that remain on the original tools. These minute polishes and marks, only properly visible using a scanning electron microscope, can be compared against evidence from modern experiments, and we can deduce the type of material a tool was used to work (such as wood, bone, hide, or meat) and the type of action used (such as piercing, cutting, or scraping).

Wood

Wood is one of the most important organic materials, and must have been used to make tools for as long as stone and bone. Indeed, many prehistoric stone tools were employed to obtain and work timber. If wood survives in good condition, it may preserve toolmarks to show how it was worked. A wide range of wooden tools can survive under special conditions. In the dry environment of ancient Egypt, for instance, numerous wooden implements for farming (rakes, hoes, grain-scoops, sickles), furniture, weapons and toys, carpentry tools such as mallets and chisels, and even whole ships have come down to us. Egyptian paintings such as those in the tomb of the nobleman Rekhmire at Thebes sometimes depict carpenters using drills and saws. But it has been waterlogged wood (including the remains of ships and boats) that has yielded the richest information about woodworking skills.

Plant and Animal Fibers

The making of containers, fabrics, and cords from skins, bark, and woven fibers probably dates back to the very earliest archaeological periods, but these fragile materials rarely survive. However, as we saw in Chapter 2, they do survive in very dry or wet conditions. In arid regions, such as Egypt or parts of the New World, such perishables have come down to us in some quantity, and the study of basketry and cordage there reveals complex and sophisticated designs and techniques that display complete mastery of these organic materials. Waterlogged conditions can also yield a great deal of fragile evidence.

Where textiles are concerned, the most crucial question is how they were made, and of what. In the New World, information on pre-Columbian weaving methods

KEY CONCEPTS: ARTIFACTS MADE FROM UNALTERED MATERIALS

- *Stone:* the archaeological record is dominated by stone artifacts. A combination of archaeological investigation, modern experimentation, and ethnographic observation can tell us a great deal about how stone artifacts were made and used

- *Wood:* wood does not survive well, apart from in very dry or waterlogged conditions, but was almost certainly as important a resource as stone

- *Plant and animal fibers:* containers, fabrics, and cords made from plant and animal fibers would also have been common objects in the past, but, again, they rarely survive in the archaeological record

- *Other materials:* bone, antler, shell, and leather are also often found by archaeologists, but, along with most other artifacts made from unaltered materials, we must be careful to establish whether an object is actually humanly made, or whether it has been created by natural processes

is available from ethnographic observation, as well as from Colonial accounts and illustrations, from depictions on Moche pottery, and from actual finds of ancient looms and other objects found preserved in the Peruvian desert. The richest New World evidence, however, comes from Peruvian textiles themselves, which have survived well in the dry conditions. The Andean **cultures** mastered almost every method of textile weaving or decoration now known, and their products were often finer than those of today – indeed, were some of the best ever made.

Other Unaltered Materials

Artifacts made from bone, antler, shell, and leather are also commonly found on archaeological sites. **Microwear analysis** combined with experimental archaeology are the most successful means of determining firstly whether the find really is humanly made (sharp bone points or pierced shells, for instance, can easily be created by natural processes), as well as reconstructing manufacturing techniques and deducing function.

SYNTHETIC MATERIALS

It is possible to consider the whole development of technology, as far as it relates to synthetic materials, in terms of the control of fire: pyrotechnology. Until very recent times, nearly all synthetic materials depended upon the control of heat; and the development of new technologies has often been largely dependent upon achieving higher and higher temperatures under controlled conditions.

Clearly the first step along this path was the mastery of fire, possible evidence for which already occurs in the Swartkrans Cave, South Africa, in layers dating to 1.5 million years ago. Cooked food and preserved meat then became a possibility, as did the use of heat in working flint, and in hardening wooden implements such as the yew spear from the Middle Paleolithic site of Lehringen, Germany.

A significant development of the Early Neolithic period in the Near East, around 8000 BC, was the construction of special ovens used both to parch cereal grains (to facilitate the threshing process) and to bake bread. These ovens consisted of a single chamber in which the fuel was burnt. When the oven was hot the fuel was raked out and the grain or unbaked bread placed inside. This represents the first construction of a deliberate facility to control the conditions under which the temperature was raised. We may hypothesize that it was through these early experiences in pyrotechnology that the possibility of making pottery by firing clay was discovered. Initially pottery was made by firing in an open fire, but the introduction of the potter's kiln meant higher temperatures could be achieved, which also spurred on the development of metallurgy.

Pottery

Throughout the earlier periods of **prehistory** containers made of light, organic materials were probably used. This does not mean, as has often been assumed, that Paleolithic people did not know how to make pottery: every fire lit on a cave floor will have hardened the clay around it, and terracotta figurines were sometimes produced. The lack of pottery vessels before the Neolithic period is mainly a consequence of the mobile way of life of Paleolithic **hunter-gatherers**, for whom heavy containers of fired clay would have been of limited usefulness.

The introduction of pottery generally seems to coincide with the adoption of a more sedentary way of life, for which vessels and containers that are durable and strong are a necessity. The almost indestructible potsherd is as common in later periods as the stone tool is in earlier ones – and just as some sites yield thousands of stone tools, others contain literally tons of pottery fragments.

How Were Pots Made? The making or "throwing" of pots on a wheel or turntable was only introduced after 3400 BC at the earliest (in Mesopotamia), but in the New World only after European contact. The previous method, still used in some parts of the world, was to build the vessel up by hand in a series of coils or slabs of clay. A simple examination of the interior and exterior surfaces of a pot usually allows us to identify the method of manufacture. Wheelthrown pots generally have a telltale spiral of ridges and marks which is absent from handmade wares. These marks are left by the fingertips as the potter draws the vessel up on the turntable.

Evidence for pot-making using a wheel. An Egyptian potter shapes a vessel on the turntable type of wheel in this limestone portrait of *c.* 2400 BC.

The firing technique can be inferred from certain characteristics of the finished product. For example, if the surfaces are vitrified or glazed (i.e. have a glassy appearance), the pot was fired at over 900°C (1652°F) and probably in an enclosed kiln. The extent of oxidization in a pot (the process by which organic substances in the clay are burnt off) is also indicative of firing methods. Complete oxidization produces a uniform color throughout the paste. If the core of a sherd is dark (grey or black), the firing temperature was too low to fully oxidize the clay, or the duration of the firing was insufficient, factors which often point to the use of an open kiln. Experimental firing of different pastes at different temperatures and in various types of kiln provides a guide to the colors and effects that can be expected.

Unlike the making of stone tools, the production of pottery by traditional methods is still widespread in the world, so a good deal can be learned from ethnoarchaeological studies not only about the technological aspects but also about the use and trade of pottery.

Metals

The study of ancient metal artifacts and manufacturing processes is known as archaeometallurgy. Many of the advances in metalworking techniques made in the past were dependent on the ability to achieve and control ever higher temperatures. **Non-Ferrous Metals.** The most important non-ferrous metal – that is, one not containing iron – used in early times was copper. In due course it was learned that a harder, tougher product could be made by **alloying** the copper with tin to produce bronze. Other elements, notably arsenic and antimony, were sometimes used in the alloying process; and in the later Bronze Age of Europe it was realized that a small amount of lead would improve the casting qualities. Gold and silver were also important, as was lead itself.

The techniques of manufacture of artifacts made from these materials can be investigated in several ways. The first point to establish is composition. Traditional laboratory methods readily allow the identification of major constituents. For instance, the alloys present in bronze may be identified in this way. However, in practice it is now more usual to utilize the techniques of **trace element analysis** (see below). The other essential approach is that of **metallographic examination**, when the structure of the material is examined microscopically. This will determine whether an artifact has been formed by cold-hammering, **annealing**, casting, or a combination of these methods. **Iron.** Iron was not used in the New World during pre-Columbian times, and makes its appearance in quantity in the Old World with the beginning in the Near East of the Iron Age around 1000 BC. Once the technique of smelting iron was well understood, it became very important, since iron is more widely found in nature

KEY CONCEPTS: ARTIFACTS MADE FROM SYNTHETIC MATERIALS

- Many of the developments in pottery and metalworking technology can be linked to developments in pyrotechnology – the ability to control fire and attain and maintain ever higher temperatures

- *Pottery:* pottery is very hard-wearing and potsherds are a common find on archaeological sites. We can learn through simple observation how pottery was made (either by hand or on a wheel) and through experiment and ethnographic studies how it was fired

- *Metals:* we can identify what metal or combination of metals an artifact is made from with simple laboratory techniques. The examination of the microscopic structure of the metal can give clues as to how an artifact was manufactured

than is copper. But it is much more difficult to reduce – i.e. to separate from oxygen with which it is found combined in nature in the form of iron oxides – requiring temperatures of about 800°C (1472°F).

It is clearly important and interesting to identify what an artifact is made of, how it was made, and what it was used for. But once an artifact has been created, it takes on a life of its own – not only in terms of being used, broken or discarded, but also in terms of being transported, bought, or exchanged. The study of these processes teaches us a great deal about past human societies and how they operated. In the next section we will discuss what can be learned from the study of trade and exchange, and examine some methods for investigating the movements of different kinds of materials.

TRADE AND EXCHANGE

Societies and economies depend upon exchanges – on exchange of information and of actual goods – between individuals and between organizations. Every social transaction implies some interaction between people, and the study of the movement and flow of goods in the course of such exchange transactions is often the most direct way for the archaeologist to monitor such interactions.

In many exchanges the relationship is more important than what is exchanged. In the Christian tradition, for instance, when presents are exchanged within a family at Christmas, the giving of presents between relatives is generally more important than the actual objects: "it's the thought that counts." There are also different kinds of exchange relationship: some where generosity is the order of the day (as in the family Christmas); others where the aim is profit, and the personal relationship is not emphasized. Moreover, there are different kinds of goods:

MATERIALS OF PRESTIGE VALUE

Nearly all cultures have valuables. Although some of these are useful (e.g. pigs in Melanesia, which can be eaten) most of them have no use at all, other than display. They are simply prestige objects.

Valuables tend to be in a limited range of materials to which a particular society attributes a high value. For instance, in our own society gold is so highly valued as to be a standard against which all other values are measured.

We tend to forget that this valuation is an entirely arbitrary one, and we speak of gold's *intrinsic* value,

as if in some way it were inherent. But gold is not a very useful material (although it is bright, and does not tarnish), nor is it the product of any special skills of the craftsperson. Intrinsic value is a misnomer: the Aztecs valued feathers more highly, unlike the Conquistadors who craved gold; both were following subjective systems of value. When we survey the range of materials to which different societies have ascribed intrinsic value we can see that many of them had the qualities of rarity, of durability, and of being visually conspicuous:

Zapotec mask from Monte Albán, Mexico, made of jade, the eyes of shell.

- The bright *feathers* favored by the Aztecs and by tribes of New Guinea fulfill two of these qualities.
- *Ivory*: elephant and walrus tusks have been valued since Upper Paleolithic times.
- *Shell*, especially of large marine molluscs, has been highly prized in many cultures for millennia.
- That very special organic material *amber* was valued in Upper Paleolithic times in northern Europe.
- *Jade* is a favored material in many cultures, from China to Mesoamerica, and was valued as long ago as 4000 BC in Neolithic Europe.
- Other naturally hard and *colorful stones* (e.g. rock crystal, lapis lazuli, obsidian, quartz, and onyx) have always been valued.
- *Gemstones* have taken on a special value in recent centuries, when the technique of cutting them to a faceted, light-catching shape was developed.
- *Gold* has perhaps pride of place (certainly in European eyes) among "intrinsically" valuable commodities, followed by *silver*.
- *Copper* and other metals have taken a comparable role: in North America copper objects had a special value.
- With the development of pyrotechnology, artificial materials such as *glass* came into full prominence.
- The finest *textiles* and other clothing materials (e.g. tapa, bark-cloth, in Polynesia) have also always been highly valued, for prestige often means personal display.

Feathered headdress (above) of the Aztec emperor Motecuhzoma II (Moctezuma). (Above center) The Portland Vase, a superb example of 1st-century AD Roman glassworking.

Woven silk robe (above) from the reign of the Chinese emperor Yung Cheng (1723–35), bearing the Imperial dragon.

(Above) Upper Paleolithic ivory female figurine (cast) from Lespugue, France (ht. 14.7 cm). (Above center) Gold mask thought by Schliemann to represent King Agamemnon, from a shaft grave at Mycenae, late 16th century BC.

Prestige objects of North America's Mississippian culture (c. AD 900–1450). (Above) Embossed copper face, with typical forked eye motif. (Left) Shell pendant (c. 14 cm) showing a panther and bird of prey.

everyday commodities that are bought and sold, and special goods, valuables (see box on previous pages), that are suitable for gifts.

Fifty years ago, when "diffusionist" explanations were popular in archaeology, the presence of objects of foreign type or material at an archaeological site was often thought to indicate significant "influence" from other, perhaps more advanced cultures. Today, however, we are more interested in finding out what those objects can tell us about social and economic interactions between distant groups. But the mere resemblance in the form of an artifact with those found elsewhere is not usually enough to be sure an exchange has occurred or that there is a definite link between two groups. We must show that the actual material the artifact is made from *must* have come from a distant source, and we can do this by **characterization**.

Discovering the Sources of Traded Goods: Characterization

The discovery of an artifact at a particular location does not mean that it originated in that place: it may, in fact, have been brought over hundreds or even thousands of miles. The study of where artifacts originated is not simple: artifact forms can be imitated, or can resemble each other by chance. So it is not always safe to recognize an import in an archaeological **context** just because it resembles objects that are known to have been made elsewhere. Much more reliable evidence for trade can be provided if the raw material of which the object is made can be reliably shown to have originated elsewhere. Characterization, or sourcing, refers to those techniques of examination by which characteristic properties of the constituent material may be identified, and so allow the source of that material to be determined. Some of the main methods for sourcing of materials by characterization are described below.

For characterization to work, there must obviously be something about the source of the material that distinguishes its products from those coming from other sources. Of course, sometimes a material is so unusual and distinctive in itself that it can at once be recognized as deriving from a given source. But in practice, there are very few materials for which the different sources can be distinguished by eye. Usually, it is necessary to use scientific techniques which allow a much more precise description of the material. During the past 40 years there have been striking advances in the ability to analyze very small samples with accuracy. A successful characterization, however, does not just depend on analytical precision: sources of some materials (e.g. flint, or some metals) are often very similar and so cannot be distinguished whatever the precision of the testing. For other materials (e.g. obsidian), the sources are all quite different and can be distinguished relatively easily.

An important point to note is that the sourcing of materials by characterization studies depends crucially on our knowledge of the distribution of the raw materials in nature. This comes mainly from the fieldwork of such specialists as geologists. For example, we might have a good knowledge of the exact kinds of rock a whole range of stone axes were made from, but this would not help us unless we could match those particular kinds of rock with their specific occurrences in nature (i.e. the quarries). Thus, good geological mapping is a necessary basis for a sound sourcing study.

Microscopic Examination of Thin Section. Since the middle of the 19th century techniques have existed for cutting a thin section of a sample taken from a stone object or a potsherd to determine the source of the material. It is made thin enough to transmit light and then, by means of petrological examination (studying the rock or mineral structure) with a light microscope, it is usually possible to recognize specific minerals that may be characteristic of a specific source. This part of the work has to be done by someone with petrological training.

This method has been applied to *stone* objects in different parts of the world – to pinpoint the sources of building stones (e.g. the special colored stones used by the ancient Greeks and Romans), monuments (e.g. Olmec heads, Stonehenge), and portable artifacts, such as stone axes (e.g. in Australia and New Guinea). One of the success stories of characterization studies is the analysis of the patterns of trade in stone axes in Neolithic times in Britain, which started before 3000 BC.

With *pottery*, the clay itself may be distinctive, but more often it is the inclusions – particles of minerals or rock fragments – that are characteristic. Sometimes the inclusions are naturally present in the clay. In other cases, the inclusions are deliberately added as "**temper**" to improve drying and firing qualities, and this can complicate characterization studies, since the pottery fabric may then consist of material from two or more separate sources. Fossil constituents, such as diatoms (see Chapter 6) can also be an aid to identification of the source of the raw materials.

The picture of the prehistoric trade in pottery in Britain that such analyses have documented is quite surprising. Until the **thin-section** work of David Peacock and his associates it was simply not realized that pottery bowls and other vessels might be traded over quite long distances (of the order of 100 km (62 miles)) in Neolithic times, before 3000 BC. Now that we know the extent of this exchange of pottery, and that of stone axes discussed above, it is clear that many individuals and settlements were linked by quite far-flung exchange systems.

Trace-Element Analysis. The basic composition of many materials is very consistent. Obsidian, a volcanic glass used in the manufacture of chipped stone tools in the same manner as flint, is a good example of this. The concentration of the main elements of which obsidian is formed (silicon, oxygen, calcium, etc.) is broadly similar whatever the source of the material. However, the *trace elements* (elements present only in very small quantities, measured in just a few parts per million) do vary according to the source, and there are a variety of useful methods for measuring their concentration.

When obsidian from New Britain and the Admiralty Islands in the Pacific was examined using trace-element analysis, it was found that obsidian from one source in New Britain (Talasea) was being traded as far as Fiji to the east and Sabah (northern Borneo) to the west, a distance of 6500 km (4000 miles), at about 3000 years ago. This is surely the widest distribution of any commodity in the global Neolithic record.

Isotopic Analysis.   Atoms of the same element, but with different numbers of neutrons in the nucleus, are called isotopes. Most elements occurring in nature consist of a number of isotopes. Particularly when we are investigating metal sources, we can analyze the sources (as well as the artifacts we are investigating) for the presence of different proportions of lead isotopes in order to characterize them. Sometimes more than one source can have the same isotope ratios, but this can usually be resolved by consideration of trace-element data.

Lead isotope analysis is of direct use not only for lead artifacts, but also for those of silver, in which lead is usually present as an impurity. Copper sources also contain at least a trace of lead, and it has been shown by experimentation that a large proportion of that lead passes into the copper metal produced during smelting. Here, then, is a characterization method applicable to lead, silver, and copper artifacts. It has been used successfully for the determination of mineral sources of Classical and medieval silver coins, Bronze Age copper and bronze tools, lead weights, as well as lead in pigments of glasses and glazes, and lead-based white paint.

Oxygen isotope ratios have also proved useful for the characterization of marine shell. The shell of *Spondylus gaederopus* was widely traded in the form of bracelets and decorations during the Neolithic in southeast Europe. Archaeologists needed to know whether it came from the Aegean, or possibly from the Black Sea. As discussed in the section on deep-sea cores in Chapter 6, the oxygen isotopic

KEY CONCEPTS: CHARACTERIZATION

- Characterization allows archaeologists to discover the source of the material from which an artifact was made

- Successful characterization depends on all the sources of a material being sufficiently different so as to be distinguishable through scientific analysis

- The main methods for sourcing materials by characterization are microscopic thin-section analysis, trace-element analysis, and isotopic analysis composition of marine shell is dependent on the temperature of the sea where the organism lives. The Black Sea is much colder than the Mediterranean, and analysis confirmed that the shells in question came from the Aegean.

The Study of Distribution

The study of the traded goods themselves, and the identification of their sources by means of characterization, are the most important procedures in the investigation of exchange. But it is the study of distribution, or the movement of goods, that allows us to get to the heart of the matter – how societies operated and how they interrelated socially and economically.

In the absence of written records it is not easy to determine what were the mechanisms of distribution, or what was the nature of the exchange relationship. However, where such records exist, they can be most informative.

Earlier evidence from pre-literate societies – societies without written records – can, however, give some clear idea of ownership and of the managed distribution of goods. For example, clay sealings, used to stopper jars, to secure boxes, and to seal the doors of storehouses, and distinguished by the impression of a carved seal, are widely found in the pre-literate phases in the Near East, and in the Aegean Bronze Age.

In some cases, however, the traded goods themselves were marked by their owner or producer. For instance, the potters who produced storage containers (amphorae) in Roman times used to stamp their name on the rim. The general pattern of export can be made clear by the production of a distribution map.

But a distribution map must be interpreted if we are to understand the processes that lay behind it: and at this point it is useful to consider how the spatial distribution of finds may depend on the exchange mechanism – or in other words, what

A distribution study. Roman storage containers (amphorae) bearing the stamp of the potter Sestius have been found in northern Italy and widely throughout central and southern France. They and their contents (no doubt wine) were probably made on an estate near Cosa. The distribution map thus indicates the general pattern of the export from the Cosa area of this commodity.

can the pattern of distribution of finds tell us about the type of exchange that was occurring? The different mechanisms can be summarized as follows:

- "Direct access": the user goes directly to the source of the material, without the intervention of any exchange mechanism
- "Down-the-line" exchange: repeated exchanges of a **reciprocal** nature, so that a commodity travels across successive territories through successive exchanges
- "Freelance (middleman)" trading: traders operate independently and for gain: usually the traders work by bargaining but instead of a fixed marketplace they are travelers who take the goods to the consumer
- "Emissary" trading: the "trader" is a representative of a central organization based in the home country

Not all of these types of transaction can be expected to leave clear and unmistakable indications in the archaeological record, although, as we shall see, down-the-line trading apparently does. And a former port of trade ought to be recognizable if the materials found there come from a wide range of sources, and it is clear that the site was not principally an administrative center, but was specialized in trading activities.

Spatial Analysis of Distribution

Several formal techniques are available for the study of distribution. The first and most obvious technique is naturally that of plotting the distribution map for finds, as in the case of the stamped Roman amphorae mentioned above. Quantitative studies of distributions are also helpful; the size of the dot or some other feature can be used as a simple device to indicate the number of finds on the map. This kind of map can give a good indication of important centers of consumption and of **redistribution**. Direct use of distribution maps, even when aided by quantitative plotting, may not, however, be the best way of studying the data, and more thorough analysis may be useful.

Recently, there has been a considerable focus of interest in "**fall-off analysis**". The quantity of a traded material usually declines as the distance from the source increases. This is not really very surprising, but in some cases (such as when a particular type of trade is happening) there are regularities in the way in which the decrease occurs. If the quantities of material are plotted against the distance from source on a graph, a *fall-off curve* is created. Although different mechanisms of distribution sometimes produce comparable end-results, down-the-line trading, for instance, produces a quite distinctive exponential curve (which on a logarithmic scale is represented by a straight line, as in the example below).

Distribution Studies of Obsidian. A good example is the obsidian found at Early Neolithic sites in the Near East. Characterization studies pinpointed two sources in central Anatolia and two in eastern Anatolia. Samples were obtained from most of

The obsidian trade in the Near East. Characterization studies revealed that Early Neolithic villages in Cyprus, Anatolia, and the Levant obtained their obsidian from two sources in central Anatolia, while villages such as Jarmo and Ali Kosh depended on two sources in Armenia (eastern Anatolia). At sites relatively close to the sources (e.g. Çatalhöyük), obsidian formed 80 percent of the chipped stone tools, suggesting that within this "supply zone" (inner lines on the distribution map) people collected obsidian directly from the source. Beyond this zone the fall-off curves (right) were indicative of down-the-line trade.

the known Early Neolithic sites in the Near East, dating from the 7th and 6th millennia BC. A rather clear picture emerged with the central Anatolian obsidians being traded in the Levant area (down to Palestine), while those of eastern Anatolia were mostly traded down the Zagros Mountain range to sites in Iran such as Ali Kosh.

A quantitative distributional study revealed a pattern of fall-off which indicated down-the-line trade. It could therefore be concluded that obsidian was being handed on down from village settlement to village settlement. Only in the area close to the sources (within 320 km (200 miles) of the sources) – termed the supply zone – was there evidence that people were going direct to the source to collect their own obsidian. Outside that area – within what has been termed the contact zone – the exponential fall-off indicates a down-the-line system. There is no indication of

- Analysis of the spatial distribution of finds can help us to understand the exchange mechanisms that were operating in the past

- The main different exchange mechanisms can be summarized as: direct access; down-the-line; freelance; and emissary trading

- Quantitative studies, for example fall-off analysis, can give a statistical indication of which method was in use

specialist middleman traders at this time, nor does it seem that there were central places which had a dominant role in the supply of obsidian.

Shipwrecks and Hoards: Trade by Sea and Land. A different approach to distribution questions is provided by the study of transport. Travel by water was often much safer, quicker, and less expensive than travel by land. The best source of information, both for questions of transport and for the crucial question of what commodity was traded against what, and on which scale, is offered by shipwrecks. From earlier times, for instance, complete cargoes of the Roman amphorae referred to above have been recovered. Our knowledge of marine trade has been greatly extended by George Bass's investigations of two important Bronze Age shipwrecks off the south coast of Turkey, at Cape Gelidonya and Uluburun (see box overleaf).

The terrestrial equivalent of the shipwreck is the trader's cache or **hoard**. When substantial assemblages of goods are found in archaeological deposits, it is not easy to be clear about the intentions of those who left them there: some hoards evidently had a votive character, left perhaps as offerings to deities, but those with materials for recycling, such as scrap metal, may well have been buried by itinerant smiths who intended to return and retrieve them.

In such cases, particularly with a well-preserved shipwreck, we come as close as we shall ever do to understanding the nature of distribution.

Exchange and Interaction: The Complete System

The archaeological evidence is rarely sufficient to permit the reconstruction of a complete exchange system. It is extremely difficult, for example, to establish without written records what was traded against what, and which particular values were ascribed to each commodity. Furthermore, exchange in perishable materials will have left little or no trace in the archaeological record. In most cases, all we can hope to do is to fit together the evidence about sources and distribution that can be established archaeologically. A good example of such a project is the work of Jane Pires-Ferreira in Oaxaca, Mexico.

An Exchange System in Ancient Mexico. Pires-Ferreira studied five materials used in Oaxaca during the Early and Middle Formative periods (1450–500 BC). The first was obsidian, of which some nine sources were identified. These were characterized and the relevant networks were established. Pires-Ferreira then proceeded to consider exchange networks for another material, mother-of-pearl shell, and concluded that two different networks were in operation here, one bringing marine material from the Pacific Coast, the other material from freshwater sources in the rivers draining into the Atlantic.

For her next study she considered the iron ore (magnetite) used to manufacture mirrors in the Formative period. Finally, she was able to bring into consideration two classes of pottery whose area of manufacture (in Oaxaca and in Veracruz, respectively) could be determined stylistically. These results were then fitted together onto a single map, showing some of the commodities that linked regions of Mesoamerica in the Early Formative period into several exchange networks. The picture is evidently incomplete, and it does not offer any notion of the relative values of the traded goods. But it does make excellent use of the available

The complete system: Pires-Ferreira's map which shows some of the commodities that linked regions of Early Formative Mesoamerica from the study of five different materials.

DISTRIBUTION: THE ULUBURUN WRECK

It is difficult for the archaeologist to learn what commodity was traded against what other commodity, and to understand the mechanics of trade. The discovery of the shipwreck of a trading vessel, complete with cargo, is thus of particular value.

In 1982, just such a wreck, dating from close to 1300 BC, was found at Uluburun, near Kas, off the south Turkish coast in 43 m (141 ft) to 60 m (198 ft) of water. It was excavated between 1984 and 1994 by George Bass and Cemal Pulak of the Institute of Nautical Archaeology in Texas.

The ship's cargo contained about 10 tons of copper in the form of over 350 of the so-called "oxhide" ingots (i.e. shaped like an oxhide) already known from wall paintings in Egypt and from finds in Cyprus, Crete, and elsewhere. The copper for these ingots was almost certainly mined on the island of Cyprus

(as suggested by lead-isotope analysis, and trace-element analysis). Also of particular importance are nearly a ton of ingots and other objects of tin found on the sea floor in the remains of the cargo. The source of the tin used in the Mediterranean at this time is not yet clear. It seems evident that at the time of the shipwreck, the vessel was sailing westwards from the east Mediterranean coast, and taking with it tin, from some eastern source, as well as copper from Cyprus.

The pottery included jars of the type known as Canaanite amphorae, because they were made in Palestine or Syria (the Land of Canaan). Most held turpentine-like resin from the terebinth tree, but several contained olives, and another glass beads.

Similar jars have been found in Greece, Egypt, and especially along the Levantine coast.

The exotic goods in the wreck included lengths of a wood

resembling ebony, which grew in Africa south of Egypt. Then there were Baltic amber beads, which came originally from northern Europe (and which probably reached the Mediterranean overland). There was also ivory in the form of elephant and hippopotamus tusks, possibly from the eastern Mediterranean, and ostrich eggshells that probably came from North Africa or Syria. Bronze

Three striking objects from the wreck: (clockwise, from top) impression of a hematite seal, cut in Mesopotamia c. 1750 BC, with a new scene carved over it some 400 years later; a gold scarab, the first ever found bearing the name of the famous Egyptian queen Nefertiti, who reigned with her consort Akhenaten during the 14th century BC; and gold pendant showing an unknown goddess with a gazelle in each upraised hand.

The map shows the probable route of the ill-fated ship found at Uluburun. Also indicated are likely sources of materials for the various artifacts found on board the wreck.

tools and weapons from the wreck show a mixture of types that include Egyptian, Levantine, and Mycenaean forms. Among other important finds were several cylinder seals of Syrian and Mesopotamian types, ingots of glass (at that time a special and costly material), and a chalice of gold.

This staggering treasure from the sea bed gives a glimpse into Bronze Age trade in the Mediterranean. Bass and Pulak consider it likely that the trader started his final voyage on the Levantine coast. His usual circuit probably involved sailing across to Cyprus, then along the Turkish coast, past Kas, and west to Crete,

or, more likely, to one of the major Mycenaean sites on the Greek mainland, or even further north, as hinted by the discovery on the wreck of spears and a ceremonial scepter/mace from the Danube region of the Black Sea. Then, profiting from seasonal winds, he would head south across the open sea to the coast of North Africa, east to the mouth of the Nile and Egypt, and, finally, home again to Phoenicia. On this occasion, however, he lost his ship, his cargo, and possibly his life at Uluburun.

Divers working on the oxhide ingots.

characterization data, and undertakes a preliminary synthesis of the area's exchange networks that is securely based on the archaeological evidence.

Symbolic Exchange and Interaction.   Interaction involves the exchange not only of material goods but of information, which includes ideas, symbols, inventions, aspirations, and values. Modern archaeology has been able to learn a quite a lot about material exchanges, using characterization studies and spatial analyses, but it has been more difficult to identify and explain the more symbolic aspects of interaction.

While similar innovations separated by long distances should not be used as indicators of contact in the absence of other evidence, the development of a striking new technology, making its appearance at a number of locations over a limited area, is usually an indication of the flow of information and hence of contact.

In the past archaeologists talked of "diffusion" when they discussed interactions between neighboring areas. The term implied that one area was dominant over the other, and that new technologies passed down to the subordinate area. The opposite approach would be to consider different areas as completely autonomous and independent. But it seems unrealistic to exclude the possibility of significant interactions between different groups.

The solution is to seek ways of analyzing interactions, including their symbolic components, that do not make assumptions about dominance and subordination, core and periphery, but consider different areas as on a more or less equal footing. When discussing such interactions between independent societies of equal status, it has been found useful to speak of **interaction spheres**.

One major interaction sphere is competition. Neighboring areas compete with one another in various ways, judging their own success against that of their neighbors. This often takes a symbolic form in periodic meetings at some major ceremonial centers where representatives of the various areas meet, celebrate ritual, and sometimes compete in games and other enterprises.

Such behavior is seen among hunter-gatherer **bands**, which meet periodically in larger units (at what in Australia are called corroborees). It is seen also in the pilgrimages and rituals of **state** societies, most conspicuously in ancient Greece at the Olympic Games and at other Panhellenic assemblies, when representatives of all the city states would meet.

At such gatherings there is a tendency for one society to try to outdo its neighbors in conspicuous consumption, such as in the expensive public feasts of the Northwest Coast American Indians, the institution of the potlatch. Very similar in some ways is the erection of magnificent monuments at regional ceremonial centers, each outdoing its neighbor in scale and grandeur. Something similar may have occurred in the ceremonial centers of Maya cities, and the same phenomenon is seen in the magnificent cathedrals in the capital cities of medieval Europe.

Warfare is, of course, an obvious form of competition. But the object of the competition is not necessarily to gain territory – for example, it might also be used to capture prisoners for sacrifice. It operated under well-understood rules, and was as much a form of interaction as the others listed here.

Innovations can also be transmitted – naturally a technical advance made in one area will soon spread to other areas. And there may also be a ceremonial exchange of valuables: although we have emphasized non-material (i.e. symbolic) interactions here, it is certainly the case that between the elites of different societies there may also be a series of material exchanges – the transfer of marriage partners and of valuable gifts. At the same time, large-scale exchanges between participating societies of everyday commodities should not, of course, be overlooked. Economies in some cases became linked together.

Such concepts, where as much emphasis is laid on symbolic aspects as on the physical exchange of material goods, can profitably be used to analyze interactions in most early societies and cultures. Systematic analysis of this kind has, however, so far been rare in archaeology.

SUMMARY

- In this chapter we have highlighted some basic questions about early technology, and considered how to find answers to them. First, one must assess whether an object is indeed an artifact, and then of what material – unaltered (primarily stone, wood, fibers) or synthetic (pottery, metals). Ethnography and archaeological context may suggest the function of a tool; but only analysis of its microwear or residues can demonstrate its likely use. Nevertheless, ethnoarchaeology is proving extremely valuable.

- Studies of characterization – i.e. the sources of the raw materials that make up artifacts – have been of enormous importance in archaeology, by shedding light on technological processes, and contact and trade between different regions and cultures. Thin-sections, as well as trace-element analysis and isotopic analysis, have played a major role in these investigations.

- Once an understanding of the whole process of making and using the artifacts has been attained, we can turn to their distribution – the spatial analysis of their places of manufacture and discovery, and hence the exchange and transportation systems which have caused these distribution patterns to come about.

FURTHER READING

Broad surveys of ancient technology, trade, and exchange include:

Earle, T.K. & Ericson, J.E. (eds.). 1977. **Exchange Systems in Prehistory**. ACADEMIC PRESS: NEW YORK & LONDON.

Ericson, J.E. & Earle, T.K. (eds.). 1982. **Contexts for Prehistoric Exchange**. ACADEMIC PRESS: NEW YORK & LONDON.

Fagan, B.M. (ed.). 2004. **The Seventy Great Inventions of the Ancient World.** THAMES & HUDSON: LONDON & NEW YORK.

Forbes, R.J. (series) **Studies in Ancient Technology.** E.J. BRILL: LEIDEN.

Gale, N.H. (ed.). 1991. **Bronze Age Trade in the Mediterranean.** (Studies in Mediterranean Archaeology 90). ÅSTRÖM: GÖTEBORG.

Lambert, J.B. 1997. **Traces of the Past: Unraveling the Secrets of Archaeology through Chemistry**.

HELIX BOOKS/ADDISON-WESLEY LONGMAN: READING, MASS.

Nicholson, P. & Shaw, I. (eds.). 2000. **Ancient Egyptian Materials and Technology.** CAMBRIDGE UNIVERSITY PRESS: CAMBRIDGE.

Pollard, A.M. (ed.). 1992. **New Developments in Archaeological Science** (Proceedings of the British Academy 77). OXFORD UNIVERSITY PRESS: OXFORD.

Scarre, C. & Healy, F. (eds.). 1993. **Trade and Exchange in Prehistoric Europe**. OXBOW MONOGRAPH 33: OXFORD.

White, K.D. 1984. **Greek and Roman Technology.** THAMES & HUDSON: LONDON; CORNELL UNIVERSITY PRESS: ITHACA, NY.

8 What Did They Think? What Were They Like?

cognitive archaeology and the archaeology of people

This chapter is about the attributes – both mental and physical – of our ancestors. Strangely, introductory books on **archaeology** generally say little or nothing about the archaeology of people themselves – about their physical characteristics and **evolution**. Yet one of archaeology's principal aims is to recreate the lives of the people who produced the archaeological record, and what more direct evidence can there be than the physical remains of past humanity? In some cases we can tell the age and sex of a person, what they looked like, and how they died; and we can deduce more general facts about groups of people rather than individuals. And, of course, the lives of ancient people were not just about the physical aspects of existence: they had mental abilities, thoughts, and spiritual lives just as we do today.

We will begin this chapter by looking at **cognitive archaeology** – the study of past ways of thought from material remains – which is in many respects one of the newer branches of modern archaeology. Rather than simply "imagining" what people in the past must have thought or believed, it is possible to use the more disciplined techniques of cognitive archaeology to gain insights into these important aspects of the past: we can analyze the concepts people had and the way they thought.

We can, for example, investigate how people went about describing and measuring their world: as we shall see, the system of weights used in the Indus Valley civilization can be understood very well today. We can investigate which material goods people valued most highly, and perhaps viewed as symbols of authority or power. And we can investigate the manner in which people conceived of the supernatural, and how they responded to these conceptions in their ritual practice.

Having examined the ways in which we can try to discover what people were thinking, we will move on to investigate how we can tell what people looked like – what were their physical attributes?

COGNITIVE ARCHAEOLOGY

It is generally agreed today that what most clearly distinguishes the human species from other life forms is our ability to use *symbols*. All intelligent thought and indeed all coherent speech are based on symbols, for words are themselves symbols, where the sound or the written letters stand for and thus represent (or symbolize) an aspect of the real world. Usually, however, meaning is attributed to a particular symbol in an arbitrary way. And that meaning is specific to a particular cultural tradition. It is usually impossible to infer the meaning of a symbol within a given **culture** from the symbolic form of the image or object alone. We have to see how that form is used, and to try to understand its meaning from the context in which it is used. Cognitive archaeology has thus to be very careful about specific contexts of discovery. There are very few symbols that have a universal meaning cross-culturally. It is the assemblage that matters, not the individual object in isolation.

Investigating How Human Symbolizing Faculties Evolved

The field of cognitive archaeology is concerned primarily with the cognitive behavior or our own species, *Homo sapiens sapiens*. Modern genetic studies suggest that we are all closely related, and that the innate cognitive abilities within any one regional group of our species, along with other behavioral attributes, are much like those in another. For instance all human groups today have the capacity of complex speech, and that is a capacity which in all probability we share with our ancestors of 80,000 to 60,000 years ago, the time of the first human dispersals out of Africa. Clearly, however, as we go back much further in time and consider earlier hominid species, whether *Homo habilis* or *Homo erectus*, we are dealing with creatures of more limited cognitive abilities. Their study represents an important subdivision of cognitive archaeology – the development of hominid cognitive abilities up to the emergence of our own species. It presents special problems, since for these earlier ancestors we cannot make the assumption that they had innate cognitive facilities much like our own. That is something which has to be investigated.

Language and Self-Consciousness.   Most physical anthropologists agree that modern human abilities have been present since the emergence of *Homo sapiens sapiens* some 100,000–40,000 years ago. But as we look earlier, scholars are less united. Some archaeologists and physical anthropologists consider that an effective language may have been developed by *Homo habilis* around 2 million years ago, along with the first chopper tools, but others think that a full language capability developed very much more recently, with the emergence of *Homo sapiens sapiens*. This would imply that the tools made by hominids in the Lower and Middle **Paleolithic** periods were produced by beings without true linguistic capacities.

The origins of self-consciousness have been debated by scientists and philosophers, but with few definite conclusions. There is little evidence available to clarify the matter, but one philosopher, John Searle, has argued that there is no sudden transition, but rather a gradual development: he asserted, for example, that his dog Ludwig has a significant degree of self-consciousness.

There are several lines of approach into other aspects of early human abilities. One way that we can try to assess early human cognitive ability is by examining the way stone tools and other **artifacts** were made.

Design in Tool Manufacture.   Whereas the production of simple pebble tools – for instance by *Homo habilis* – may perhaps be considered a simple, habitual act, not unlike a chimpanzee breaking off a stick to poke at an ant hill, the fashioning by *Homo erectus* of so beautiful an object as an Acheulian **hand-axe** seems more advanced.

So far, however, that is just a subjective impression. How do we investigate it further? One way is to measure, by experiment, the amount of time taken in the manufacturing process. A more rigorous quantitative approach, as developed by Glynn Isaac, is to study the range of variation in an assemblage of artifacts. For if the toolmaker has, within his or her **cognitive map**, some enduring notion of what the end-product should be, one finished tool should be much like another. Isaac distinguished a tendency through time to produce an increasingly well-defined variety or assemblage of tool types. This implies that each person making tools had a notion of different tool forms, no doubt destined for different functions. Planning and design in tool manufacture thus become relevant to our consideration of the cognitive abilities of early hominids, abilities that moreover distinguish them from higher apes such as the chimpanzee.

The production of a stone tool, a pot, a bronze artifact, or any product of a well-defined manufacturing process involves a complicated and often highly standardized sequence of events. For early periods, such as the Paleolithic, the study of the processes involved in making artifacts offers one of the few insights available into the way cognitive structures underlay complex aspects of human behavior. French prehistorians Claudine Karlin and Michèle Julien analyzed the sequence of events necessary for the production of blades in the Magdalenian period of the French Upper Paleolithic; many other production processes can be investigated along similar lines.

Procurement of Materials and Planning Time. Another way of investigating the cognitive behavior of early hominids is to consider planning time, defined as the time between the planning of an act and its execution. For instance, if the raw material used to manufacture a stone tool comes from a specific rock outcrop, but the tool itself is produced some distance away (as documented by waste flakes produced in its manufacture), that would seem to indicate some enduring intention or foresight by the person who transported the raw material. Similarly, the transport of natural or finished objects, whether tools, seashells, or attractive fossils, as has been documented, indicates at least a continuing interest in them, or the intention of using them, or a sense of "possession." The study of such objects, by the techniques of characterization discussed in Chapter 7 and other methods, has now been undertaken in a systematic way.

Deliberate Burial of Human Remains. From the Upper Paleolithic period there are many well-established cases of human burial, where the body or bodies have been deliberately laid to rest within a dug grave, sometimes accompanied by ornaments of personal adornment. Evidence is emerging, however, from even earlier periods. The

Deliberate burial of the dead: an elderly man buried at Sungir, near Moscow, *c.* 25,000 years ago, with thousands of ivory beads across his chest and a cap sewn with fox canines.

act of burial itself implies some kind of respect or feeling for the deceased individual, and perhaps some notion of an afterlife (although that point is less easy to demonstrate). The adornment seems to imply the existence of the idea that objects of decoration can enhance the individual's appearance, whether in terms of beauty or prestige or whatever. A good Upper Paleolithic example is the discovery made at Sungir, some 200 km (125 miles) northeast of Moscow and dating from *c.* 25,000 years ago: burials of a man and two children together with mammoth ivory spears, stone tools, ivory daggers, small animal carvings, and thousands of ivory beads.

In assessing such finds, we must be sure to understand the formation processes – in particular what may have happened to the burial after it was made. For example, animal skeletons have been discovered alongside human remains in graves. Traditionally this would have been taken as proof that animals were deliberately buried with the humans as part of some ritual act. Now, however, it is thought possible that in certain cases animals scavenging for food found their way into these burials and died accidentally – thus leaving false clues to mislead archaeologists.

Representations. Any object, and any drawing or painting on a surface that can be unhesitatingly recognized as a depiction – that is, a representation of an object in the real world (and not simply a mechanical reproduction of one, as a fossil is) – is a symbol. General questions about representations and depictions for all time periods are discussed in a later section. For the Paleolithic period, there are two issues of prime importance: evaluating the date (and hence in some cases the authenticity), and confirming the status as a depiction. Although it has long been believed that the earliest depictions are of Upper Paleolithic date and produced by *Homo sapiens sapiens*, increasing numbers of earlier examples are forcing us to re-examine this supposition.

KEY CONCEPTS: EARLY HUMAN SYMBOLIZING FACULTIES

- The development of language and self-consciousness

- Evidence of design in tool manufacture

- Evidence of the procurement of materials and planning

- The deliberate burial of human remains

- Representations and "art"

Piece of red ocher with abstract engravings, from Blombos Cave, South Africa, dating to *c.* 77,000 years ago.

So far the earliest well-dated product which might securely be described as "art", or at least as "graphic design" (of however modest a kind) is a piece of red ocher with an incised network pattern, from the Blombos Cave, South Africa, dating to 77,000 years ago. It is believed to be the work of our own species *Homo sapiens sapiens.*

We should, however, note the enormous cognitive significance of the act of depiction itself, in all the vividness seen in the art of Chauvet or Lascaux in France, or Altamira in Spain. We do not yet understand very well, however, why such representation was rare in the Pleistocene (Ice Age) period, or what the significance to their creators of the remarkable depiction of animals in the painted caves of France and Spain may have been (see box overleaf).

WORKING WITH SYMBOLS

We are interested in studying *how symbols were used.* Perhaps we cannot fully understand their meaning, if that implies the full meaning they had for the original users. Without going into a profound analysis, we can define "meaning" as "the relationship between symbols." As researchers today we can hope to establish some, but by no means all, of the original relationships between the symbols observed.

In the pages that follow we shall consider cognitive archaeology in terms of five different uses to which symbols are put.

1 A basic step is the *establishment of place* by marking and delimiting territory and the territory of the community, often with the use of symbolic markers and monuments, thereby constructing a perceived landscape, generally with a sacred as well as a secular dimension, a land of memories.
2 A fundamental cognitive step was the development of symbols of *measurement* – as in units of time, length, and weight – which help us organize our relationships with the natural world.

PALEOLITHIC CAVE ART

The Ice Age caves of western Europe are decorated with images of animals and with abstract markings. Clustered in specific regions – most notably the Périgord and Pyrenees in southwest France and Cantabria in northern Spain – they span the whole of the Upper Paleolithic, from about 30,000 BC onward. The majority of the art, however, dates to the latter part of the Ice Age, to the Solutrean and especially the Magdalenian period, ending around 10,000 BC.

The cave artists used a great range of techniques, from simple finger tracings and modeling in clay to engravings and bas-relief sculpture, and from hand stencils to paintings using two or three colors. Much of the art is unintelligible – and

(Above) Principal locations of Paleolithic cave art in western Europe.

(Right) Lascaux is one of the most famous sites of Paleolithic cave art: here we see the position of the major figures in Lascaux's Axial Gallery: mainly horses, aurochs (wild cattle), deer, ibex, and enigmatic dots and rectangles. These paintings are about 17,000 years old.

Axial Gallery

The spectacular paintings of Chauvet Cave, southern France, discovered in 1994, depict over 440 animals.

therefore classified by scholars as "signs" or abstract marks – but of the figures that can be identified, most are animals. Very few humans and virtually no objects were drawn on cave walls. Figures vary greatly in size, from tiny to over 5 m (16.5 ft) in length. Some are easily visible and accessible, while others are carefully hidden in recesses of the caves.

New finds continue to be made – an average of one cave per year, including major discoveries in France, such as Cosquer Cave (1991) near Marseilles, whose Ice Age entrance is now drowned beneath the sea, and the spectacular Chauvet Cave (1994) in the Ardèche, with its unique profusion of depictions of rhinoceroses and big cats.

However, in the 1980s and 1990s a series of discoveries also revealed that "cave art" was produced in the open air. Indeed this was probably the most common form of art production in the Ice Age, but the vast majority of it has been erased by weathering over many millennia, leaving us with the heavily skewed sample of figures that survived more readily inside caves. Only a dozen sites are known so far, in Spain, Portugal, and France, but they comprise hundreds of figures, mostly pecked into rocks, which by their style and content are clearly Ice Age in date.

3 Symbols allow us to cope with the future world, as instruments of *planning*. They help us define our intentions more clearly, by making models for some future intended action, for example plans of towns or cities.

4 Symbols are used to regulate and organize *relations between human beings*. Money is a good example of this, and with it the whole notion that some material objects have a higher value than others. Beyond this is a broader category of symbols, such as the badges of rank in an army, that have to do with the exercise of power in a society.

5 Symbols are used to represent and to try to regulate *human relations with the Other World*, the world of the supernatural or the transcendental – which leads on to the archaeology of **religion** and cult.

No doubt there are other kinds of uses for symbols, but this rather simplistic listing will help us in our discussion of how we should set about analyzing them.

Establishing Place: The Location of Memory

One of the fundamental aspects of the cognition of the individual is the establishment of place, often through the establishment of a center, which in a permanent settlement is likely to be the hearth of the home. For a community another significant place is likely to be the burial place of the ancestral dead, whether within the house or at some collective tomb or shrine. For a larger community, whether sedentary or mobile, there may be some communal meeting place, a sacred center for periodic gatherings.

These various **features**, some of them deliberate symbolic constructions, others more functional works which nonetheless are seen to have meaning – the home, the tilled agricultural land, the pasture – together constitute a constructed landscape in which the individual lives. As some archaeologists have pointed out, this landscape structures the experience and the world view of that individual. These observations are just as relevant to small-scale societies as to **state** societies. Many great cities from China to Cambodia and from Sri Lanka to the Maya Lowlands and Peru are laid out on cosmological principles, allowing the ruler to ensure harmony between his subjects and the prevailing sacred and supernatural forces. But the sacred center can be important in smaller societies also, and many of those which appear to have had a corporate structure rather than a powerful central leader, were capable of major public works – the temples of Malta and the megalithic centers of Carnac and of Orkney are good examples, as well as Stonehenge and Chaco Canyon. Such monuments can also be used to structure time and can operate to facilitate access to the other, sacred world.

The ceremonial center of Orkney, a ritual landscape in which individuals lived and which in turn shaped their experience and world view. The Ring of Brodgar (left) was one element of a complex and rich sacred landscape (right) which demonstrates that not only large, organized state societies were capable of creating major public works.

But these things operate also at a local level, not only at great centers. So the entire countryside becomes a complex of constructed landscapes, with meaning as well as of practical use. The landscape is composed of places bringing memories, and the history of the community is told with reference to its significant places.

Landscape archaeology thus has a cognitive dimension, which takes it far beyond the preoccupation with productive land-use characteristic of a purely materialist approach: the landscape has social and spiritual meaning as well as utility.

Measuring the World

One aspect of an individual's cognition we can readily reconstruct is the way in which it copes with measurement or quantitative description. The development of units was a fundamental cognitive step. In many cases, they can be recovered archaeologically, especially in the case of units of time, length, and weight.

The measurement of time is implied whenever a calendrical system can be documented. It is implied also when alignment, preserving the direction of the sun (or moon) at one of the major turning points can be documented. That is well known to be the case for the major axis of Stonehenge, the great **Neolithic** monument in England, which is oriented towards the midsummer sunrise. Such is also the case for the stone tomb of Newgrange in Ireland, dating from 3200 BC, whose entrance passage is oriented towards the midwinter sunrise.

The existence of measurements of weight can be demonstrated by the discovery of objects of standard form that prove to be multiples of a recurrent quantity (by weight), which we can assume to be a standard unit. Such finds are made in many early civilizations. Sometimes the observations are reinforced by the discovery of markings on the objects themselves, that accurately record how many times the standard the piece in question weighs. Systems of coinage are invariably graded using measurement by weight, as well as by material (gold, silver etc.), although their purpose is to measure differences in value, discussed in a later section. More directly relevant here are discoveries of actual weights.

An excellent example comes from the **site** of Mohenjodaro, a major city of the Indus Valley civilization around 2500–2000 BC. Attractive and carefully worked

Units of weight: stone cubes from Mohenjodaro, Pakistan, were produced in multiples of 0.836 g (0.03 oz). Scale pans indicate the practical use to which the cubes were put.

cubes of colored stone were found there. They proved to be multiples of what we may recognize as a constant unit of mass (namely 0.836 g, or 0.03 oz), multiplied by integers such as 1 or 4 or 8 up to 64, then 320 and 1600.

It can be argued that this simple discovery indicates:

1 that the society in question had developed a concept equivalent to our own notion of weight or mass;

2 that the use of this concept involved the operation of units of measure;

3 that there was a system of numbering, involving hierarchical numerical categories (e.g. tens and units), in this case apparently based on the fixed ratio of 16:1;

4 that the weight system was used for practical purposes (as the finding of scale pans indicates);

5 that there probably existed a notion of equivalence, on the basis of weight among different materials, and hence, it may follow, a ratio of value between them;

6 that this inferred concept of value may have entailed some form of constant rate of exchange between commodities

Items 5 and 6 are more hypothetical than the others in the list. But it seems a good example of the way that superficially simple discoveries can, when subjected to analysis, yield important information about the concepts and procedures of the communities in question.

Symbols of Organization and Power

Symbols are used for regulating and organizing people as well as the material world. They may simply convey information from one person to another, as with language or, as in the case of archival records, from one point in time to another. But sometimes they are symbols of power, commanding obedience and conformity, for example the giant statues of rulers found in many civilizations.

Power relations are sometimes documented graphically, as in the great statues of the Egyptian pharaohs, or on the splendid stelae and reliefs of the Maya. For example Lintel 24 from Yaxchilán shows the ruler ("Shield Jaguar") and his wife during a blood-letting ritual. The glyphs which frame their images give details of their names, the calendar date, and a description of the rite. The images do of course have religious significance, but they also emphasize the role of the ruler and his family in subjecting themselves to this painful ritual for the good of the community. Shield Jaguar holds aloft a flaming torch. He has a magnificent headdress, with feathers at the rear and the shrunken head of a past sacrificial victim tied to the top of his head by a headband. The inscription indicates a date in the Maya Long Count calendar equivalent to October 28, AD 709.

5 Eb 15 Mac
9.13.17.15.12
28 Oct.
AD 709

he is letting blood   ?   ?   4 Katun Lord

Shield Jaguar the captor of

name of captive

Lord of Yaxchilán

she is letting blood

name or titles

Lady K'abal Xoc

Lady Batab

Lintel 24 from Yaxchilán showing Shield Jaguar and his wife, Lady K'abal Xoc, during a bloodletting ritual. The glyphs which frame their images give details of their names, the calendar date, and a description of the rite.

More often, however, power relations are not documented pictorially but have to be inferred from the association of prestigious artifacts made, often with beautiful craftsmanship, from exotic materials.

Archaeological evidence on its own can in fact yield evidence of scales of value, as work on the analysis of finds from the late Neolithic cemetery at Varna in Bulgaria, dating from *c.* 4000 BC, has shown. Numerous golden artifacts were discovered in the cemetery, constituting what is the earliest known major find of gold anywhere in the world. But it cannot simply be assumed that the gold is of high value (its relative abundance in the cemetery might imply the opposite).

Three arguments, however, can be used to support the conclusion that the gold here was indeed of great worth:

1 Its use for artifacts with evidently symbolic status: e.g. to decorate the haft of a perforated stone axe which, through its fine work and delicate nature, was clearly not intended for use.

2 Its use for ornaments at particularly significant parts of the body: e.g. for face decorations, for a penis sheath.

Deducing scales of value: the great worth of the gold from Varna, Bulgaria, is suggested by, among other things, its use to decorate significant parts of the body.

3 Its use in simulation: sheet gold was used to cover a stone axe to give the impression of solid gold; such a procedure normally indicates that the material hidden is less valuable than the covering material.

The demonstration that gold objects were highly valued by society at this time in ancient Bulgaria also implies that the individuals with whom the gold finds were associated had a high social status. The importance of burials as sources of evidence for social status and ranking was discussed in Chapter 5. Here we are more interested in the use of grave-goods like the Varna gold-covered axes, and other discoveries, as *symbols of authority and power*. The display of such authority is not very pronounced in a society like that excavated at Varna, but it becomes more blatant the more hierarchical and stratified the society becomes.

The Archaeology of Religion

One leading English dictionary defines religion as: "Action or conduct indicating a belief in, or reverence for, and desire to please, a divine ruling power." Religion thus involves a framework of beliefs, and these relate to supernatural or superhuman beings or forces that go beyond the everyday material world. In other words superhuman beings are conceptualized by humans, and have a place in the shared cognitive map of the world.

One problem that archaeologists face is that these belief systems are not always given expression in material culture. And when they are – in what can be termed the **archaeology of cult** – there is the problem that such actions are not always clearly separated from the other actions of everyday life: cult can be embedded within everyday functional activity, and thus difficult to distinguish from it archaeologically.

The first task of the archaeologist is to recognize the evidence of cult for what it is, and not make the old mistake of classifying as religious activity every action in the past that we do not understand.

Recognition of Cult   If we are to distinguish cult from other activities, such as the largely secular ceremonial that may attend a head of state (which can also have very elaborate symbolism), it is important not to lose sight of the transcendent or supernatural object of the cult activity. Religious ritual involves the performance of expressive acts of worship toward the deity or transcendent being. In this there are generally at least four main components (we will see below how these may then help us draw up a list of aspects that are identifiable archaeologically):

• *Focusing of attention* The act of worship both demands and induces a state of heightened awareness or religious excitement in the human celebrant. In communal acts of worship, this invariably requires a range of attention-focusing devices, including the use of a sacred location, architecture (e.g. temples), light, sounds, and smell to ensure that all eyes are directed to the crucial ritual acts.

• *Boundary zone between this world and the next* The focus of ritual activity is the boundary area between this world and the Other World. It is a special and mysterious region with hidden dangers. There are risks of pollution and of failing to comply with the appropriate procedures: ritual washing and cleanliness are therefore emphasized.

• *Presence of the deity* For ritual to be effective, the deity or supernatural force must in some sense be present. It is the divine as well as human attention that needs to be heightened. In most societies, the deity is symbolized by some material form or image: this need be no more than a very simple symbol – for instance, the outline of a sign or container whose contents are not seen – or it may be a three-dimensional cult image such as a statue.

• *Participation and offering* Worship makes demands on the celebrant. These include not only words and gestures of prayer and respect, but often active participation involving movement, perhaps eating and drinking. Frequently, it involves also the offering of material things to the deity, both by sacrifice and gift.

An excellent example of cult activity visible in the archaeological record is offered by the great ceremonial center at Chavín de Huantar in north-central Peru, which flourished from 850 to 200 BC.

The most immediately obvious feature of the site is its imposing architecture, comprising a complex of stone-faced platforms built in the earliest phase on a U-shaped plan and set apart from living areas at the site. Ritual involving both conspicuous public display and hidden mysteries is implied by the presence of an open circular sunken plaza that could hold 300 participants, and hidden underground passageways, the most important of which led to a narrow chamber dominated by a 4.5 m (14 ft 9 in) high granite shaft know as the Lanzón (Great Image).

The carving on this shaft of a fanged anthropomorphic being, its location in a central chamber facing east along the temple's main axis, and its size and workmanship all suggest that this was the principal cult image of the site. Moreover, some 200 other finely carved stone sculptures were discovered in and around the temple, the **iconography** of which was dominated by images of caymans, jaguars, eagles, and snakes. A cache of over 500 broken high-quality pots containing food found in an underground gallery may have been offerings (though the excavator believes they were used for storage). There is some evidence for drug-induced rituals and the possibility that canals beneath the site were used for ritual cleansing and to create roaring sounds to heighten the impact of ceremonies.

(Right) Perspective and plan views of the early U-shaped platforms at the site, with a section through the central passageway showing the narrow chamber dominated by the Lanzón or Great Image.

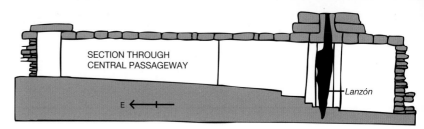

SECTION THROUGH
CENTRAL PASSAGEWAY

Lanzón

E ←

(Below) Two views of the Lanzón or Great Image (a side view, left, and a rollout drawing, right), depicting a fanged anthropomorphic being.

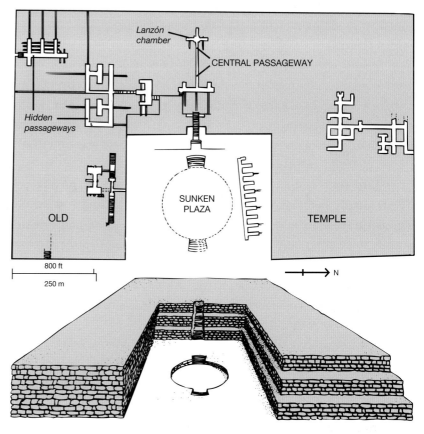

Lanzón chamber

CENTRAL PASSAGEWAY

Hidden passageways

SUNKEN PLAZA

OLD

TEMPLE

800 ft

250 m

N

SOUTH AMERICA

Chavín de Huantar

(Right) Transformation of a masked shaman (left) into a jaguar (right). These sculptures were displayed on the outer wall of the temple, and hint at drug-induced rituals.

KEY CONCEPTS: WORKING WITH SYMBOLS

The human species is distinguished from other life forms by its use of symbols

Symbols are used by humans for a variety of purposes, some of which can be recognized in the archaeological record:

• The marking of place and the definition of territory

• The construction of systems of measurement

• Design, mapping, and the planning of future actions

• Shaping and reflecting social realities, including identity and power relationships

• Communicating with supernatural powers in the Other World

The study of Chavín thus demonstrates that a careful archaeological and art historical analysis of different kinds of evidence can produce sound proof of cult activity – even for a site and society concerning which there are no written records whatsoever.

THE IMPACT OF LITERACY

Symbols of depiction provide us with perhaps our most direct insight into the cognition of an individual or a society for pre-literate periods. Among literate communities, however, written words – those deceptively direct symbols used to describe the world – inevitably dominate the evidence. The locations and dates of the world's earliest writing systems are summarized on the map overleaf.

Ancient literature in all its variety, from poems and plays to political statements and early historical writings, provides rich insights into the cognitive world of the great civilizations. But, to use such evidence accurately and effectively, we need to understand something of the social context of the use of writing in different societies.

The very existence of writing implies a major extension of human cognitive processes. Written symbols have proved the most effective system ever devised by humans not only to describe the world around them, but to communicate with and control people, to organise society as a whole, and to pass on to posterity the accumulated knowledge of a society.

Literacy in Classical Greece

The importance of literacy is well illustrated by the case of Classical Greece, where literacy was widespread among the population. In several ancient civilizations writing was practised only by a small segment of the population, notably scribes – for

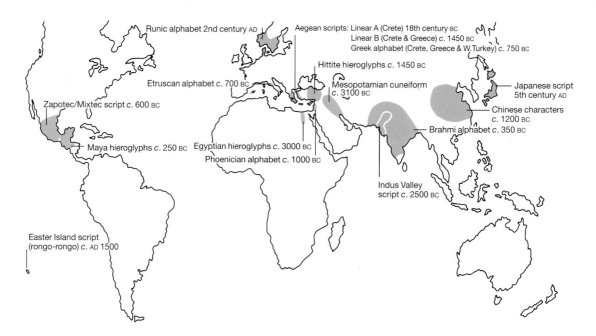

Runic alphabet 2nd century AD

Aegean scripts: Linear A (Crete) 18th century BC
Linear B (Crete & Greece) c. 1450 BC
Greek alphabet (Crete, Greece & W.Turkey) c. 750 BC

Hittite hieroglyphs c. 1450 BC

Etruscan alphabet c. 700 BC

Mesopotamian cuneiform c. 3100 BC

Japanese script 5th century AD

Zapotec/Mixtec script c. 600 BC

Chinese characters c. 1200 BC

Brahmi alphabet c. 350 BC

Maya hieroglyphs c. 250 BC

Egyptian hieroglyphs c. 3000 BC

Phoenician alphabet c. 1000 BC

Indus Valley script c. 2500 BC

Easter Island script (rongo-rongo) c. AD 1500

Map to show locations of the world's earliest writing systems.

instance in Ancient Egypt or Mesopotamia, and the same was probably true in Mesoamerica. In Greece, however, it is likely that many of the people who had the status of citizens were able to read.

For extended texts, whether works of literature or accounts, the Greeks wrote on papyrus. Examples of such texts have been found at Pompeii and in the very dry conditions of the Faiyum depression in Egypt. For public inscriptions, the Greeks used stone or bronze, although notices that were not of permanent interest were put on display on whitened boards (the simple alphabetic script of the Greeks favored such relatively casual use).

Among the functions of Greek inscriptions carved on stone or bronze were:
- Public decree by the ruling body (council or assembly)
- Award of honors by the ruling body to an individual or group
- Treaty between states
- Letters from a monarch to a city
- List of taxes imposed on tributary states
- Inventories of property and dedications belonging to a deity
- Rules for divination (understanding omens), e.g. from the flight of birds
- Building accounts, records of specifications, contracts, and payments
- Public notices: e.g. list for military service
- Boundary stones and mortgage stones
- Epitaph
- Curse laid on whoever might disturb a particular tomb.

It is clear from this list what an important role writing had within the democratic government of the Greek states.

A better indication of literacy and of the role of writing in Greek daily life is given by the various objects bearing inscriptions, and by comments scrawled on walls (graffiti). One type of object, the *ostrakon*, was a voting ticket in the form of a fragment of pottery with the name of the individual – for (or against) whom the vote was being cast – incised on it. Many have been found in Athens where (by the system of "ostracism") public men could, by a vote of the assembly, be driven into exile.

Other Greek uses of writing on a variety of objects were:

- On coins, to show the issuing authority (city)
- To label individuals shown in scenes on wall paintings and painted vases
- To label prizes awarded in competitions
- To label dedications made to a deity
- To indicate the price of goods
- To give the signature of the artist or craftsperson
- To indicate jury membership (on a jury ticket)

Many of these simple inscriptions enable us to glimpse aspects of everyday life in Ancient Greece, and even to identify and learn things about individuals. The British Museum has a black-figure drinking cup of *c.* 530 BC, made in Athens and imported to Taranto, Italy, bearing the inscription: "I am Melousa's prize: she won the maiden's carding contest."

It can be seen from this brief summary that writing touched nearly every aspect of Classical Greek life, private as well as public. The cognitive archaeology of ancient Greece thus inevitably draws to a great extent on the insights provided by such literary evidence – as will become apparent, for example, in our discussion of procedures for identifying supernatural beings in art and individual artists. But we should not imagine that cognitive archaeology is thus necessarily dependent on literary sources to generate or test its theories.

Textual evidence is indeed of paramount importance in helping us understand ways of thought among literate societies but, as we saw above for the Paleolithic period, there are in addition purely archaeological sources that may be used to create theories about the thought processes of ancient individuals and peoples, and purely archaeological criteria to judge their validity. Moreover, literary sources may themselves be biased in ways which need to be fully assessed before any attempt can be made to match such sources with evidence from the archaeological record.

Potsherds (ostraka) inscribed with two famous Greek names: above, Themistokles; below, Perikles.

THE ARCHAEOLOGY OF PEOPLE

We have seen how archaeological evidence can help us to understand – at least to some degree – the mental capabilities of ancient people, as well as some of the ways in which they thought about their world and their everyday lives. The archaeological record also provides us with much more tangible evidence – complete skeletons, bones, and bone fragments, and sometimes preserved corpses that have been preserved in special circumstances – that enables us to reconstruct the physical attributes of past individuals and groups. If sufficient evidence has survived, archaeologists can determine, for example, the sex and age of an individual, perhaps how that person died, and even their physical appearance.

The Variety of Human Remains. How does the archaeologist know that human remains are present? This is relatively easy where intact bodies, complete skeletons, or skulls are found. Archaeologists can usually reliably identify individual bones and large fragments as human. Even small fragments may include diagnostic features by which human beings can be recognized. In some recent, careful **excavations**, individual hairs have been recovered which can be identified under the microscope as human.

Even where the physical remains of the body have disappeared, evidence may sometimes survive. The best-known examples are the hollows left by the bodies of the people of Pompeii as they disintegrated inside their hardened casing of volcanic ash. Modern plaster casts of these bodies show not only the general physical appearance, hairstyles, clothing, and posture, but even such fine and moving detail as the facial expression at the moment of death.

Nevertheless the vast majority of human remains are in the form of actual skeletons and bone fragments, which yield a wide range of information, as we shall see. Indirect physical evidence about people also comes from ancient art, and provides important evidence about what people looked like.

Identifying Physical Attributes

Once the presence and abundance of human remains have been established, how can we attempt to reconstruct physical characteristics – sex, age at death, build, appearance, and relationships? A good example of what we can learn from human remains is provided by the Lindow Man bog body (see box overleaf). The techniques for assessing each different physical characteristic are described below.

Which Sex? Where *intact bodies* and *artistic depictions* are concerned, sexing is usually straightforward from the genitalia. If these are not present, secondary characteristics such as breasts and beards and moustaches provide fairly reliable indicators. Where *human skeletons* and *bone remains* without soft tissue are

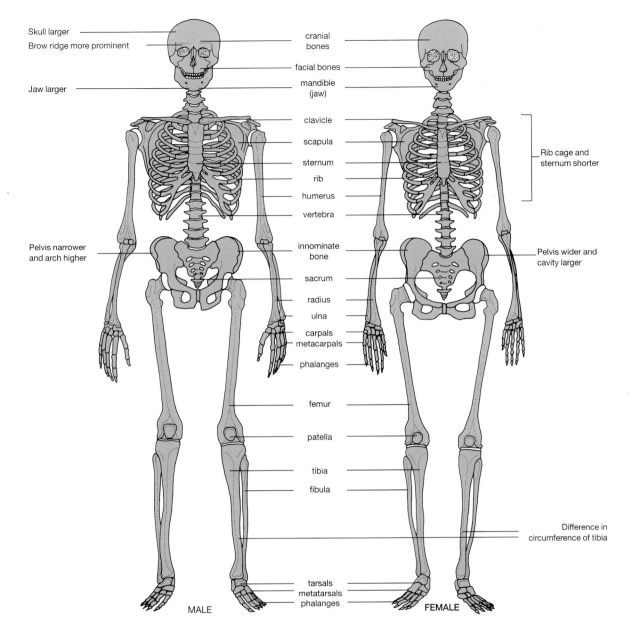

Skull larger
Brow ridge more prominent

cranial bones

facial bones

mandible (jaw)

Jaw larger

clavicle

scapula

sternum

rib

humerus

vertebra

Rib cage and sternum shorter

Pelvis narrower and arch higher

innominate bone

sacrum

radius

ulna

carpals
metacarpals

phalanges

Pelvis wider and cavity larger

femur

patella

tibia

fibula

Difference in circumference of tibia

tarsals
metatarsals
phalanges

MALE

FEMALE

concerned, however, there are lots more sources of evidence. The best indicator of sex is the shape of the pelvis, since this is visibly different in males and females (see diagram, above).

Other parts of the skeleton can also be used in sex differentiation. Male bones are generally bigger, longer, more robust, and have more developed muscle markings than those of females, which are slighter.

For *children* it is worth noting that, with the exception of preserved bodies and artistic depictions showing genitalia, their remains cannot be sexed with the same degree of reliability as adults, although analysis of teeth can provide some evidence.

Bones of the human skeleton, with salient differences between the sexes.

LINDOW MAN: THE BODY IN THE BOG

In 1984, part of a human leg was found by workers at a peat-shredding mill in northwest England. Subsequent investigation of the site at Lindow Moss, Cheshire, where the peat had been cut, revealed the top half of a human body still embedded in the ground. This complete section of peat was removed and later "excavated" in the laboratory by a multi-disciplinary team of scientists. The various studies made of the body have yielded remarkable insights into the life and death of this ancient individual, now dated to the late Iron Age or Roman period – perhaps the 1st century AD.

Despite the missing lower half, it was obvious from the beard, sideburns, and moustache that this was the body of a male. The age of Lindow Man (as he is now called) has been estimated at around the mid–20s. He appears to have been well-built, and probably weighed around 60 kg (132 lb). His height, calculated from the length of his humerus (upper arm bone), was estimated to be between 1.68 and 1.73 m (5 ft 6 in to 5 ft 8 in) – average today, but fairly tall for the period.

Lindow Man wore no clothing apart from an armband of fox fur. His brown/ginger hair and whiskers were cut, and analysis by scanning electron microscopy indicated that their ends had a stepped surface, implying that they had probably been cut by scissors or shears. His manicured fingernails indicate that he did not do any heavy or rough work – he was clearly not a laborer.

The bog acid had removed the enamel from his teeth, but what survived seemed normal and quite healthy – there were no visible cavities.

Lindow Man appears to have had very slight osteoarthritis; and a CAT-scan revealed changes in some vertebrae caused by stresses and strains. Parasite eggs show that he had a relatively high infestation of whipworm and maw worm, but these would have caused him little inconvenience. Overall, therefore, he was fairly healthy.

His blood group was found to be O, like the majority of modern Britons. The food residues in the part of his upper alimentary tract that survived revealed that his last meal had consisted of a griddle cake.

X-rays confirmed that his head had been fractured from behind – they revealed splinters of bone in the vault of the skull. A forensic scientist deduced from the two lacerated wounds joined together that the skull had been driven in twice by a narrow-bladed weapon. There may also have been a blow (from a knee?) to his back, because X-rays showed a broken rib.

The blows to the head would have rendered him unconscious, if not killed him outright, so that he cannot have felt the subsequent garotting or the knife in his throat. A knotted thong of sinew, 1.5 mm thick, around his throat had broken his neck and strangled him, and his throat had been slit with a short, deep cut at the side of the neck that severed the jugular. Once he had been bled in this way, he was dropped face-down into a pool in the bog.

We do not know why he died – perhaps as a sacrifice, or as an executed criminal – but we have been able to learn a great deal about the life and death of Lindow Man.

Cleaning the back of Lindow Man in the laboratory. Distilled water is being sprayed to keep the skin moist.

Fully conserved remains of Lindow Man photographed in ultra-violet light to enhance the details.

When we examine subadult skeletal remains we can often only guess – though the odds of being right are 50:50.

How Long Did They Live?   However confidently some scholars may indicate the exact age at death of particular deceased human beings, it should be stressed that what we can usually establish with any certainty is biological age at death – young, adult, old – rather than any accurate measurement in years and months. The best indicators of age, as with animals, are the *teeth*. We can study the eruption and replacement of the milk teeth; the sequence of eruption of the permanent

18–30

16–25

13–19

15–20

15–23

16–23

16–20
16–20

Assessing age: the years at which bone ends fuse.

dentition; and finally the degree of wear, allowing as best one can for the effects of diet and method of food preparation.

A timescale for age at death derived from this kind of dental information in modern people works reasonably well for recent periods, despite much individual variation. But can it be applied to the dentition of our remote ancestors? New work on the microstructure of teeth suggests that old assumptions may not be correct. Tooth enamel grows at a regular, measurable rate, and its microscopic growth lines form ridges that can be counted from epoxy resin replicas of the tooth placed in a scanning electron microscope. In modern populations a new ridge grows approximately each week, and a similar rate of growth has to be assumed in analyses of our hominid ancestors.

By measuring tooth growth ridges in fossil specimens, Tim Bromage and Christopher Dean have concluded that previous investigators overestimated the age at death of many early hominids. The famous 1–2 million-year-old australopithecine skull from Taung, South Africa, for example, belonged to a child who probably died at just over 3 years of age, not at 5 or 6 as had been believed. This suggests that our earliest ancestors grew up more quickly than we do, and that their development into maturity was more like that of the modern great apes.

Bones are also used in assessing age. The sequence in which the articulating ends of bones become fused to the shafts gives a timescale that can be applied to the remains of young people. One of the last bones to fuse is the inner end of the clavicle (collar bone) at about 26; after that age, different criteria are needed to age bones.

Skull thickness in immature individuals bears a rough relationship to age – the thicker the skull the older the specimen – and in old age all bones usually get thinner and lighter, although skull bones actually get thicker in about 10 percent of elderly people.

But what if the bone remains are small fragments? The answer lies under the microscope, in *bone microstructure.* As we get older, the architecture of our bones changes in a distinct and measurable way. A young longbone, at about 20, has rings around its circumference, and a relatively small number of circular structures called osteons. With age the rings disappear, and more and smaller osteons appear.

Assessing age: changes in bone structure are visible under the microscope as humans grow older. The circular osteons become more numerous and extend to the edge of the bone.

By this method, even a fragment can provide an age. Putting a thin section of a femur (thigh bone) under the microscope and studying the stage of development is a technique which, in tests with modern specimens, has achieved accuracy to within 5 years.

What Did They Look Like?   Once again, it is preserved bodies that provide us with our clearest glimpses of faces. Tollund Man, one of the remarkable Iron Age bog bodies from Denmark, is the best-known prehistoric example. Discoveries at Thebes in Egypt in 1881 and 1898 of two royal burial caches have given us a veritable gallery of mummified pharaohs, their faces still vivid, even if some shrinkage and distortion has taken place.

Thanks to artists from the Upper Paleolithic onward, we also have a huge array of portraits. Some of them, such as images painted on mummy cases, are directly associated with the remains of their subject. Others, such as Greek and Roman busts, are accurate likenesses of well-known figures whose remains may be lost for ever. The extraordinary life-size terracotta army found near Xi'an, China, is made up of thousands of different models of soldiers of the 3rd century BC. Even though only the general features of each are represented, they constitute an unprecedented "library" of individuals, as well as providing invaluable information on hairstyles, armor, and weaponry. From later periods we have many life- or death-masks, sometimes used as the basis for life-size funerary effigies or tomb-figures, such as those of European royalty and other notables from medieval times onward.

Attempts to reconstruct faces were already being carried out in the 19th century by German anatomists in order to produce likenesses from the skulls of celebrities such as Schiller, Kant, and Bach. But the best-known exponent of the technique in the 20th century was the Russian Mikhail Gerasimov, who worked on specimens ranging from fossil humans to Ivan the Terrible. It is now felt that much of his work represented "inspired interpretation," rather than factual reconstruction. Currently, the process has reached a higher degree of accuracy.

Faces from the past.
(Far left) Bronze head of the Roman emperor Hadrian (reigned AD 117–138), from the Thames river.
(Second left) Moche portrait vase, *c.* 6th century AD , from Peru. (Second right) Head of Tollund Man, the Iron Age bog body from Denmark.
(Right) Mummified head of a man, perhaps the pharaoh Tuthmosis I (1504–1492 BC), from Deir el-Bahri, Egypt.

The reconstruction made from the skull found in the sarcophagus.

One of the most intriguing recent facial reconstructions has been of the best-preserved Etruscan skeleton known today, that of a noblewoman called Seianti Hanunia Tlesnasa, who died about 2200 years ago in central Italy. Since 1887 her remains have been housed in the British Museum inside a splendid painted terracotta sarcophagus which bears her name engraved on it. The lid of this sarcophagus features a life-size image of the dead woman, reclining on a soft pillow, with a bronze mirror in her jewelled hand. This is perhaps the earliest identifiable portrait in western art, but is it really Seianti?

Anthropologists deduced from the skeleton that the woman was about 1.5 m (4 ft 11 in) tall, and middle-aged at death. Damage and wear on her bones, and the fact that she was almost toothless, had at first suggested old age, but in fact she had incurred severe injuries, most likely a riding accident which had crushed her right hip and knocked out the teeth of her right lower jaw. The bone was damaged where the jaw joins the skull, and opening her mouth wide would have been painful. This prevented her from eating anything but soups and gruels, and from keeping her remaining teeth clean – most of them subsequently fell out. Seianti would also have had painful arthritis and increasing disabilities.

Two of the surviving teeth confirmed, from analysis of the dentine, that she was about 50 when she died. And **radiocarbon dating** of the bones produced a result

The terracotta sarcophagus of Seianti Hanunia Tlesnasa, which contained her bones; the lid takes the form of a life-size image of the dead woman – but how accurately did it represent her appearance?

of 250–150 BC, which proved that the skeleton was genuinely ancient and of the right period. The facial reconstruction showed a middle-aged woman who had grown rather obese. How did it compare with the coffin image?

From the side, there were differences, since the artist had given Seianti a prettier nose, but from the front the resemblances were clearer. The final confirmation came from a computerized technique for matching facial proportions and features – the computer photocomparison of the reconstruction and the portrait left no doubt that this was the same person. The sarcophagus image showed her as some years younger, with fewer chins, and a smaller, more girlish mouth. In other words, the sculptor had made flattering improvements to the portrait of this short, portly, middle-aged woman, but also captured Seianti's likeness extremely well.

How Were They Related? In certain cases it is possible to assess the relationship between two individuals by comparing skull shape or analyzing the hair. There are other methods of achieving the same result, primarily by study of dental morphology. Some dental anomalies (such as enlarged or extra teeth, and especially missing wisdom teeth) run in families.

Blood groups can be determined from soft tissue, bone, and even from tooth dentine up to more than 30,000 years old. Since blood groups are inherited in a simple fashion from parents, different systems – of which the best known is the A-B-O system in which people are divided into those with blood types A, B, O, AB etc. – can sometimes help clarify physical relationships between different bodies. For example, it was suspected that Tutankhamun was somehow related to the unidentified body discovered in Tomb 55 at Thebes in 1907. The shape and

KEY CONCEPTS: ASSESSING HUMAN PHYSICAL ATTRIBUTES

- *Sex:* intact bodies can be sexed from the genitalia; skeletons and bone remains, much more common in the archaeological record, are sexed from size and form differences between male and female bones. Children are difficult to sex

- *Age:* the main methods of establishing the age of a skeleton are by examinations of the growth patterns of bones and teeth and of bone microstructure

- *Appearance:* it is now possible to make accurate facial reconstructions of ancient individuals, as long as their skull or fragments of it survive

- *Relationships:* examinations of skull shape, hair type, teeth, and blood group can help to establish whether two individuals were related diameter of the skulls were very similar, and when X-rays of the two crania were superimposed there was almost complete conformity. Robert Connolly and his colleagues therefore analyzed tissue from the two mummies, which showed that both had blood of group A, subgroup 2 with antigens M and N, a type relatively rare in ancient Egypt. This fact, together with the skeletal similarities, makes it almost certain that the two were closely related. The exact identity of the mysterious Tomb 55 body is still unresolved, however, some scholars holding that it is Tutankhamun's father, Akhenaten, others that it is his possible brother, Smenkhkare.

SUMMARY

- In this chapter we have shown how archaeological evidence can be used to provide insights into the way of thinking of cultures and civilizations long dead, as well as into the physical attributes of our ancestors.

- Whether it be evidence for measurement, means of organization and power, or cult activity – there are good archaeological procedures for analyzing and testing cognitive hypotheses about the past. An archaeological project may focus on one aspect of the way ancient people thought (for example, in the search for a possible standard unit of measurement), or it may be much broader (for example, the work at Chavín). While textual evidence may be of crucial importance in supporting or helping to assess cognitive claims – as in Mesoamerica or Mesopotamia – cognitive archaeology does not depend on literary sources for its validity.

- In addition to these aspects of the ancient mind, we are also deeply interested in some of the physical attributes of our ancestors. Since archaeology studies the relics of the human past, it follows that the archaeologist's ultimate interest must lie in the remains of the very people who produced the archaeological record. A huge range of very varied information can now be extracted from even minor fragments of humanity. We can assess age, sex, appearance and inter-relationships.

FURTHER READING

The following provide an introduction to the study of the attitudes and beliefs of ancient humans, as well as to the study of their physical remains:

Arsuaga, J.L. 2003. **The Neanderthal's Necklace: In Search of the First Thinkers.** FOUR WALLS EIGHT WINDOWS: NEW YORK.

Aufderheide, A. C. 2003. **The Scientific Study of Mummies.** CAMBRIDGE UNIVERSITY PRESS: CAMBRIDGE.

Brothwell, D. 1986. **The Bog Man and the Archaeology of People.** BRITISH MUSEUM PUBLICATIONS: LONDON; HARVARD UNIVERSITY PRESS: CAMBRIDGE, MASS.

Chamberlain, A.T. & Parker Pearson, M. 2001. **Earthly Remains. The History and Science of Preserved Human Bodies.** BRITISH MUSEUM PRESS: LONDON; OXFORD UNIVERSITY PRESS: NEW YORK.

Johnson, M. 1999. **Archaeological Theory.**

BLACKWELL: OXFORD.

Larsen, C.S. 2000. **Skeletons in our Closet: Revealing our Past through Bioarchaeology.** PRINCETON UNIVERSITY PRESS: CAMBRIDGE & NEW YORK.

Marshack, A. 1991. **The Roots of Civilization.** (2nd ed.) MOYER BELL: NEW YORK.

Mays, S. 1998. **The Archaeology of Human Bones.** ROUTLEDGE: LONDON.

Renfrew, C. & Zubrow E.B.W. (eds.). 1994. **The Ancient Mind: Elements of Cognitive Archaeology.** CAMBRIDGE UNIVERSITY PRESS: CAMBRIDGE & NEW YORK.

9 Why Did Things Change?

explanation in archaeology

To answer the question "why?" is the most difficult task in **archaeology**. We must go beyond simply describing the appearance of things and try to *understand* the pattern of events.

This is the goal motivating many who take up the study of the human past. There is a desire to learn something from a study of what is dead and gone that is relevant for the conduct of our own lives and our societies today. Archaeology, which allows us to study early and remote prehistoric periods as well as the more recent historical ones, is unique among the human sciences in offering a considerable time depth. Thus, if there are patterns to be found among human affairs, the archaeological timescale may reveal them.

There is no agreed and accepted way of setting out to understand the human past. A chapter such as this is therefore bound to be inconclusive, and certain to be controversial. But it is a chapter worth writing and worth thinking about, for it is in this area of inquiry that archaeological research is now most active. The main debates have developed over the past 40 years or so.

Traditional explanations of change in the past focused on the concepts of diffusion and migration – they assumed that changes in one group must have been caused either by the influence or influx of a neighboring and superior group. But in the 1960s the development of the **processual** approach of the New Archaeology exposed the shortcomings of the earlier explanations. It was realized that there was no well-established body of theory to underpin archaeological inquiry (to a large extent this is still true, although there have been many attempts).

The early New Archaeology involved the explicit use of theory and of models, and above all of generalization. However, it was criticized as being too much concerned with ecological aspects of adaptation and with efficiency, and with the purely utilitarian and functional aspects of living (in other words, it was too "functionalist"). Meanwhile, an alternative perspective, inspired by Marxism, was laying more stress on social relations and the exercise of power.

From the 1970s, in reaction to the processual "functionalists," some archaeologists favored a **structuralist** archaeology, then a post-structuralist, and, finally, a **postprocessual** one. These approaches stressed that the ideas and beliefs of past societies should not be overlooked in archaeological explanation.

Since that time archaeologists have given more systematic attention to the way humans think, how they make and use symbols, and to what may be described as cognitive issues. One approach, today termed "**cognitive archaeology**," seeks to work in the tradition of processual archaeology while stressing social and cognitive aspects.

So far there is no single, widely agreed approach.

KEY CONCEPTS: STRATEGIES OF EXPLANATION

- *Migrationist and Diffusionist:* explanations rely on rather simple ideas of the supposed migrations of peoples, or the often ill-defined spread of ideas

- *Processual:* attempts to provide more general explanations (using, for instance, evolutionary theory), sometimes using law-like formulations, and (more successfully) framing hypotheses and testing deductions from these against the data

- *Postprocessual or Interpretive:* emphasizes the specific context, drawing sometimes on structuralist or neo-Marxist ideas, stressing often the role ("agency") of the individual, and avoiding the generalizations of the processual approach

MIGRATIONIST AND DIFFUSIONIST EXPLANATIONS

The New Archaeology made the shortcomings of traditional archaeological explanations much more apparent. These shortcomings can be made clearer in an example of the traditional method – the appearance of a new kind of pottery in a given area and period, the pottery being distinguished by shapes not previously recognized and by new decorative motifs. The traditional approach will very properly require a closer definition of this pottery style in space and time. The archaeologist will be expected to draw a distribution map of its occurrence, and also to establish its place in the stratigraphic sequence at the **sites** where it occurs. The next step is to assign it to its place within an archaeological **culture**.

Using the traditional approach, it was argued that each archaeological culture is the manifestation in material terms of a specific *people* – that is, a well-defined ethnic group, detectable by the archaeologist by the method just outlined. This is an ethnic classification, but of course the "people," being prehistoric, were given an arbitrary name. Usually, they were named after the place where the pottery was first recognized (e.g. the Mimbres people in the American Southwest), or sometimes after the pottery itself (e.g. the Beaker Folk).

Next it was usual to see if it is possible to think in terms of a folk *migration* to explain the changes observed. Could a convenient homeland for this group of people be located? Careful study of the ceramic assemblages in adjoining lands might suggest such a homeland, and perhaps even a migration route.

Alternatively, if the migration argument did not seem to work, a fourth approach was to look for specific features of the cultural assemblage that have *parallels* in more distant lands. If the whole assemblage cannot be attributed to an external source, there may be specific features of it that can. Links may be found with more civilized lands. If such "parallels" can be discovered, the traditionalist would argue that these were the points of origin for the features in our assemblage, and were transmitted to it by a process of cultural *diffusion*. Indeed, before the advent of **radiocarbon dating**, these parallels could also be used to date the pottery finds in our hypothetical example, because the features and traits lying closer to the heartlands of civilization would almost certainly already be dated through comparison with the historical chronology of that civilization.

It would be easy to find many actual examples of such explanations. For instance, in the New World, the very striking developments in architecture and other crafts in Chaco Canyon in New Mexico have been explained by comparisons of precisely this kind with the more "advanced" civilizations of Mexico to the south.

Traditional explanations rest, however, on assumptions that are easily challenged today. First, there is the notion among traditionalists that archaeological "cultures" can somehow represent real entities rather than merely the classificatory terms devised for the convenience of the scholar. Second is the view that ethnic units or "peoples" can be recognized from the archaeological record by equation with these notional cultures. It is in fact clear that ethnic groups do not always stand out clearly in archaeological remains. Third, it is assumed that when resemblances are noted between the cultural assemblages of one area and another, this can be most readily explained as the result of a migration of people. Of course, migrations did indeed occur (see below), but they are not so easy to document archaeologically as has often been supposed.

Finally, there is the principle of explanation through the diffusion of culture. Today, it is felt that this explanation has sometimes been overplayed, and nearly always oversimplified. For although contact between areas, not least through trade, can be of great significance for the developments in each area, the effects of this contact have to be considered in detail: explanation simply in terms of diffusion is not enough.

Nevertheless it is worth emphasizing that migrations did take place in the past, and on rare occasions this can be documented archaeologically. The colonization of the Polynesian islands in the Pacific offers one example. A complex of finds – especially pottery with incised decoration – known as the Lapita culture provides a record of the rapid movement of islanders eastward across a vast uninhabited area, from the northern New Guinea region to as far as Samoa, between 1600 and 1000 BC (see overleaf). Also, innovations are frequently made in one place and adopted in neighboring areas, and it is still perfectly proper to speak of the mechanism as one of diffusion (see illustration of the origins of the Roman alphabet overleaf). A good example of what was first a migrationist explanation, and then became a diffusionist explanation, until it was subsequently rejected, is offered by the case of Great Zimbabwe (see box on p. 251).

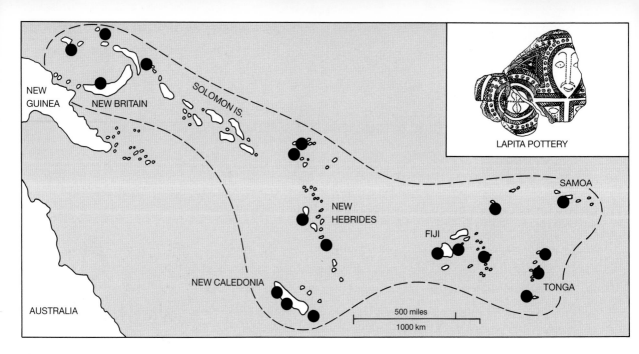

Migration: a positive example. The question of first settlement of the Polynesian islands has apparently been resolved by the discovery of the Lapita culture, which is characterized in particular by pottery with incised decoration. Lapita sites providea record of the rapid movement of islanders by boat, eastwards from the northern New Guinea region to as far as Samoa in western Polynesia, between 1600 and 1000 BC.

Diffusion: a positive example. One instance where an innovation in one place is known to have spread widely elsewhere through diffusion is that of the alphabet. Around the 12th century BC, on the Levantine coast, the Phoenicians developed a simplified phonetic script to write their Semitic language. By the early 1st millennium BC, the script had been adapted by the Greeks to write their language. Then the Greek alphabet was modified in Italy, to write Etruscan and Latin, the Roman language. It was through Latin that our own alphabet (known as the Roman alphabet) came to much of Europe, and later the rest of the world.

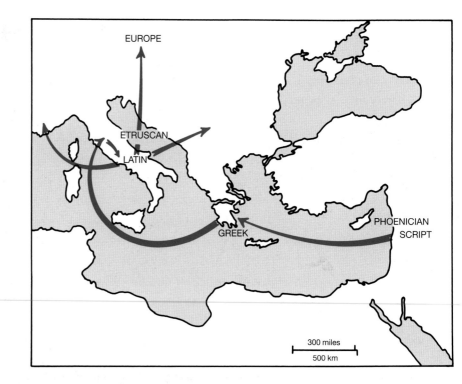

DIFFUSIONIST EXPLANATION REJECTED: GREAT ZIMBABWE

The remarkable monument of Great Zimbabwe, near Masvingo in modern Zimbabwe, has been the object of intense speculation ever since this region of Africa was first explored by Europeans in the 19th century. For here was an impressive structure of great sophistication, with beautifully finished stonework.

Early scholars followed the traditional pattern of explanation in ascribing Great Zimbabwe to architects and builders from "more civilized" lands to the north. On a visit to the site by the British explorer Cecil Rhodes, the local Karange chiefs were told that "the Great Master" had come "to see the ancient temple which once upon a time belonged to white men."

This was thus a migrationist view.

Systematic excavations were undertaken by Gertrude Caton-Thompson (p. 32), and she concluded her report in 1931: "Examination of all the existing evidence, gathered from every quarter, still can produce not one single item that is not in accordance with the claim of Bantu origin and medieval date." Despite her carefully documented conclusions, however, other archaeologists continued to follow the typical pattern of diffusionist explanation in speaking of "influences" from "higher centers of culture." Portuguese traders were one favored source of inspiration.

Subsequent research has backed up the conclusions of Gertrude Caton-Thompson. Great Zimbabwe is now seen as the most notable of a larger class of monuments in this area.

Although the site has an earlier history, the construction of a monumental building probably began there in the 13th century AD, and the site reached its climax in the 15th century. Various archaeologists have now been able to give a coherent picture of the economic and social conditions in the area that made this great achievement possible.

Significant influence – diffusion – from more "advanced" areas is no longer part of that picture. Today a processual framework of explanation has replaced the diffusionist one.

Carved soapstone bird found in the Great Zimbabwe Eastern Enclosure in 1889, and later sold to Cecil Rhodes.

Site plan: Great Zimbabwe, with its series of enclosed areas, platforms, and impressive conical tower.

An aerial view of Great Zimbabwe.

THE PROCESSUAL APPROACH

The processual approach attempts to isolate and study the different processes at work within a society, and between societies, placing emphasis on relations with the environment, on subsistence and the economy, on social relations within the society, on the impact which the prevailing ideology and belief system have on these things, and on the effects of the interactions taking place between the different social units.

It is a characteristic of processual explanations that they have usually focused on ecological and social factors whose operation can be analyzed in some detail. Sometimes a systems model is used, looking at the interaction of what may be defined as the subsystems of the culture system. A good early example of a processual explanation, even though today it is regarded as incomplete, is offered by Lewis Binford's explanation for the origins of sedentary society and of a farming economy.

In 1968, Binford published an influential paper, "Post-Pleistocene Adaptations," in which he set out to explain the origins of farming, or food production. Attempts to do this had been made by earlier scholars. But Binford's explanation had one important feature that distinguished it from earlier explanations and made it very much a product of the New Archaeology: its generality. For he was setting out to explain the origins of farming not just in the Near East or the Mediterranean – although he focused on these areas – but worldwide. He drew attention to global events at the end of the last Ice Age (i.e. at the end of the Pleistocene epoch, hence the title of his paper).

Binford centered his explanation on demography: he was concerned with population dynamics within small communities, stressing that once a formerly mobile group becomes sedentary – ceases to move around – its population size will increase markedly. For in a settled village the constraints no longer operate that, in a mobile group, severely limit the number of small children a mother can rear. There is no longer the difficulty, for instance, of carrying small children from place to place. Crucial to the question was the fact that in the Near East some communities (of the Natufian culture around 9000 BC) did indeed become sedentary before they were food-producing. He could see that, once settled, there would be considerable population pressure, in view of the greater number of surviving children. This would lead to increasing use of locally available plant foods such as wild cereals that had hitherto been considered marginal and of little value. From the intensive use of cereals, and the introduction of ways of processing them, would develop the regular cycle of sowing and harvesting, and thus the course of plant-human involvement leading to domestication would be well under way.

But why did these pre-agricultural groups become sedentary in the first place? Binford's view was that rising sea levels at the end of the Pleistocene (caused by the melting of polar ice) had two significant effects. First, they reduced the extent of the coastal plains available to the **hunter-gatherers**. And second, the new habitats created by the rise in sea level offered to human groups much greater access to migratory fish and to migrant fowl. Using these rich resources, rather as the inhabitants of the Northwest Coast of North America have done in more recent times, the hunter-gatherer groups found it possible for the first time to lead a sedentary existence. They were no longer obliged to move.

In some respects Binford's explanation is seen today as rather too simple. Nevertheless, it has many strengths. Although the focus was on the Near East, the same arguments can equally be applied to other parts of the world. Binford avoided migration or diffusion, and analyzed the origins of farming in processual terms.

Marxist Archaeology

Following the upsurge in theoretical discussion that followed the initial impact of the New Archaeology, there has been a reawakening of interest in applying to archaeology some of the implications of the earlier work of Karl Marx. Marx was an extremely influential 19th-century philosopher and political economist. Although his work covered a wide range of issues, he is most famous for his analysis of history in terms of conflicts between social classes.

The key feature of "**Marxist archaeology**," then, is that change within a past society was caused mainly by the *contradictions* that arise between the forces of production and social organization. Characteristically these contradictions emerge as a struggle between classes (if this is a society where distinct social classes have already developed). Emphasis on class struggle and internal differences is a feature of most Marxist explanations: this is a view of the world where change comes about through the resolution of internal dissent. It may be contrasted with the "functionalist" view favored by the early New Archaeology where selective pressures towards greater efficiency are seen to operate, and changes are often viewed as mutually beneficial.

In traditional Marxism the ideology of a society – the whole system of knowledge and belief – is seen as largely determined by the nature of the economic base. This point is disputed by the "neo-Marxists" who regard ideology and economics as interrelated and mutually influential, rather than one as dominant and the other subordinate.

There are many positive features that Marxist analyses share with processual archaeology, but, in comparison with the processual studies of the New Archaeologists, many such Marxist analyses seem rather short on the handling of concrete archaeological data. The gap between theoretical archaeology and field archaeology is not always effectively bridged, and the critics of Marxist archaeology sometimes observe that since Karl Marx laid down the basic principles more than a century ago, all that remains for the Marxist archaeologists to do is to elaborate them: research in the field is superfluous. Despite these differences, processual archaeology and Marxist archaeology have much in common.

Evolutionary Archaeology

Evolutionary archaeology explores the notion that the processes responsible for biological **evolution** (as set out by Charles Darwin) also drive culture change.

Some evolutionary anthropologists see the modern mind as the product of biological evolution, and argue that the only way so complex an entity can have arisen is by natural selection. In particular they argue that the human mind evolved under the selective pressures faced by hunter-gatherers during the Pleistocene (Ice Age) period, and that our minds remain adapted to that way of life.

Evolutionary archaeologists in the United States advocate the application of Darwinian evolutionary theory to the archaeological record. They can justifiably point to long-standing cultural traditions in different parts of the world which reflect the inheritance of cultural traits from generation to generation. It could be argued that they have shown how the transmission of human culture can validly be seen in Darwinian evolutionary terms. However, it is less clear that to analyze culture change in those terms offers fresh insights not already available to archaeologists. Evolutionary archaeology has not yet produced case studies of culture change which explain its processes more coherently or persuasively than other approaches: that is the challenge which it currently faces.

THE FORM OF EXPLANATION: SPECIFIC OR GENERAL

To understand these debates within archaeology it is useful to consider what exactly we mean by "explanation." The different things we try to explain might require different kinds of explanation.

There are two completely opposite forms of explanation. The first approach is specific: it seeks to know more and more of the details surrounding an event. It assumes that if we can establish enough of what led up to the event we hope to explain, then that event itself will become much clearer for us. Such explanation has sometimes been called "historical."

Some historical explanations lay great stress on any insights we can gain into the ideas of the historical people in question, and for that reason are sometimes termed *idealist*. If you want to know why an action was taken it is necessary to get inside the mind of the decision-maker, and thus to know as many of the surrounding details, and as much about their life, as possible.

The second form of explanation, that of the New Archaeology, lays much more stress on generalization. The early New Archaeologists sought for "regularities," for patterns in the data, and turned to the philosophy of science (of the time) for help. Unluckily, perhaps, they turned to the American philosopher Carl Hempel, who argued that all explanations should be framed in terms of *natural laws*. A lawlike statement is a universal statement, meaning that in certain circumstances (and other things being equal) *X* always implies *Y*, or that *Y* varies with *X* according to a certain definite relationship. Hempel argued that the events we might be seeking to explain could be accounted for by bringing together two things: the detailed circumstances leading up to the event, and the "law" which would allow us to forecast what actually happened.

A few New Archaeologists tried to write archaeology in the form of universal laws. Most, however, saw that it is very difficult to make universal laws about human behavior that are not either very trivial, or untrue. Some archaeologists, such as Kent Flannery, saw that when Hempel's approach was applied to archaeology, it produced only "Mickey Mouse laws" of little conceivable value. Flannery's favorite example was: "as the population of a site increases, the number of storage pits will go up."

One of the positive contributions of the New Archaeology, however, was in fact to follow the scientific convention of making specific and explicit, as far as is possible, the assumptions on which an argument rests. It makes very good sense to formulate a hypothesis, establish by **deduction** what would follow from it if it were true, and then to see if these consequences are in fact found in the archaeological record by testing the hypothesis against fresh data. Processual archaeologists argued that it is this willingness to test our beliefs and assumptions against real data that separates a scientific approach from mere uncontrolled speculation.

EXPLANATION: ONE CAUSE OR SEVERAL?

As soon as we start to address the really big questions in archaeology, explanation becomes a very complicated matter: many of the big questions refer not to a single event, but to a class of events.

One of the biggest questions, for example, is the development of urbanization and the emergence of **state** societies. This process apparently happened in different parts of the world independently. Each case was, in a sense, no doubt unique. But each was also a specific instance of a more general process. In just the same way, a biologist can discuss (as Darwin did) the process by which the different species emerged without denying the uniqueness of each species, or the uniqueness of each individual within a species.

If we focus now on the origins of urbanization and the state as an example, we shall see that this is a field where many different explanations have been offered. Broadly speaking, we can distinguish between explanations that concentrate largely on one cause (**monocausal explanations**) and those that consider a number of factors (**multivariate explanations**).

Monocausal Explanations: The Origins of the State

If we look at different monocausal explanations in turn, we shall find that some of them are in their way very plausible. Often, however, one explanation works more effectively than another when applied to a particular area – to the emergence of the state in Mesopotamia, for instance, or in Egypt, but not necessarily in Mexico or in the Indus Valley. Each of the following examples today seems incomplete. Yet each makes a point that remains valid.

The Hydraulic Hypothesis.   The historian Karl Wittfogel, writing in the 1950s, explained the origin of the great civilizations in terms of the large-scale irrigation of the alluvial plains of the great rivers. It was, he suggested, this alone that brought about the fertility and the high yields, which led to the considerable density of population in the early civilizations, and hence to the possibility of urbanism. At the same time, however, irrigation required effective management – a group of people in authority who would control and organize the labor needed to dig and maintain irrigation ditches, etc. So irrigation and "hydraulic organization" had to go together, and from these, Wittfogel concluded, emerged a system of differentiated leadership, greater productivity and wealth, and so on.

Wittfogel categorized the system of government characteristic of those civilizations founded on irrigation agriculture as one of "oriental despotism." Among the civilizations to which this line of thinking has been applied are:

- Mesopotamia: the Sumerian civilization from *c.* 3000 BC and its successors
- Ancient Egypt: the Valley of the Nile from *c.* 3000 BC
- India/Pakistan: the Indus Valley civilization from *c.* 2500 BC
- China: the Shang civilization, *c.* 1500 BC, and its successors

Internal Conflict.   In the late 1960s the Russian historian Igor Diakonoff developed a different explanation for state origins. In his model, the state is seen as an organization that imposes order on class conflict, which itself arises from increased wealth. Internal differentiation within the society is here seen as a major causative element, from which other consequences follow.

Warfare.   Warfare between adjacent groups is increasingly seen as an agent of change. While in some cases there were cyclical conflicts with little long-term effect, in others the result was conquest and the formation of larger, inclusive state societies. Kent Flannery has recently emphasized the historically documented role of individual military leaders in the initial formation of state societies (an example of the "agency" of the individual, see below).

Population Growth. An explanation much favored by many archaeologists focuses on the question of population growth. The 18th-century English scholar Thomas Malthus argued that human population tends to grow to the limit permitted by the food supply. When the limit or "carrying capacity" is reached, further population increase leads to food shortage, and this in turn leads to increased death rate and lower fertility (and in some cases to armed conflict). That sets a firm ceiling on population.

population growth → food shortage → increased death rate & lower fertility

Esther Boserup, in her influential book *The Conditions of Agricultural Growth* (1965), effectively reversed the position of Malthus. He had viewed food supply as essentially limited. She argued that agriculture will intensify – farmers will produce more food from the same area of land – if population increases. In other words, by shortening the periods during which land is left to lie fallow, or by introducing the plow, or irrigation, farmers can increase their productivity. Population growth can then be sustained to new levels.

population growth → introduction of new farming methods → increase in agricultural production

So increase of population leads to intensification of agriculture, and to the need for greater administrative efficiencies and economies of scale, including the development of craft specialization. People work harder because they have to, and the society is more productive. There are larger units of population, and consequent changes in the settlement pattern. As numbers increase, any decision-making machinery will need to develop a hierarchy. Centralization ensues, and a centralized state is the logical outcome.

Environmental Circumscription. A different approach, although one that uses some of the variables already indicated, is offered by Robert Carneiro. Taking as his example the formation of state society in Peru, he developed an explanation that laid stress on the constraints ("circumscription") imposed by the environment, and on the role of warfare. Population increase is again an important component of his model, but the model is put together in a different way, and the development of strong leadership in time of war is one of the key factors.

External Trade. The importance of trading links with communities outside the homeland area has been stressed by several archaeologists seeking explanations for the formation of the state. One of the most elaborate of these is the model put forward by the American archaeologist William Rathje for the emergence of state societies in the Maya Lowlands. He argued that in lowland areas lacking basic raw materials there will be pressure for the development of more integrated and highly organized communities able to ensure the regular supply of those materials. He used this hypothesis to explain the rise of the Classic Maya civilization in the lowland rainforest.

Multivariate Explanations: The Classic Maya Collapse

All the preceding explanations for the origins of the state primarily emphasize one chief variable, a principal strand in the explanation, even though there are several strands involved. In reality, when there are so many factors at work, there is something rather too simplified about such monocausal explanations. It is necessary somehow to be able to deal with several factors at once: that is why such explanations are termed multivariate. Of course, none of the explanations summarized above is so naive as to be truly monocausal: each involves a number of factors. But these factors are not systematically integrated. Several scholars have therefore sought for ways of coping with a large number of variables that simultaneously vary.

One example of a multivariate explanation has been developed for the collapse of Classic Maya society in the 9th century AD (see box overleaf).

POSTPROCESSUAL OR INTERPRETIVE EXPLANATION

After the mid-1970s, the early New Archaeology we have termed here functional-processual archaeology came under criticism from several quarters. For example, early on it was criticized by Bruce Trigger in his book *Time and Tradition* (1978), who found the approach which sought to formulate explanatory laws too constraining. He preferred the broadly descriptive approach of the traditional historian. It was also criticized by Kent Flannery, who was scornful of the trivial nature of some of the so-called laws proposed and felt that more attention should be focused on the ideological and symbolic aspects of societies. Ian Hodder, likewise, felt that archaeology's closest links were with history, and wanted to see the role of the individual in history more fully recognized.

Hodder also very validly stressed what he called "the active role of material culture," emphasizing that the **artifacts** and the material world we construct are not simply the reflections of our social reality that become embodied in the material record. On the contrary, material culture and actual objects are a large part of what makes society work: wealth, for instance, is what spurs many to work in a modern society. Hodder goes on to assert that material culture is "meaningfully constituted," or in other words that it is the result of deliberate actions by individuals whose thoughts and actions should not be overlooked.

Discussions of these issues led some archaeologists in Britain and in the United States to create the postprocessual archaeology of the 1990s, overcoming some of what they saw as the limitations of processual archaeology (and indeed much of traditional Marxist archaeology also). These debates are now largely over, but the result is a series of interesting approaches which together will shape the interpretive archaeologies of the early 21st century, operating alongside the continuing processual or **cognitive-processual** tradition.

Structuralist Approaches

Several archaeologists have been influenced by the structuralist ideas of the French anthropologist Claude Lévi-Strauss, and by the advances in linguistics of the American Noam Chomsky. Structuralist archaeologists stress that human actions are guided by beliefs and symbolic concepts, and that the proper object of study is the structures of thought – the ideas – in the minds of human actors who made the artifacts and created the archaeological record. These archaeologists argue that there are recurrent patterns in human thought in different cultures, many of which can be seen in such polar opposites as: cooked/raw; left/right; dirty/clean; man/woman, etc. Moreover, they argue that thought categories seen in one sphere of life will be seen also in other spheres, so that, for example, a preoccupation with boundaries in the field of social relations is likely to be detectable in other areas such as "boundaries" visible in pottery decoration.

Critical Theory

Critical Theory is the term given to the approach developed by the so-called "Frankfurt School" of German social thinkers, which came to prominence in the 1970s. This stresses that any claims to seek "objective" knowledge are illusory. By their interpretive approach these scholars seek a more enlightened view, which will break out of the limitations of existing systems of thought. They see research workers (including archaeologists) who claim to be dealing in a scientific way with social matters as tacitly supporting the "ideology of control" by which domination is exercised in modern society.

This overtly political critique has serious implications for archaeology. For the philosophers of this school stress that there is no such thing as an objective fact. Facts only have meaning in relation to a view of the world, and in relation to theory. Followers of this school are critical of the criterion of testing as used by processual archaeologists, seeing this procedure as merely the importing into archaeology and

THE CLASSIC MAYA COLLAPSE: A MULTIVARIATE APPROACH

Ever since the impressive remains of ancient states and cities were first discovered and studied by western scholars, the collapse of long-gone civilizations has been a focus of debate and inquiry. In the 1830s the explorations of Stephens and Catherwood in Central America led to the discovery of a then unknown civilization: the Maya.

The last 30 years have witnessed a number of theories seeking to account for the Classic Maya collapse in the 9th century AD, most of them based broadly on the concept of civilization as a system, and seeing collapse as the result of disequilibrium between different parts of the system.

Evidence for a Collapse

The first evidence for a crisis in the Maya Lowlands came from the monumental record. Here the cessation of activity at each site could be dated with some accuracy, with the assumption that this represented the collapse of its ruling dynasty. Such failures in the southern Lowlands began just after AD 800 and, although some centers clung to existence for a time, none survived to erect monuments beyond 909. Subsequent excavation demonstrated that there was a corresponding halt to major construction and building maintenance. The number of formal burials declined and the grave offerings were fewer and of lower quality. Demographic studies consistently showed that political disintegration coincided with a dramatic decline in population. This fall continued until, by the 10th century, the southern lowlands held only a fraction of the millions it once supported. During the ensuing Postclassic period the homes of the former elite were re-occupied by squatters and simple pole-and-thatch houses were erected on the great ceremonial plazas. For a time there was a renaissance to the north, which saw rising populations and major construction, especially in the Puuc region and cities like Uxmal. However, this was shortlived and by the mid-10th century only Chichén Itzá continued elite traditions on any scale, and by now these were heavily modified by contact with Central Mexico.

Causal Factors

If these were the effects of the collapse, what were the causal factors that lay behind it? In the absence of any definitive data scholars in the 1970s devised a variety of theoretical models, in some cases constructing computer simulations to test them. While early explanations had emphasized single factors, whether epidemic disease, drought, peasant revolt, foreign invasion, etc., there

Temple I at Tikal, Guatemala, built around AD 740–750. Tikal was one of the great Maya centers where large and impressive ceremonial complexes were built. However, the site seems to have been almost completely deserted after AD 950. It is possible that high population densities and overcultivation may have had disastrous effects on the environment.

was a growing recognition that the collapse must be viewed as a system failure, with a number of contributing factors. It was also widely accepted that since the highest populations and most conspicuous signs of cultural florescence directly preceded the collapse, the very same processes that had created one had led to the other.

There was a broad division between those modeling a system failure and those emphasizing a greater element of social conflict. In the former, rising populations forced the society into more intensive forms of agriculture. In the short term, yields increased and allowed the rise in population to escalate, but such methods over-exploited the soils and were not sustainable. The result was falling yields exactly when demand was at its greatest. At the very least, a subsistence system under such stress would have been especially vulnerable to crop diseases or drought.

On the social front, a percentage increase of the elite class (who would reproduce more successfully than the less well-nourished peasantry) led to social imbalance and ever greater demands on the lower orders. Competition between elite groups would have expressed itself in larger and more magnificent construction projects and production was increasingly funneled into such activity and away from basic farming. This ultimately led to social strife and disintegration.

There was also work on the impact of trade, seen either in terms of a technological shift from riverine to sea-going transport that took routes away from the southern Lowlands, or competition between the Maya and better-organized

traders in Mexico. Our very poor understanding of Maya economics hampers any reconstruction of this kind.

Simulation Study
One of the most interesting simulations of the Classic Maya collapse is that by John Lowe (see diagram below). His work is based on the chronological patterning of the collapse, as determined from the latest dates of monument construction at different Maya centers. From this Lowe reconstructs a collapse which started in the peripheral areas and moved inward, with sites in the northeast being the last to feel the effects. By correlating this pattern with site density and site hierarchy, Lowe is led to the conclusion that it was population pressure coupled with a top-heavy elite

administration which precipitated the collapse.

The basic mechanism was pressure on land creating the need for more intensive agriculture, which in turn placed greater demands on the ruling elites for the regulation of food distribution and the allocation of manpower. Competition within and between the elites themselves placed still further strains on the system, requiring increasing labor inputs for the construction of ceremonial monuments.

The model owes much to earlier work. It is, however, the most thorough attempt so far to account for the details of the Classic Maya collapse within a systems framework.

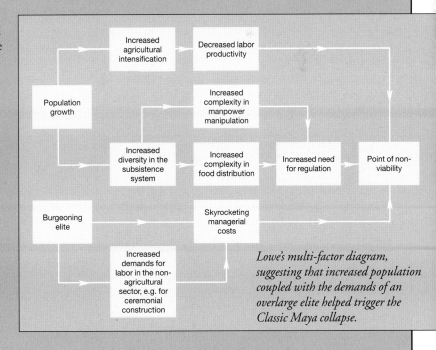

Lowe's multi-factor diagram, suggesting that increased population coupled with the demands of an overlarge elite helped trigger the Classic Maya collapse.

history of "positivistic" approaches from the sciences. They call into question most of the procedures of reasoning by which archaeology has operated.

The processualists' response to these ideas is to point out that to follow them seems to imply that one person's view of the past is as good as another's (so-called "relativism"), without any hope of choosing systematically between them. This would open the way to the "fringe" or "alternative" archaeologies discussed in Chapter 10, where explanations can be offered in terms of flying saucers, or extra-terrestrial forces or any fantasies which the human mind may conjure up. It is not entirely clear how the Critical Theorists can answer this criticism.

Neo-Marxist Thought

Neo-Marxist thought places a much greater emphasis on the significance of ideology in shaping change in societies than does traditional Marxism (which treats ideology as subordinate to economy).

One example of a neo-Marxist approach is offered by the work of Mark Leone at Annapolis in Maryland, as part of a research project concerned with establishing a deeper historical identity for the area. His example is the 18th-century garden of William Paca, a wealthy landowner: the garden has been studied archaeologically and has now been reconstructed.

Leone examines the Annapolis garden in detail, and emphasizes the contradiction represented between a slave-owning society and one proclaiming independence in order to promote individual liberty, a contradiction seen also in Paca's life. "To mask this contradiction," Leone writes, "his position of power was placed in law and in nature. This was done both in practicing law and in gardening."

This neo-Marxist outlook has its echo in the emerging local archaeologies of some Third World countries, where there is an understandable desire to construct a history (and an archaeology) that lays stress on the local population and its achievements before the colonial era.

COGNITIVE ARCHAEOLOGY

During the 1980s and 1990s a new perspective emerged, which transcends some of the limitations of functional-processual archaeology of the 1970s. This new synthesis, known as cognitive archaeology (or "cognitive-processual" archaeology), while willingly learning from any suitable developments in postprocessual archaeology, remains in the mainstream of processual archaeology. It still wishes to explain rather than merely describe. It also still emphasizes the role of generalization within its theoretical structure, and stresses the importance not only of formulating hypotheses but of testing them against the data. It rejects the total relativism that seems to be the end point of Critical Theory, and it is suspicious of structuralist (and other) archaeologists who claim privileged insight into "meaning" in ancient societies, or proclaim "universal principles of meaning."

Cognitive-processual archaeology differs from its functional-processual predecessor in several ways:

1 It seeks actively to incorporate information about the cognitive and symbolic aspects of early societies into its formulations (see below).

2 It recognizes that ideology is an active force within societies and must be given a role in many explanations, as neo-Marxist archaeologists have argued, and that ideology acts on the minds of individuals.

3 Material culture is seen as an active factor in constituting the world in which we live. Individuals and societies construct their own social reality, and material culture has an integral place within that construction, as effectively argued by Ian Hodder and his colleagues.

4 The role of internal conflict within societies is a matter to be more fully considered, as Marxist archaeologists have always emphasized.

5 The rather limited view of historical explanation being entirely related to the human individual should be revised.

6 It can take account of the creative role of the individual without relying on intuition or becoming extremely subjective.

7 "Facts" can no longer be viewed as having an objective existence independent of theory.

This last point needs further discussion. Philosophers of science have long contrasted two approaches to the evaluation of the truth of a statement. One approach evaluates the statement by comparing it with relevant facts, to which, if true, it should correspond. The other approach evaluates the statement by judging whether or not it is consistent with the other statements that we believe to be true within our framework of beliefs. Although it might be expected that the scientist would follow the first of these two procedures, in practice any assessment is based on a combination of the two. For it is accepted that facts have to be based on observations, and observations themselves cannot be made without using some framework of inference, which itself depends on theories about the world. It is more appropriate to think of facts modifying theory, yet of theory being used in the determination of facts.

Cognitive-processual archaeologists, like their functional-processual predecessors, believe that theories must be tested against facts. They reject the relativism of the Critical Theory and postprocessual archaeology of the 1990s. They do, however, accept that the relationship between fact and theory is more complicated than some philosophers of science 40 years ago recognized. Cognitive-processual archaeology at present appears to be exploring two main directions: investigation of the role of symbols within processes of change, and exploration of the structure of transformations.

Symbol and Interaction

The point has already been made that the early New Archaeology aspired to investigate social structures. But it was slow to explore symbolic aspects of culture, which is why cognitive-processual archaeology is a recent development.

The role of religious ritual within society has been investigated in a new way over the past 30 years by the cultural anthropologist Roy Rappaport. Instead of seeking to immerse himself in the agricultural society in New Guinea under study, becoming totally familiar with the meanings of its symbolic forms, he followed instead a strategy of distancing himself – of looking at the society from the outside, at what it actually does (not what it says it does) in its ritual behavior. This position is a convenient one for the archaeologist who is always outside the society under study, and unable to discuss issues of meaning with its participants. Rappaport has studied the way ritual is used within society and his focus is on the functioning of symbols rather than on their original meaning.

His work influenced Kent Flannery, one of the few of the original generation of New Archaeologists to concern himself in detail with symbolic questions. The book written by Joyce Marcus and Kent Flannery, *Zapotec Civilization* (1996), is one of those rare archaeological studies where symbolic and cognitive questions are integrated with subsistence, economic, and social ones to form an integrated view of society.

Quite clearly **religion** and other ideologies such as modern Communism have brought about great changes, not just in the way societies think but in the way they act and behave – and this will leave its mark in the archaeological record. The whole field of official symbolism, and of religious symbolism within it, is now the focus of archaeological research in several parts of the world.

Postprocessual archaeology has not shown itself adept at explaining classes of events or general processes, since the focus in postprocessual thought is upon the specific conditions of the context in question, and the validity of wider or cross-cultural generalizations is not accepted. Cognitive-processual archaeology on the other hand is very willing to generalize, and indeed to integrate the individual into the analysis as an active agent.

Two recent works in the mainstream processual tradition exemplify well the emphasis that is now placed upon the cognitive dimension. Timothy Earle in *How*

KEY CONCEPTS: COGNITIVE ARCHAEOLOGY

Cognitive archaeology is the study of the ways of thought and structures of belief of past societies on the basis of their material remains. It:

- attempts to use the more rigorous and explicit methods of the processual approach

- applies these to symbolic and ideological issues many of which were first addressed by postprocessual or interpretive approaches (e.g. questions of identity, gender, and religious belief in the past)

- shows willingness to address the symbolizing and reasoning abilities of hominids before the emergence of *Homo sapiens sapiens*, sometimes within an evolutionary framework

- accepts the postprocessual emphasis on the active role of material culture

- recognizes that cognitive developments are also social developments

Chiefs Come to Power devotes successive chapters to economic power, military power, and ideology as a source of power, utilizing three widely separated case studies situated in Denmark, Hawaii, and the Andes.

And, likewise treating the subject within a comparative perspective, Richard Blanton has examined the sources of power in early states, contrasting the "cognitive-symbolic base of power" with what he terms the "objective base of power." The study fully integrates the cognitive dimension into the analysis, alongside economic issues. In such works the limitations of the earlier processual archaeology have been transcended and the roots of change are investigated with full weight being given to the cognitive and the symbolic dimensions.

AGENCY AND MATERIAL ENGAGEMENT

In the past decade or so archaeologists working in different conceptual traditions have sought in various ways to reconcile the cognitive and symbolic on the one hand with the practical and productive on the other. One aim is to reconcile the short-term intentions or **agency** of the individual with the long-term and often unintended consequences of cumulative actions. Archaeologists who take this approach hope to combine a broad outline of processes of change with the finer texture of specific culture histories.

The concept of agency has been introduced to permit discussion of the role of the individual in promoting change, but the scope of the term is not always clear, particularly when used, as by some anthropologists, as a quality which can be assigned to artifacts as well as to people. The various discussions of agency attempt to illuminate the role of the individual, but it is very difficult to determine clearly how the actions of one individual had a wider and longer-term impact.

A related notion, that change arises from conscious and often purposeful human activities, is associated with the recently developed concepts of material engagement or materialization. They seek, as others have, to overcome the duality in discussions of human affairs between the practical and the cognitive, the material and the conceptual. Indeed most innovations and long-term changes in human societies, even technical ones, have a symbolic dimension as well as a material one, involving what the philosopher John Searle terms "institutional facts," which are themselves social creations.

There is still a tension also between those using archaeology to write culture history (usually of a single society) and those using evolutionary thinking to analyze long-term change. Each perspective has clear coherence and validity, but the two rarely seem to mesh together.

In these different approaches to the explanation of change there is some commonality of aspiration and this may yet lead to interesting new developments. But there is no single theoretical perspective which commands universal or even widespread respect.

SUMMARY

- It is difficult to explain *why* things happened in the past, yet this must be one of the key tasks of archaeology.

- Explanations in terms of the migrations of people or using the rather vague idea of the "diffusion" of culture used to be very popular: today they are less frequent.

- The processual approach has consistently tried to see broader patterns and general explanations. In general multivariate (several factor) explanations work better than monocausal (single factor) explanations for complex outcomes such as the origins of state societies.

- Interpretive explanations, on the other hand, usually emphasize the specific context. Both approaches converge towards a cognitive archaeology which acknowledges the role of human intelligence, creativity, and initiative.

- Yet there remain several different approaches to the difficult task of explanation. Some scholars advocate the notion of human agency, others analyze the knowledgable engagement between humans and the material world. This remains an under-developed area of archaeological theory. Watch this space!

FURTHER READING

The broad topics covered in this chapter are explored in:

DeMarrais, E., Gosden, C. & Renfrew, C. (eds.). 2004. **Rethinking Materiality, the Engagement of Mind with the Material World**. MCDONALD INSTITUTE: CAMBRIDGE.

Daniel, G. & Renfrew, C. 1988. **The Idea of Prehistory**. EDINBURGH UNIVERSITY PRESS: EDINBURGH; COLUMBIA UNIVERSITY PRESS: NEW YORK.

Earle, T. 1997. **How Chiefs Come to Power, the Political Economy in Prehistory**. STANFORD UNIVERSITY PRESS.

Hodder, I. 1991. **Reading the Past**. (2nd ed.) CAMBRIDGE UNIVERSITY PRESS: CAMBRIDGE & NEW YORK. (The contextual and postprocessual alternative.)

Mithen, S. 1996. **The Prehistory of the Mind**. THAMES & HUDSON: LONDON & NEW YORK.

Renfrew, C. 1982. Explanation Revisited, in Renfrew, C., Rowlands, M., & Seagraves, B.A. **Theory and Explanation in Archaeology**. ACADEMIC PRESS: NEW YORK, 5–24.

Renfrew, C. 2003. **Figuring It Out – the Parallel Visions of Artists and Archaeologists**. THAMES & HUDSON: LONDON & NEW YORK.

Renfrew, C. & Zubrow, E.B.W. (eds.). 1994. **The Ancient Mind: Elements of Cognitive Archaeology**. CAMBRIDGE UNIVERSITY PRESS: CAMBRIDGE & NEW YORK.

Shanks, M. & Tilley, C. 1987. **Social Theory and Archaeology**. POLITY PRESS: OXFORD; UNIVERSITY OF NEW MEXICO PRESS: ALBUQUERQUE 1988.

Shennan, S. 2002. **Genes, Memes and Human History**. THAMES & HUDSON: LONDON & NEW YORK.

10 Whose Past?
archaeology and the public

In this chapter:

THE MEANING OF THE PAST: THE ARCHAEOLOGY OF IDENTITY
Nationalism and its Symbols
Archaeology and Ideology

WHO OWNS THE PAST?
Museums and the Return of Cultural Property

CONSERVATION AND DESTRUCTION
The Rise of CRM in the United States

THE RESPONSIBILITY OF COLLECTORS AND MUSEUMS

POPULAR ARCHAEOLOGY VERSUS PSEUDOARCHAEOLOGY

Summary
Further Reading

This book is concerned with the way that archaeologists investigate the past, with the questions we can ask and our means of answering them. But the time has come to address much wider questions: Why, beyond reasons of scientific curiosity, do we want to know about the past? What does the past mean to us? What does it mean to others who have different viewpoints? And whose past is it anyway?

These issues lead us to questions of responsibility, public as well as private. For surely a national monument, such as Great Zimbabwe or the Parthenon in Athens, means something special to the modern descendants of its builders? Does it not also mean something to all humankind? If so, should it not be protected from destruction, in the same way as endangered plant and animal species? If the looting of ancient **sites** is to be deplored, should it not be stopped, even if the sites are on privately owned land? Who owns, or should own, the past?

These very soon become ethical questions – of right and wrong, of appropriate action and reprehensible action. The archaeologist has a special responsibility because **excavation** itself entails destruction. Future workers' understanding of a site can never be much more than our own, because we will have destroyed the evidence and recorded only those parts of it we considered important and had the energy to publish properly.

Destruction on a much larger scale comes from another quarter, far exceeding anything suffered in earlier centuries. The earth's surface is now being exploited more exhaustively than ever before, for commercial, industrial, and agricultural purposes, and any fragile vestiges of earlier human activity are often swept away if they hinder that exploitation. Moreover, the very interest that **archaeology** has generated in our past has created new destructive forces: not only looters and illegal excavators – whose plunder finds its way into private collections and public museums – but also tourists, who by their numbers threaten the sites they seek to enjoy.

The past is big business – in tourism and in the auction rooms. The past is politically highly charged, ideologically powerful, and significant. And the past, or what remains of it, is subject to increasing destruction. What can we do about these problems?

THE MEANING OF THE PAST: THE ARCHAEOLOGY OF IDENTITY

When we ask what the past means, we are asking what the past means for *us*, for it means different things to different people. An Australian Aborigine, for example, may attach a very different significance to fossil human remains from an early site like Lake Mungo or to paintings in the Kakadu National Park, than a white Australian. Different communities have very different conceptions about the past which often draw on sources well beyond archaeology.

At this point we go beyond the question of what actually happened in the past, and of the explanation of why it happened, to issues of meaning, significance, and interpretation. And it is at this point, therefore, that many of the concerns which have become explicit in archaeology over the past couple of decades become entirely relevant. How we interpret the past, how we present it (for instance in museum displays), and what lessons we choose to draw from it, are to a considerable extent matters for subjective decision, often involving ideological and political issues.

For in a very broad sense the past is where we came from. Individually we each have our personal, genealogical past – our parents, grandparents, and earlier kinsfolk from whom we are descended. Increasingly in the western world there is an interest in this personal past, reflected in the enthusiasm for family trees and for "roots" generally. Our personal identity, and generally our name, are in part defined for us in the relatively recent past, even though those elements with which we choose to identify are largely a matter of personal choice. Nor is this inheritance purely a spiritual one. Most land tenure in the world is determined by inheritance, and much other wealth is inherited: the material world in this sense comes to us from the past, and is certainly, when the time comes, relinquished by us to the future.

Nationalism and its Symbols

Collectively our cultural inheritance is rooted in a deeper past: the origins of our language, our faith, our customs. Increasingly archaeology plays an important role in the definition of national identity. This is particularly the case for those nations which do not have a very long written history, though many consider oral histories of equal value to written ones. The national emblems of many recently emerged nations are taken from **artifacts** seen as typical of some special and early local golden age: even the name of the state of Zimbabwe comes from the name of an archaeological site.

Yet sometimes the use of archaeology and of images recovered from the past to focus and enhance national identity can lead to conflict. A major crisis related to the name and national emblems adopted by the then newly independent Former Yugoslav Republic of Macedonia. For in Greece, immediately to the south, the name Macedon refers not only to contemporaneous provinces within Greece, but to the ancient kingdom of that famous Greek leader, Alexander the Great. The affront which the name caused in Greece was compounded by the use by the FYR Macedonia of a star as a national symbol, using the image on a gold casket found among the splendid objects in a tomb from the 4th century BC at Vergina, a tomb located well within modern Greek territory, thought to have belonged to Philip of Macedon, the father of Alexander. Territorial claims can

Philip II of Macedon, father of Alexander the Great, was probably buried in this gold casket decorated with an impressive star. This was adopted as the national symbol of the former Yugoslav republic of Macedonia, as seen on a stamp.

sometimes be based on contentious histories, and some Greeks thought that the FYR Macedonia was seeking to appropriate not only the glorious history of Macedonia but perhaps also to incorporate Greece's second city, Thessaloniki, within its territorial boundaries. Riots ensued, based, however, more on inflamed ethnic feelings than upon political reality.

Archaeology and Ideology

The legacy of the past goes beyond sentiments of nationalism and ethnicity. Sectarian sentiments often find expression in major monuments, and many Christian churches were built on the site of deliberately destroyed "pagan" temples. In just a few cases they actually utilized such temples – the Parthenon in Athens is one example – and one of the best preserved Greek temples is now the Cathedral in Syracuse in Sicily.

Religious extremism is responsible for many acts of destruction. The destruction in March 2001 by the Taliban of the two giant Buddhas carved into the sandstone cliffs at Bamiyan, in the Hindu Kush, perhaps in the 3rd century AD, shocked the world as an act of senseless destruction. The only motivation seems to have been that these were religious images not in accordance with the faith of the Taliban. Despite a delegation from the Islamic Conference, at which 55 Islamic nations were represented, the destruction went ahead. Standing 53 and 36 m high (174 and 118 ft), these were the tallest standing Buddhas in the world; explosive charges destroyed them almost totally.

These are cases of religious ideology leading to the destruction of important symbols which are part of the world's archaeological heritage. In war the sentiments are sometimes national or ethnic, rather than religious. Such was the case in the

The larger of the colossal Buddhas of Bamiyan, carved from the cliff face in perhaps the 3rd century AD, and now destroyed.

The shocking sequence of images recording the destruction of the colossal Buddha statue. Such historical monuments have now become targets in politics and war.

The bridge at Mostar, in Bosnia, dating from the 16th century, was destroyed in fighting in 1993 but has now been rebuilt.

civil war in Yugoslavia, although it also had religious overtones. The bridge at Mostar in Bosnia, built by the Ottoman Turks in 1566 and a symbol of Bosnian identity, was destroyed by Croatian forces in 1993. Although it has now been rebuilt, the loss of the original structure was one of the most tragic acts in Europe since World War II: the deliberate destruction of the cultural heritage on purely ethnic grounds.

WHO OWNS THE PAST?

Until recent decades, archaeologists gave little thought to the question of the ownership of past sites and antiquities. Most archaeologists themselves came from western, industrialized societies whose economic and political domination seemed to give an almost automatic right to acquire antiquities and excavate sites around the world. Since World War II, however, former colonies have grown into independent nation states eager to uncover their own past and assert control over their own heritage. Difficult questions have therefore arisen. Should antiquities acquired for western museums during the colonial era be returned to their lands of origin? And should archaeologists be free to excavate the burials of groups whose modern descendants may object on religious or other grounds?

Museums and the Return of Cultural Property

At the beginning of the 19th century Lord Elgin, a Scottish diplomat, removed many of the marble sculptures that adorned the Parthenon, the great 5th-century BC temple that crowns the Acropolis in Athens. Elgin did so with the permission of the then Turkish overlords of Greece, and later sold the sculptures to the British Museum, where they still reside, displayed in a special gallery. The Greeks now want the "Elgin Marbles" back. That in essence is the story so far of perhaps the best-known case where an internationally famous museum is under pressure to return cultural property to the country of origin.

But there are numerous other claims directed at European and North American museums. The Berlin Museum, for example, holds the famous bust of the Egyptian queen Nefertiti, which was shipped out of Egypt illegally. The Greek government

Part of the "Elgin Marbles" in the British Museum: a horse-man from the frieze of the Parthenon in Athens, *c.* 440 BC.

has officially asked France for the return of the Venus de Milo, one of the master-works of the Louvre, bought from Greece's Ottoman rulers. And Turkey has recently been successful in recovering art treasures, including the "Lydian Hoard," from New York's Metropolitan Museum (which has also agreed to return the now infamous "Euphronios Vase" to Italy, see below), and may now pursue Turkish statuary and objects in European countries, including the British Museum.

Excavating Burials: Should We Disturb the Dead?   The question of excavating burials can be equally complex. For prehistoric burials the problem is not so great, because we have no direct written knowledge of the relevant **culture**'s beliefs and wishes. For burials dating from historic times, however, religious beliefs are known to us in detail. We know, for example, that the ancient Egyptians and Chinese, the Greeks, Etruscans, and Romans, and the early Christians all feared disturbance of the dead. Yet it has to be recognized that tombs were falling prey to the activities of robbers long before archaeology began. Egyptian pharaohs in the 12th century BC had to appoint a commission to inquire into the wholesale plundering of tombs at Thebes. Not a single Egyptian royal tomb, including that of Tutankhamun, escaped the robbers completely. Similarly, Roman carved gravestones became building material in cities and forts; and at Ostia, the port of ancient Rome, tomb inscriptions have even been found serving as seats in a public latrine!

The American Indians.   For some Indians in North America, archaeology has become a focal point for complaints about wrongdoings of the past. They have expressed their grievances strongly in recent years, and their political influence has resulted in legal mechanisms that sometimes restrict or prevent archaeological excava-tions, or provide for the return to Indian peoples of some collections now in museums. Apart from the question of returning and/or reburying material, sometimes there

Seminole Indian bones from Florida are reburied in 1989 by archaeologists and American Indians at Wounded Knee.

have been vehement objections to new excavations. The Chumash Indians, for example, refused permission for scientists to remove what may be the oldest human remains in California, even though an offer was made to return and rebury the bones after a year's study. The bones, thought to be about 9000 years old, were eroding out of a cliff on Santa Rosa Island, 100 km (62 miles) west of Los Angeles. Under California's Antiquities Act the fate of the bones lay with their most likely descendants – and the Chumash were understandably angry about past treatment of their ancestors' skeletons, with hundreds of remains scattered in various universities and museums. Like many Maori, they preferred to see the bones destroyed "in accordance with nature's law" than to have other people interfere with them. In other cases, however, American Indian communities have provided for the systematic curation of such remains once they have been returned to them.

As in Australia (see below), there is no single, unified indigenous tradition. American Indians have wide-ranging attitudes toward the dead and the soul. Nonetheless demands for reburial of ancestral remains are common. The solution to the problem has been found to lie in acquiescence, compromise, and collaboration. Often archaeologists have supported or acquiesced in the return of remains of fairly close ancestors of living people. Material has also been returned that had no archaeological **context** and was thus of minimal value to science.

Repatriation of older and more important material is a difficult issue. The longstanding position of the Society for American Archaeology is that scientific and traditional interests in archaeological materials must be balanced, weighted by the closeness of relationship to the modern group making a claim and the scientific value of the remains or objects requested. With the Society's support, in 1990 the Native American Graves Protection and Repatriation Act (NAGPRA) was passed. It requires some 5000 federally funded institutions and government agencies to inventory their collections and assess the "cultural affiliation" of Native American skeletons, funerary and sacred objects, and items of cultural patrimony. If cultural affiliation can be shown, the human remains and objects must, on request, be returned to the affiliated American Indian **tribe** or Native Hawaiian organization. Difficult problems lie in interpreting key terms in the law, such as "cultural affiliation," and in weighing diverse forms of evidence in the context of prehistoric material. In addition to archaeological and historical information, the law explicitly recognizes the validity of oral traditions. This has led to broad expectations by tribes that prehistoric remains can be claimed if their oral traditions say that its people were created in the same region where the remains were found. However, when these expectations were tested in court it was found that the law requires a balanced consideration of oral tradition with scientific evidence.

An archaeologist and a sculptor work on the reconstruction of the head of Kennewick Man (with the aid of a cast of the original skull).

The most prominent controversy and legal battle concerned the bones of "Kennewick Man," found in 1996 in Washington State, and radiocarbon dated to 9300 BP. When the US Army Corps of Engineers, which has jurisdiction over the site, announced that it would hand over the skeleton to the local Native American Umatilla tribe for reburial, eight prominent anthropologists sued them for permission to study the bones. A preliminary examination had suggested that Kennewick Man was a 19th-century white settler, so its early date raised fascinating questions (although it is now known that Kennewick Man was *not* Caucasian). While the scientists were anxious to examine the remains, the Umatilla, on the other hand, adamantly opposed any investigation. They insisted that their oral tradition says their tribe has been part of this land since the beginning of time, and so all bones recovered from here are necessarily their ancestors – and must not be damaged for dating or genetic analysis. In 2002 a magistrate affirmed the right of the scientists to study the bones, but the US Department of the Interior with the support of a coalition of four Native American tribes promptly appealed against the decision. Their objections were, however, overruled by the appeals court and the scientists have proceeded with extensive study.

The Australian Aborigines.   In Australia, the present climate of Aboriginal emancipation and increased political power has focused attention on wrongdoings during the colonial period, when anthropologists had little respect for Aboriginal feelings and beliefs. Sacred sites were investigated and published, burial sites desecrated, and cultural and skeletal material exhumed, to be stored or displayed in museums. The Aborigines were thus, by implication, seen as laboratory specimens. Inevitably, the fate of all this material, and particularly of the bones, has assumed great symbolic significance. Unfortunately, here as in other countries, archaeologists are being blamed for the misdemeanors of the non-archaeologists who obtained most of the human remains in question.

The view of Aborigines in some parts of Australia is that all human skeletal material (and occasionally cultural material too) must be returned to them, and then its fate will be decided. In some cases they themselves wish the remains to be curated in conditions that anthropologists would consider to be satisfactory, usually under Aboriginal control. Since the Aborigines have an unassailable moral case, the Australian Archaeological Association (AAA) is willing to return remains which are either quite modern or of "known individuals where specific descendants can be traced," and for these to be reburied. However, such remains are somewhat the exception. The University of Melbourne's Murray Black Collection consists of skeletal remains from over 800 Aborigines ranging in date from several hundred years to at least 14,000 years old. They were dug up in the 1940s without any consultation with local Aborigines. Owing to a lack of specialists the collection has still by no means been exhaustively studied – but nevertheless it has been returned to the relevant Aboriginal communities. In 1990 the unique series of burials from Kow Swamp, 19,000 to 22,000 years old, were handed back to the Aboriginal community and reburied; more recently the first skeleton found at Lake Mungo, the world's oldest known cremation (26,000 years BP), was returned to the custody of the Aborigines of the Mungo area; and Aboriginal elders have announced they may rebury all the skeletal material (up to 30,000 years old) from Mungo.

Archaeologists are understandably alarmed at the prospect of having to hand over material many thousands of years old. Some also point out that the Aborigines – like indigenous peoples elsewhere – tend to forget that not all of their recent forebears took pious care of the dead. But, not least in the light of Aboriginal sufferings at European hands, their views are entitled to respect.

CONSERVATION AND DESTRUCTION

Most nations of the world now recognize that it is the public duty of a government to have some policy with regards to conservation. That policy will apply to natural resources and wildlife, but it will also apply to archaeological remains. So most nations now have some protective legislation – which is not all equally effective – for their ancient sites, minor as well as major, and government programs. In the United States these are organized under the rubric of **Cultural Resource Management**, and in other countries under Archaeological Heritage Management.

There are two principal stages in archaeological conservation everywhere. The first is the gathering of information, so that relevant sites and areas may be recognized and properly recorded. The second is the conservation of those sites and areas that can be effectively protected. Sometimes damage or destruction cannot be prevented, in which case a policy of **salvage** or rescue archaeology can be adopted, partially excavating or at least recording the site before it vanishes for good.

There are two main agencies of destruction, both of them human. One is the construction of roads, quarries, dams, office blocks, etc. These are conspicuous and the threat is at least easily recognizable. A different kind of destruction – agricultural intensification – is slower but much wider in its extent, thus in the long term much more destructive.

Elsewhere, reclamation schemes are transforming the nature of the environment, so that arid lands are being flooded, and the wetlands of say Florida are being reclaimed through drainage. The result is destruction of remarkable archaeological evidence. More ancient remains have been lost in the last two decades than ever before in the history of the world.

There are two further human agencies of destruction, which should not be overlooked. The first is tourism, which, while economically having important effects on archaeology, makes the effective conservation of archaeological sites more difficult. The second is not new, but has grown dramatically in scale: the looting of archaeological sites by those who dig for monetary gain, seeking only saleable objects and destroying everything else in their search.

Agricultural Damage. Ever increasing areas of the earth, once uncultivated or cultivated by traditional non-intensive methods, are being opened up to mechanized farming. The tractor and the deep plow have replaced the digging stick and the ard. In other areas, forest plantations now cover what was formerly open land, and tree roots are destroying settlement sites and field monuments.

Although most countries keep some control over the activities of developers and builders, the damage to archaeological sites from farming is much more difficult to assess. The few published studies make sober reading. One shows that in Britain even those sites that are notionally protected – by being listed on the national Schedule of Ancient Monuments – are not, in reality, altogether safe. The position may be much better in Denmark and in certain other countries, but elsewhere only the most conspicuous sites are protected. The more modest field monuments and open settlements are not, and these are the sites that are suffering from mechanized agriculture.

Damage in War. Among the most distressing outrages of recent years has been the continuing destruction, sometimes deliberate, of monuments and of archaeological materials in the course of armed conflict. Already, during World War II, historic buildings in England were deliberately targeted in German bombing raids.

The Warka Vase was looted from the Iraqi National Museum, Baghdad, during the 2003 invasion of Iraq. Fortunately it was recovered (right) and, though in pieces, these were probably ancient breaks.

The failure of Coalition forces in the 2003 invasion of Iraq to secure the Iraqi National Museum in Baghdad allowed the looting of the collections, including the celebrated Warka Vase, one of the most notable finds from the early Sumerian civilization – although, like many other important antiquities, this was later returned to the Museum. The failure was all the more shocking since archaeologists in the United States had met with representatives of the Defense Department some months prior to the war to warn of the risk of looting in museums and at sites, and archaeologists in Britain had similarly indicated the dangers to the Prime Minister's office and the Foreign Office months before the war began. Only parts of the collection were taken, and it seems that it was the work both of looters from the street, who smashed cases, decapitated statues, and trashed offices, but also perhaps some well-informed individuals who knew what they were looking for and who had access to keys to the storerooms. It is these who are likely to have taken the Museum's collection of Mesopotamian cylinder seals, the finest in the world, for sale to collectors overseas.

It seems all the more extraordinary that the United States and the United Kingdom have still not ratified the 1954 Hague Convention for the Protection of Cultural Property in the Event of Armed Conflict, or its protocols. The British Government has announced its intention of doing so, but claims – some 50 years after the initial drafting of the Convention – that "to do so will require extensive consultation on legal, operational, and policy issues relating to the implementation of the Protocol."

Damage from Looting and the Market in Illicit Antiquities. The saddest kind of damage is that by clandestine excavators, concerned only to find objects of high saleable value, and quite untroubled by the loss of information when the finds are divorced from their original context. Many of these looters use metal detectors, even on legally protected sites.

One such *clandestino*, Luigi Perticarari, a robber in Tarquinia, Italy, published his memoirs in 1986 and makes no apology for his trade. He has more first-hand knowledge of Etruscan tombs than any archaeologist, but his activity destroys the chance of anyone sharing that knowledge. He claims to have emptied some 4000 tombs dating from the 8th to the 3rd centuries BC in 30 years. So it is that, while the world's store of Etruscan antiquities in museums and private collections grows larger, our knowledge of Etruscan burial customs and social organization does not.

The same is true for the remarkable marble sculptures of the Cycladic islands of Greece, dating to around 2500 BC. We admire the breathtaking elegance of these works in the world's museums, but we have little idea of how they were produced or of the social and religious life of the Cycladic communities that made them. Again, the contexts have been lost.

In the American Southwest, 90 percent of the Classic Mimbres sites (*c.* AD 1000) have now been looted or destroyed (see box overleaf). In southwestern Colorado, 60 percent of prehistoric Anasazi sites have been vandalized. Pothunters work at night, equipped with two-way radios, scanners, and lookouts. They can be prosecuted under the present legislation only if caught red-handed, which is almost impossible.

The *huaqueros* of Central and South America, too, are interested only in the richest finds, in this case gold – whole cemeteries are turned into fields of craters, with bones, potsherds, mummy wrappings, and other objects smashed and scattered. The remarkable tombs excavated between 1987 and 1990 at Sipán, northwest Peru, of the Moche civilization, were rescued from the plunderers only by the persistence and courage of the local Peruvian archaeologist, Walter Alva.

The Rise of CRM in the United States

Over the past four decades North American archaeology has become embedded in Cultural Resource Management (CRM), a complex of laws, regulations, and professional practice designed to manage historic buildings and sites, cultural landscapes, and other cultural and historic places.

Building on earlier laws like the Antiquities Act of 1906 and the Historic Sites Act of 1935, the National Historic Preservation Act of 1966 and the National Environmental Policy Act of 1969 are the major legal bases for CRM in the USA. These laws require agencies of the US government to consider the environmental impacts of their actions, including impacts on historical, archaeological and cultural values. They also created an administrative system featuring CRM program leadership by the National Park Service and the independent Advisory Council on Historic Preservation, and a "State Historic Preservation Officer" (SHPO) in each US state.

Construction and land use projects in which US government agencies are involved – whether on federal land or on other lands but federally funded or requiring a federal permit, must be reviewed to determine their effects on

DESTRUCTION AND RESPONSE: MIMBRES

The Mimbres potters of the American Southwest created a unique art tradition in the prehistoric period, painting the inside of hemispherical bowls with vigorous animalian and human forms. These bowls are now much prized by archaeologists and art lovers. But this fascination has led to the systematic looting of Mimbres sites on a scale unequaled in the United States, or indeed anywhere in the world.

The Mimbres people lived along a small river, the Rio Mimbres, in mud-built villages, similar in some respects to those of the later Pueblo Indians. Painted pottery began, as we now know, around AD 550, and reached its apogee in the Classic Mimbres period, from about AD 1000 to 1130.

Systematic archaeological work on Mimbres sites began in the 1920s, but it was not in general well published. Looters soon found, however, that with pick and shovel they could unearth Mimbres pots to sell on the market for primitive art. Nor was this activity necessarily illegal. In United States law there is nothing to prevent excavation of any kind by the owner on private land, and nothing to prevent the owner permitting others to destroy archaeological sites in this way.

In the early 1960s, a method of bulldozing Mimbres sites was developed which did not destroy all the pottery. The operators found that by controlled bulldozing they could remove a relatively small depth of soil at a time and extract many of the pots unbroken. In the process sites were of course completely destroyed, and all hope of establishing an archaeological context for the material was lost.

Since 1973 there has at last been a concerted archaeological response. The Mimbres Foundation, under the direction of Steven LeBlanc, was able to secure funding from private sources to undertake excavations in the remains of some of the looted sites. They also made good progress in explaining to the owners of those sites how destructive this looting process was to any hope of learning about the Mimbres past. From 1975 to 1978 a series of field seasons at several partially looted sites succeeded in establishing at least the outlines of Mimbres archaeology, and in putting the chronology upon a sure footing.

The Mimbres Foundation also reached the conclusion that archaeological excavation is an expensive form of conservation, and decided to purchase a number

A masked coyote dancer is the subject of this fine Mimbres bowl, dating from AD 1100–1250.

of surviving (or partially surviving) Mimbres sites in order to protect them. Moreover, this is a lesson that has been learned more widely. Members of the Mimbres Foundation have joined forces with other archaeologists and benefactors to form a national organization, the Archaeological Conservancy. Several sites in the United States have now been purchased and conserved in this way. The story thus has, in some sense, a happy ending. But nothing can bring back the possibility of really understanding Mimbres culture and Mimbres art, a possibility which did exist at the beginning of the 20th century before the wholesale and devastating looting.

Unfortunately, in other parts of the world there are similar stories to tell.

Funerary bowl of the 10th century AD. The figures may be male and female, or life and death. The "kill" hole at the base allowed the object's spirit to be released.

environmental, cultural, and historical resources. CRM programs in state and local governments, federal agencies, academic institutions and private consulting firms have grown out of this requirement. The SHPOs coordinate many CRM activities, and keep files on historic and prehistoric sites, structures, buildings, districts and landscapes.

Section 106 of the National Historic Preservation Act (NHPA) is the legal basis for most CRM work in the USA. Its regulations require federal agencies to identify historic places of all kinds (archaeological sites, historic buildings, Indian tribal sacred sites, etc.) that may be affected by their actions, in consultation with SHPOs, tribes, and others. They are then required to determine what to do about project effects – all in consultation with SHPOs and other interested parties. Identification often requires archaeological surveys both to find and evaluate archaeological sites. Evaluation involves applying published criteria to determine eligibility for the National Register of Historic Places – the US schedule of significant historic and cultural land areas, sites, structures, neighborhoods and communities.

If the agency and its consulting partners find that significant sites are present and will be adversely affected, they seek ways to "mitigate" the effect. Often this involves redesigning the project to reduce, minimize, or even avoid the damage. Often where archaeological sites are concerned, the decision is to conduct excavations to recover significant data before they are destroyed. If the parties cannot agree on what to do, the Advisory Council on Historic Preservation makes a final recommendation and then the responsible federal agency makes its final decision.

Most surveys and data recovery projects in the USA are carried out by private firms – sometimes companies that specialize in CRM work, other times by branches of large engineering, planning, or environmental impact assessment companies. Some academic institutions, museums, and non-profit organizations also carry out CRM work. CRM-based surveys and excavations now comprise at least 90 percent of the field archaeology carried out in the USA.

The review system under Section 106 can produce excellent archaeological research, but research interests must be balanced with other public interests, especially the concerns of Indian tribes and other communities. The quality of work depends largely on the integrity and skill of the participants – agency employees, SHPOs, tribal and community representatives, and private-sector archaeologists. Among the recurring problems are quality control in fieldwork, applying the results of fieldwork to important research topics, publication and other dissemination of results, and the long-term preservation and management of recovered

An aerial view of the Lubbub Creek site on the Tombigbee River, Alabama. The smaller photograph shows two of the salvage archaeologists carefully cleaning a large pottery vessel.

artifacts. Treatment of ancestral Native American remains and associated artifacts is also a contentious issue, and is the subject of another law, the Native American Graves Protection and Repatriation Act.

One good example of this process is the vast Tennessee-Tombigbee Waterway project. Of the 682 sites revealed by survey, it was determined that 27 would be affected by waterway construction. Of these, 17 had good research potential, and another 24 sites were selected for data recovery. 12 sites could be preserved by altering the construction program.

Excavation was designed to investigate the evolution of cultures in the area, with emphasis on sampling a good range of sites. The largest site was Lubbub Creek, the only major settlement in the threatened area belonging to the Mississippian culture (AD 900–1450). It includes a major ceremonial mound surrounded by a fortified village. The work undertaken in mitigation of environmental impact gave an excellent opportunity for systematic excavation of both settlement and cemeteries.

Not all CRM projects are so well or responsibly managed. Particularly in the case of small projects, which are carried out by the thousands, it is easy for very shoddy work to be done and little useful data to be produced. The Society for American Archaeology has organized a Registry of Professional Archaeologists in an attempt to improve standards.

KEY CONCEPTS: CRM IN THE USA

- CRM (Cultural Resource Management) accounts for over 90 percent of the field archaeology carried out in the USA today

- *Legal Basis:* under Section 106 of the National Historic Preservation Act (NHPA), archaeological investigation is often carried out in advance of projects on federal land, using federal funds, or requiring a federal permit

- *Funding:* generally speaking, the proponent of the construction or land use project pays for the work, whether that party is a federal, state, or local agency, or a private developer

- *Activation:* project proponents fund identification work, often including archaeological surveys. If sites will be adversely affected, consultation often leads to their preservation in place, but if this is not feasible then data recovery is usually undertaken through excavation and analysis of results

- *Outcome:* the fieldwork typically results in at least a report filed with the SHPO and data entered in government and other databases. Many CRM projects also result in published journal articles, monographs, and books

THE RESPONSIBILITY OF COLLECTORS AND MUSEUMS

So far as illicit antiquities are concerned, the spotlight has turned upon museums and private collectors. Many of the world's great museums, following the lead of the University Museum in Philadelphia in 1970, now decline to purchase or receive by gift any antiquities which cannot be shown to have been exported legally from their country of origin. But others, such as the Metropolitan Museum of New York, have in the past had no such scruples: Thomas Hoving, at that time Director of the museum, was quoted as saying: "We are no more illegal in anything we have done than Napoleon was when he brought all the treasures to the Louvre." The Getty Museum, with its great wealth, has a heavy responsibility in this, and at present its policies are still not entirely clear.

Museums like the Metropolitan Museum of Art, which in 1990 put on display the collection of Shelby White and Leon Levy, and the J. Paul Getty Museum which in 1994 exhibited (and then acquired) that of Barbara Fleischman and the late Lawrence Fleischman – both collections with a high proportion of antiquities of unknown provenience – must share some responsibility for the prevalence of collecting in circumstances where much of the money paid inevitably goes to reward dealers who are part of the ongoing cycles of destruction, and thus ultimately the looters. And the responsibility borne by collectors who, in buying such works, indirectly fund the looting process, is now being recognized. It has been argued that "Collectors are the real looters." The exhibition of the George Ortiz collection of antiquities at the Royal Academy in London in 1994 excited controversy and was felt by many archaeologists to have brought no credit to the Royal Academy. The art critic Robert Hughes has correctly observed that "Part of the story is the renewed cult of the collector as celebrity and of the museum as spectacle, as much concerned with show business as with scholarship."

It remains a real paradox that collectors, who often have a real feeling for the antiquities which they amass, are ultimately funding the looting which is the main threat to the world's archaeological heritage.

However, there are signs that things may be improving. The Dealing in Cultural Objects (Offences) Act was approved by the United Kingdom Parliament in 2003. For the first time it is now a criminal offence in UK knowingly to deal in illicitly excavated antiquities, whether from Britain or overseas. And in New York in June 2003 the United States Court of Appeals upheld the conviction of the antiquities dealer Frederick Schultz for conspiring to deal in antiquities stolen from Egypt. Frederick Schultz is a former president of the National Association of Dealers in Ancient, Oriental, and Primitive Art and has in the past sold antiquities to some leading museums in the United States. A jail term for so prominent a dealer will send a clear message to some conspicuous collectors and museum directors that they should be more attentive in future in the exercise of "due diligence" when acquiring unprovenienced antiquities.

Recent cases include:

The "Euphronios Vase." In 2006 the Metropolitan Museum of Art in New York felt obliged to give in to demands from the Italian government that it return the now infamous "Euphronios Vase," an Ancient Greek vase painted by the artist Euphronios in the 5th century BC. The vase had been imprudently purchased in 1972 for a price of one million dollars from a dealer giving a false provenience.

The "Weary Herakles." Two parts of a Roman marble statue of the 2nd century AD are now separate. The lower part was excavated at Perge in Turkey in 1980 and is in the Antalya Museum, while the joining upper part was purchased by the late Leon Levy shortly afterwards, and is currently on view at the Boston Museum of Fine Arts, to which Levy gave a half share. The Museum and Levy have declined to return the piece to Turkey.

The Sevso Treasure. A splendid late Roman assemblage of silver vessels was acquired as an investment by the Marquess of Northampton, but was subsequently

The "Weary Herakles": the lower part, excavated in Turkey in 1980, is now in the Antalya Museum while the upper part is in the Boston Museum of Fine Arts, which has so far failed to return it to Turkey.

A splendid silver dish from the looted Sevso Treasure, one of the major scandals in the recent story of illicit antiquities.

claimed in a New York court action by Hungary, Croatia, and Lebanon. Possession was awarded to Lord Northampton, who then found the treasure unsaleable and sued his former legal advisors in London for their poor advice at the time of purchase; an out-of-court settlement, reportedly in excess of £15 million, was agreed on confidential terms in 1999. Hungary is now seeking to obtain this material, and perhaps Lord Northampton will sell his treasure after all.

The Getty Affair. The J.P. Getty Museum in Los Angeles found itself in the spotlight of publicity in 2005 when its Curator of Antiquities, Marion True (subsequently fired), went on trial in Italy on charges relating to the purchase by the Getty of antiquities allegedly illegally excavated in Italy.

POPULAR ARCHAEOLOGY VERSUS PSEUDOARCHAEOLOGY

The purpose of archaeology is to learn more about the past, and archaeologists believe that it is important that everyone should have some knowledge of the human past – of where we have come from, and how we have come to be where we are. Archaeology is not just for archaeologists. For that reason it is crucially important that we communicate effectively with the wider public. But there are several ways in which this important mission can be subverted. The first is the development of **pseudoarchaeology**, often for commercial purposes – that is to say the formulation of extravagant but ill-founded stories about the past. Sometimes those telling these stories may actually believe them, but often, as with Dan Brown's popular novel *The Da Vinci Code*, it is suspected that the primary motive of the author is just to make money. Archaeology can be subverted, also, when people actually manufacture false evidence, and perpetrate archaeological fraud.

Archaeology at the Fringe. In the later years of the 20th century "Other Archaeologies" grew up at the fringe of the discipline, offering alternative interpretations of

Stonehenge has generated innumerable theories about its origins and meaning. Several groups, including Druids and New Agers claim it as a monument central to their beliefs.

the past. To the scientist these seem fanciful and extravagant – manifestations of a postmodern age in which horoscopes are widely read, New Age prophets preach alternative lifestyles, and when many members of the public are willing to believe that "corn circles" and megalithic monuments are the work of aliens. Many archaeologists label such populist approaches as "pseudoarchaeology," and place them on a par with archaeological frauds such as Piltdown Man, where deliberate deception can be demonstrated or inferred.

But how does an archaeologist persuade the self-styled Druids who perform their rituals at Stonehenge at the summer solstice (if the governing authority, English Heritage, allows them access) that their beliefs are not supported by archaeological evidence? This brings us back to the central question of this chapter: "Whose Past?" It is not clear that we should question the reality of the Dreamtime of the Australian Aborigines, even if aspects of their belief effectively clash with current scientific interpretations. Where do we distinguish between respect for deeply held beliefs and the role of the archaeologist to inform the public and to dismiss credulous nonsense?

One of the most popular and durable myths concerns a "lost Atlantis," a story narrated by the Greek philosopher Plato in the 5th century BC, and attributed by him to the Greek sage Solon, who had visited Egypt and consulted with priests, the heirs to a long religious and historical tradition. They told him of a legend of the lost continent beyond the Pillars of Hercules (the modern Straits of Gibraltar), hence in the Atlantic Ocean, with its advanced civilization, which vanished centuries earlier "in a night and a day." In 1882 Ignatius Donnelly published *Atlantis, the Antediluvian World*, elaborating this legend. His work was one of the first to seek a simple explanation of all ancient civilizations of the world by a single marvellous means. Such theories often share characteristics:

1 They celebrate a remarkable lost world whose people possessed many skills surpassing those of the present.
2 They account for most of the early accomplishments of prehistoric and early state societies with a single explanation: all were the work of the skilled inhabitants of that lost world.
3 That world vanished in a catastrophe of cosmic proportions.
4 Nothing of that original homeland is available for scientific examination, nor are any artifacts surviving.

The basic structure of Donnelly's argument was repeated with variants by Immanuel Velikovsky (meteors and astronomical events) and recently by Graham Hancock (who sites his lost continent in Antarctica). A popular alternative, elaborated with great financial profit by Erich von Däniken, is that the source of progress is outer space, and that the advances of early civilizations are the work of aliens visiting earth. Ultimately, however, all such theories trivialize the much more remarkable story which archaeology reveals – the history of humankind.

Fraud in Archaeology. Fraud in archaeology is nothing new and takes many forms – from the manipulation of evidence by Heinrich Schliemann to the infamous cases of fakery such as Britain's Piltdown Man. It has been suggested that more than 1200 fake antiquities are displayed in some of the world's leading museums. A particularly serious example came to light as recently as 2000 when a leading Japanese archaeologist admitted planting artifacts at excavations. Shinichi Fujimura – nicknamed "God's hands" for his uncanny ability to uncover ancient objects – had been videotaped burying his "discoveries" before digging them up again as new finds. He admitted having buried dozens of artifacts in secret, claiming that it was the pressure of having to discover older sites which forced him to fake them by using artifacts from his own collections.

Of 65 pieces unearthed at the Kamitakamori site north of Tokyo, Fujimura admitted to having faked 61, together with all 29 pieces found in 2000 at the Soshinfudozaka site in northern Japan. He later admitted having tampered with evidence at 42 sites; but since Fujimura, deputy director of the Tohoku **Paleolithic** Institute, had been involved in researching at least 180 sites, Japanese

A cluster of handaxes at Kamitakamori faked by Japanese archaeologist Shinichi Fujimura.

archaeological authorities are understandably worried about the potential impact on evidence for the Early Paleolithic period in Japan unearthed since the mid-1970s.

It seems that this phenomenon may currently be on the rise. Some of this can be blamed on the increased "mediatization" of the field, where, as in Japan, it can be important to generate publicity to further one's career and scientific publication often takes a back seat to press conferences where the latest finds are trumpeted. Spectacular discoveries are now sometimes seen as more important than scholarly debate or critical review. Nevertheless, the actual fabrication or planting of fake objects is an extreme form of fraud. Japanese archaeologists are worried that there may be other fraudulent artifacts, yet to be unearthed, a situation which has been likened to "archaeological landmines," ready to wreak havoc on future generations of scholars.

The Wider Audience. Although the immediate aim of most research is to answer specific questions, the fundamental purpose of archaeology must be to provide people with a better understanding of the human past. Skillful popularization – site and museum exhibits, books, television, and increasingly the Internet – is therefore required, but not all archaeologists are prepared to devote time to it, and few are capable of doing it well.

Excavators often regard members of the public as a hindrance to work on-site. More enlightened archaeologists, however, realize the financial and other support to be gained from encouraging public interest, and they organize information sheets, open days, and on long-term projects even fee-paying daily tours, as at the Bronze Age site of Flag Fen in eastern England. In Japan, on-the-spot presentations of excavation results are given as soon as a dig is completed. Details are released to the press the previous day, so that the public can obtain information from the morning edition of the local paper before coming to the site itself.

Clearly, there is an avid popular appetite for archaeology. In a sense, the past has been a form of entertainment since the early digging of burial mounds and the public unwrapping of mummies in the 19th century. The entertainment may now take a more scientific and educational form, but it still needs to compete with rival popular attractions if archaeology is to thrive.

SUMMARY

- Archaeology can be made to serve many masters – it can be used for economic ends, or it can be popularized and sold to a willing public, curious to know more of vanished cities and lost civilizations. Or it can be used for national ends, to provide a sense of national identity by tracing back a link from an uncertain present to a past whose achievements are seen as significant and admirable.

- The ultimate value of archaeology goes beyond these specific concerns. For world archaeology is something in which we can all share. Archaeology can document the trajectory of growth of the population of every country on earth. The archaeology of every land has its own contribution to make to the understanding of human diversity and hence of the human condition. Although earlier scholars behaved with flagrant disregard for the feelings and beliefs of native peoples, and some may continue to do so, interest in these matters today is not an attempt further to appropriate the native past. It is an assertion that this past has a legitimate wider significance, in which others may properly be interested than those who inhabit the areas in question. That is not a negative message, nor a disparaging one.

- If we are to have an adequate perception of our place as human beings in the modern world, the past matters. It is where we have come from, and it has determined what we are. For that reason, it is necessary for us to face up to the lunatics and the fringe archaeologists who seek (sometimes for their own gain, but sometimes simply from an inability to think straight) to confuse or corrupt our view of the past. We cannot simply dismiss the alternative theories as farcical, because they have been so widely believed.

- The objection to this kind of nonsense is not simply that it differs from the conventional archaeological wisdom. No one has a monopoly of the truth – not even the archaeologist. The objection is that such works gloss over the difficulties, and fail to submit their evidence to scientific scrutiny. Anyone who has read this book, and who understands how archaeology proceeds, will already see why such writings are a delusion. The real antidote is a kind of healthy skepticism: to ask "where is the evidence?" Knowledge advances by asking questions – that is the central theme of this book, and there is no better way to disperse the lunatic fringe than by asking difficult questions, and looking skeptically at the answers.

FURTHER READING

Brodie, N. & Tubb, K.W. (eds.). 2002. **Illicit Antiquities. The Theft of Culture and the Extinction of Archaeology**. ROUTLEDGE: LONDON.

Greenfield, J. 1996. (2nd ed.). **The Return of Cultural Treasures**. CAMBRIDGE UNIVERSITY PRESS: CAMBRIDGE & NEW YORK.

Lynott, M.J. & Wylie, A., 2002. (2nd ed.). **Ethics in American Archaeology**. SOCIETY FOR AMERICAN ARCHAEOLOGY: WASHINGTON D.C.

Renfrew, C. 2000. **Loot, Legitimacy and Ownership: The Ethical Crisis in Archaeology.** DUCKWORTH: LONDON.

Watson, P. 2006. **The Medici Conspiracy**. PUBLICAFFAIRS: NEW YORK.

Glossary

(Terms in *italics* are defined elsewhere in the glossary)

absolute dating The determination of age with reference to a specific time scale, such as a fixed calendrical system; also referred to as chronometric dating.

aerial reconnaissance An important survey technique in the discovery and recording of archaeological sites (see also *reconnaissance survey*).

alloying Technique involving the mixing of two or more metals to create a new material, e.g. the fusion of copper and tin to make bronze.

annealing In copper and bronze metallurgy, this refers to the repeated process of heating and hammering the material to produce the desired shape.

anthropology The study of humanity – our physical characteristics as animals, and our unique non-biological characteristics we call *culture*. The subject is generally broken down into three subdisciplines: *biological* (*physical*) *anthropology*, *cultural* (*social*) *anthropology*, and *archaeology*.

archaeobotany See *paleoethnobotany*.

archaeological culture A constantly recurring *assemblage* of artifacts assumed to be representative of a particular set of behavioral activities carried out at a particular time and place (*cf. culture*).

archaeology A subdiscipline of anthropology involving the study of the human past through its material remains.

archaeology of cult The study of the material indications of patterned actions undertaken in response to religious beliefs.

archaeomagnetic dating Sometimes referred to as paleomagnetic dating, it is based on the fact that changes in the earth's magnetic field over time can be recorded as remanent magnetism in materials such as baked clay structures (ovens, kilns, and hearths).

archaeozoology Sometimes referred to as zooarchaeology, this involves the identification and analysis of faunal species from archaeological sites, as an aid to the reconstruction of human diets and to an understanding of the contemporary environment at the time of deposition.

artifact Any portable object used, modified, or made by humans; e.g. stone tools, pottery, and metal weapons.

assemblage A group of artifacts recurring together at a particular time and place, and representing the sum of human activities.

association The co-occurrence of an artifact with other archaeological remains, usually in the same *matrix*.

attribute A minimal characteristic of an artifact such that it cannot be further subdivided; attributes commonly studied include aspects of form, style, decoration, color, and raw material.

Australopithecus A collective name for the earliest known hominids emerging about 5 million years ago in East Africa.

band A term used to describe small-scale societies of hunters and gatherers, generally less than 100 people, who move seasonally to exploit wild (undomesticated) food resources. Kinship ties play an important part in social organization.

biological anthropology See *physical anthropology*.

characterization (sourcing) The application of techniques of examination by which characteristic properties of the constituent material of traded goods can be identified, and thus their source of origin; e.g. petrographic *thin-section analysis*.

chiefdom A term used to describe a society that operates on the principle of ranking, i.e. differential social status. Different *lineages* are graded on a scale of prestige, calculated by how closely related one is to the chief. The chiefdom generally has a permanent ritual and ceremonial center, as well as being characterized by local specialization in crafts.

chronometric dating See *absolute dating*.

classification The ordering of phenomena into groups or other classificatory schemes on the basis of shared attributes (see also *type* and *typology*).

cognitive archaeology The study of past ways of thought and symbolic structures from material remains.

cognitive map An interpretive framework of the world which, it is argued, exists in the human mind and affects actions and decisions as well as knowledge structures.

cognitive-processual approach An alternative to the materialist orientation of the functional-processual approach, it is concerned with (1) the integration of the cognitive and symbolic with other aspects of early societies; (2) the role of ideology as an active organizational force.

computerized (computed) axial tomography (CAT or CT scanner) The method by which scanners allow detailed internal views of bodies such as mummies. The body is passed into the machine and images of cross-sectional "slices" through the body are produced.

conjoining See *refitting*.

context An artifact's context usually consists of its immediate *matrix* (the material around it e.g. gravel, clay, or sand), its provenience (horizontal and vertical position in the matrix), and its *association* with other artifacts (with other archaeological remains, usually in the same matrix).

contract archaeology Archaeological research conducted under the aegis of federal or state legislation, often in advance of highway construction or urban development, where the archaeologist is contracted to undertake the necessary research.

coprolites Fossilized feces; these contain food residues that can be used to reconstruct diet and subsistence activities.

core A lithic artifact used as a blank from which other tools or flakes are made.

Critical Theory A theoretical approach developed by the so-called "Frankfurt School" of German social thinkers, which stresses that all knowledge is historical, and in a sense biassed communication; thus, all claims to "objective" knowledge are illusory.

cultural anthropology A subdiscipline of anthropology concerned with the non-biological, behavioral aspects of society; i.e. the social, linguistic, and technological components underlying human behavior. Two important branches of cultural anthropology are *ethnography* (the study of living cultures) and *ethnology* (which attempts to compare cultures using ethnographic evidence). In Europe, it is referred to as *social anthropology*.

cultural ecology A term devised by Julian Steward to account for the dynamic relationship between human society and its environment, in which *culture* is viewed as the primary adaptive mechanism.

cultural resource management (CRM) The safeguarding of the archaeological heritage through the protection of sites and through salvage archaeology (rescue archaeology), generally within the framework of legislation designed to safeguard the past.

culture A term used by anthropologists when referring to the non-biological characteristics unique to a particular society (*cf. archaeological culture*).

culture-historical approach An approach to archaeological interpretation which uses the procedure of the traditional historian (including emphasis on specific circumstances elaborated with rich detail, and processes of *inductive* reasoning).

deduction A process of reasoning by which more specific consequences are inferred by rigorous argument from more general propositions (*cf. induction*).

deep-sea cores Cores drilled from the sea bed that provide the most coherent record of climate changes on a worldwide scale. The cores contain shells of microscopic marine organisms (foraminifera) laid down on the ocean floor through the continuous process of sedimentation. Variations in the ratio of two oxygen isotopes in the calcium carbonate of these shells give a sensitive indicator of sea temperature at the time the organisms were alive.

dendrochronology The study of tree-ring patterns; annual variations in climatic conditions which produce differential growth can be used both as a measure of environmental change, and as the basis for a chronology.

diatom analysis A method of environmental reconstruction based on plant microfossils. Diatoms are unicellular algae, whose silica cell walls survive after the algae die, and they accumulate in large numbers at the bottom of rivers and lakes. Assemblages directly reflect the floristic composition of the water's extinct communities, as well as the water's salinity, alkalinity, and nutrient status.

diffusionist approach The theory popularized by V.G. Childe that all the attributes of civilization from architecture to metalworking had diffused from the Near East to Europe.

DNA (Deoxyribonucleic acid) The material which carries the hereditary instructions (the "blueprint") which determine the formation of all living organisms.

ecofacts Non-artifactual organic and environmental remains which have cultural relevance, e.g. faunal and floral material as well as soils and sediments.

electrical resistivity See *soil resistivity*.

electrolysis A standard cleaning process in archaeological conservation. Artifacts are placed in a chemical solution, and by passing a weak current between them and a surrounding metal grill, the corrosive salts move from the cathode (object) to the anode (grill), removing any accumulated deposit and leaving the artifact clean.

electron spin resonance (ESR) Enables trapped electrons within bone and shell to be measured without the heating that *thermoluminescence* requires. As with TL, the number of trapped electrons indicates the age of the specimen.

environmental archaeology A field of inter-disciplinary research – archaeology and natural science – which is directed at the reconstruction of human use of plants and animals, and how past societies adapted to changing environmental conditions.

environmental circumscription An explanation for the origins of the state propounded by Robert Carneiro that emphasizes the fundamental role exerted by environmental constraints and by territorial limitations.

ethnicity The existence of ethnic groups, including tribal groups. Though these are difficult to recognize from the archaeological record, the study of language and linguistic boundaries shows that ethnic groups are often correlated with language areas.

ethnoarchaeology The study of contemporary cultures with a view to understanding the behavioral relationships which underlie the production of material culture.

ethnography A subset of *cultural anthropology* concerned with the study of contemporary cultures through first-hand observation.

ethnology A subset of *cultural anthropology* concerned with the comparative study of contemporary cultures, with a view to deriving general principles about human society.

evolution The process of growth and development generally accompanied by increasing complexity. In biology, this change is tied to Darwin's concept of natural selection as the basis of species survival. Darwin's work laid the foundations for the study of artifact *typology*, pioneered by such scholars as Pitt-Rivers and Montelius.

evolutionary archaeology The idea that the processes responsible for biological evolution also drive culture change, i.e. the application of Darwinian evolutionary theory to the archaeological record.

excavation The principal method of data acquisition in archaeology, involving the systematic uncovering of archaeological remains through the removal of the deposits of soil and the other material covering them and accompanying them.

experimental archaeology The study of past behavioral processes through experimental reconstruction under carefully controlled scientific conditions.

fall-off analysis The study of regularities in the way in which quantities of traded items found in the archaeological record decline as the distance from the source increases. This may be plotted as a fall-off curve, with the quantities of material (Y-axis) plotted against distance from source (X-axis).

feature A non-portable *artifact*; e.g. hearths, architectural elements, or soil stains.

fission-track dating A dating method based on the operation of a radioactive clock, the spontaneous fission of an isotope of uranium present in a wide range of rocks and minerals. As with *potassium-argon dating*, with whose time range it overlaps, the method gives useful dates from rocks adjacent to archaeological material.

flotation A method of screening (sieving) excavated *matrix* in water so as to separate and recover small *ecofacts* and *artifacts*.

fluxgate magnetometer A type of magnetometer used in *subsurface detection*, producing a continuous reading.

formation processes Those processes affecting the way in which archaeological materials came to be buried, and their subsequent history afterwards. Cultural formation processes include the deliberate or accidental activities of humans; natural formation processes refer to natural or environmental events which govern the burial and survival of the archaeological record.

frequency seriation A *relative dating* method which relies principally on measuring changes in the proportional abundance, or frequency, observed among finds (e.g. counts of tool types, or of ceramic fabrics).

functional-processual approach See *processual archaeology.*

Geographic Information Systems/GIS GIS are software-based systems designed for the collection, organizing, storage, retrieval, analysis, and displaying of spatial/digital geographical data held in different "layers." A GIS can also include other digital data.

geomagnetic reversals An aspect of archaeomagnetism relevant to the dating of the Lower Paleolithic, involving complete reversals in the earth's magnetic field.

gift exchange See *reciprocity.*

ground reconnaissance A collective name for a wide variety of methods for identifying individual archaeological sites, including consultation of documentary sources, place-name evidence, local folklore, and legend, but primarily actual fieldwork.

half-life The time taken for half the quantity of a radioactive isotope in a sample to decay (see also *radioactive decay*).

hand-axe A Paleolithic stone tool usually made by modifying (chipping or flaking) a natural pebble.

hoards Deliberately buried groups of valuables or prized possessions, often in times of conflict or war, and which, for one reason or another, have not been reclaimed. Metal hoards are a primary source of evidence for the European Bronze Age.

hunter-gatherers A collective term for the members of small-scale mobile or semi-sedentary societies, whose subsistence is mainly focused on hunting game and gathering wild plants and fruits; organizational structure is based on *bands* with strong kinship ties.

hypothetico-deductive explanation A form of explanation based on the formulation of hypotheses and the establishment from them by *deduction* of consequences which can then be tested against the archaeological data.

ice cores Borings taken from the Arctic and Antarctic polar ice caps, containing layers of compacted ice useful for reconstructing paleoenvironments and as a method of *absolute dating.*

iconography An important component of *cognitive archaeology*, this involves the study of artistic representations which usually have an overt religious or ceremonial significance; e.g. individual deities may be distinguished, each with a special characteristic, such as corn with the corn god, or the sun with a sun goddess etc.

induction A method of reasoning in which one proceeds by generalization from a series of specific observations so as to derive general conclusions (*cf. deduction*).

interaction sphere A regional or inter-regional exchange system, e.g. the Hopewell interaction sphere.

isotopic analysis An important source of information on the reconstruction of prehistoric diets, this technique analyzes the ratios of the principal isotopes preserved in human bone; in effect the method reads the chemical signatures left in the body by different foods. Isotopic analysis is also used in *characterization* studies.

landscape archaeology The study of individual features including settlements seen as single components within the broader perspective of the patterning of human activity over a wide area.

lineage A group claiming descent from a common ancestor.

market exchange A mode of exchange which implies both a specific location for transactions and the sort of social relations where bargaining can occur. It usually involves a system of price-making through negotiation.

Marxist archaeology Based principally on the writings of Karl Marx and Friedrich Engels, this posits a materialist model of societal change. Change within a society is seen as the result of contradictions arising between the forces of production (technology) and the relations of production (social organization). Such contradictions are seen to emerge as a struggle between distinct social classes.

material culture The buildings, tools, and other artifacts that constitute the material remains of former societies.

matrix The physical material within which artifacts are embedded or supported.

Mesolithic An Old World chronological period beginning around 10,000 years ago, between the *Paleolithic* and the *Neolithic*.

metallographic examination A technique used in the study of early metallurgy involving the microscopic examination of a polished section cut from an artifact, which has been etched so as to reveal the metal structure.

microwear analysis The study of the patterns of wear or damage on the edge of stone tools, which provides valuable information on the way in which the tool was used.

Midwestern taxonomic system A framework devised by McKern (1939) to systematize sequences in the Great Plains area of the United States, using the general principle of similarities between artifact *assemblages*.

monocausal explanation Explanations of culture change (e.g. for *state* origins) which lays stress on a single dominant explanatory factor or "prime mover."

multivariate explanation Explanation of culture change, e.g. the origin of the state, which, in contrast to monocausal approaches, stresses the interaction of several factors operating simultaneously.

Neolithic An Old World chronological period characterized by the development of agriculture and, hence, an increasing emphasis on sedentism.

Neolithic Revolution A term coined by V.G. Childe in 1941 to describe the origin and consequences of farming (i.e. the development of stock raising and agriculture), allowing the widespread development of settled village life.

New Archaeology A new approach advocated in the 1960s which argued for an explicitly scientific framework of archaeological method and theory, with hypotheses rigorously tested, as the proper basis for explanation rather than simply description (see also *processual archaeology*).

non-probabilistic sampling A non-statistical sampling strategy (in contrast to *probabilistic sampling*) which concentrates on sampling areas on the basis of intuition, historical documentation, or long field experience in the area.

obsidian A volcanic glass whose ease of working and characteristically hard flint-like edges allowed it to be used for the making of tools.

off-site data Evidence from a range of information, including scatters of artifacts and features such as plowmarks and field boundaries, that provides important evidence about human exploitation of the environment.

Oldowan industry The earliest toolkits, comprising flake and pebble tools, used by hominids in the Olduvai Gorge, East Africa.

open-area excavation The opening up of large horizontal areas for *excavation*, used especially where single period deposits lie close to the surface as, for example, with the remains of American Indian or European Neolithic long houses.

paleoentomology The study of insects from archaeological contexts. The survival of insect exoskeletons, which are quite resistant to decomposition, is important in the reconstruction of paleo-environments.

paleoethnobotany (archaeobotany) The recovery and identification of plant remains from archaeological *contexts*, used in reconstructing past environments and economies.

Paleolithic The archaeological period before *c.* 10,000 BC, characterized by the earliest known stone tool manufacture.

paleomagnetism See *archaeomagnetic dating*.

palynology The study and analysis of fossil pollen as an aid to the reconstruction of past vegetation and climates.

physical anthropology A subdiscipline of anthropology dealing with the study of human biological or physical characteristics and their evolution.

plating A method of bonding metals together, for instance silver with copper or copper with gold.

polity A politically independent or autonomous social unit, whether simple or complex, which may in the case of a complex society (such as a state) comprise many lesser dependent components.

pollen analysis See *palynology*.

postprocessual explanation Explanation formulated in reaction to the perceived limitations of functional-processual archaeology. It eschews generalization in favor of an "individualizing" approach that is influenced by *structuralism, Critical Theory*, and neo-Marxist thought.

potassium-argon dating A method used to date rocks up to thousands of millions of years old, though it is restricted to volcanic material no more recent than *c.* 100,000 years old. One of the most widely used methods in the dating of early hominid sites in Africa.

prehistory The period of human history before the advent of writing.

prestige goods A term used to designate a limited range of exchange goods to which a society ascribes high status or value.

probabilistic sampling Sampling method, using probability theory, designed to draw reliable general conclusions about a site or region, based on small sample areas; 4 types of sampling strategies are recognized: (1) *simple random sampling*; (2) *stratified random sampling*; (3) *systematic sampling*; (4) *stratified systematic sampling*.

processual archaeology An approach that stresses the dynamic relationship between social and economic aspects of culture and the environment as the basis for understanding the processes of culture change. Uses the scientific methodology of problem statement, hypothesis formulation, and subsequent testing. The earlier functional-processual archaeology has been contrasted with *cognitive-processual archaeology*, where emphasis is on integrating ideological and symbolic aspects.

proton magnetometer A device used in *subsurface detection* which records variation in the earth's magnetic field.

pseudoarchaeology The use of selective archaeological evidence to promulgate nonscientific, fictional accounts of the past.

pyrotechnology The intentional use and control of fire by humans.

radioactive decay The regular process by which radioactive isotopes break down into their decay products with a half-life which is specific to the isotope in question (see also *radiocarbon dating*).

radiocarbon dating An absolute dating method that measures the decay of the radioactive isotope of carbon (^{14}C) in organic material (see *half-life*).

ranked societies Societies in which there is unequal access to prestige and status e.g. *chiefdoms* and *states*.

reciprocity A mode of exchange in which transactions take place between individuals who are symmetrically placed, i.e. they are exchanging as equals, neither being in a dominant position.

reconnaissance survey A broad range of techniques involved in the location of archaeological sites, e.g. the recording of surface artifacts and features, and the sampling of natural and mineral resources.

redistribution A mode of exchange which implies the operation of some central organizing authority. Goods are received or appropriated by the central authority, and subsequently some of them are sent by that authority to other locations.

refitting Sometimes referred to as conjoining, this entails attempting to put stone tools and flakes back together again, and provides important information on the processes involved in the knapper's craft.

relative dating The determination of chronological sequence without recourse to a fixed time scale; e.g. the arrangement of artifacts in a typological sequence, or *seriation* (*cf. absolute dating*).

religion A framework of beliefs relating to supernatural or superhuman beings or forces that transcend the everyday material world.

remote sensing The imaging of phenomena from a distance, primarily through airborne and satellite imaging. "Ground-based remote sensing" links geophysical methods such as radar with remote sensing methods applied at ground level, such as thermography.

rescue archaeology See *salvage archaeology*.

research design Systematic planning of archaeological research, usually including (1) the formulation of a strategy to resolve a particular question; (2) the collection and recording of the evidence; (3) the processing and analysis of these data and their interpretation; and (4) the publication of results.

resistivity meter See *soil resistivity*.

salvage archaeology The location and recording (usually through excavation) of archaeological sites in advance of highway construction, drainage projects, or urban development.

segmentary societies Relatively small and autonomous groups, usually of agriculturalists, who regulate their own affairs; in some cases, they may join together with other comparable segmentary societies to form a larger ethnic unit.

seriation A relative dating technique based on the chronological ordering of a group of artifacts or assemblages, where the most similar are placed adjacent to each other in the series. See *frequency seriation*.

side-scan sonar A survey method used in underwater archaeology which provides the broadest view of the sea-floor. An acoustic emitter is towed behind a vessel and sends out sound waves in a fan-shaped beam. These pulses of sonic energy are reflected back to a transducer – return time depending on distance traveled – and recorded on a rotating drum.

simple random sampling A type of *probabilistic sampling* where the areas to be sampled are chosen using a table of random numbers. Drawbacks include (1) defining the site's boundaries initially; (2) the nature of random number tables results in some areas being allotted clusters of sample squares, while others remain untouched.

simulation The formulation and computer implementation of dynamic models, i.e. models concerned with change through time.

site A distinct spatial clustering of *artifacts*, *features*, structures, and organic and environmental remains – the residue of human activity.

social anthropology See *cultural anthropology*.

soil resistivity A method of *subsurface detection* which measures changes in conductivity by passing electrical current through ground soils. This is generally a consequence of moisture content, and in this way, buried features can be detected by differential retention of groundwater.

state A term used to describe a social formation defined by distinct territorial boundedness, and characterized by strong central government in which the operation of political power is sanctioned by legitimate force. In cultural evolutionist models, it ranks second only to the empire as the most complex societal development stage

stela (pl. stelae) A free-standing carved stone monument.

step-trenching *Excavation* method used on very deep sites, such as Near Eastern *tell* sites, in which the excavation proceeds downwards in a series of gradually narrowing steps.

stratification The laying down or depositing of strata or layers (also called deposits) one above the other. A succession of layers should provide a relative chronological sequence, with the earliest at the bottom and the latest at the top.

stratified random sampling A form of *probabilistic sampling* in which the region or site is divided into natural zones or strata such as cultivated land and forest; units are then chosen by a random number procedure so as to give each zone a number of squares proportional to its area, thus overcoming the inherent bias in *simple random sampling*.

stratified systematic sampling A form of *probabilistic sampling* which combines elements of (1) *simple random sampling*, (2) *stratified random sampling*, and (3) *systematic sampling*, in an effort to reduce sampling bias.

stratigraphy The study and validation of *stratification*; the analysis in the vertical, time dimension, of a series of layers in the horizontal, space dimension. It is often used as a *relative dating* technique to assess the temporal sequence of artifact deposition.

structuralist approaches Interpretations which stress that human actions are guided by beliefs and symbolic concepts, and that underlying these are structures of thought which find expression in various forms. The proper object of study is therefore to uncover the structures of thought and to study their influence in shaping the ideas in the minds of the human actors who created the archaeological record.

style According to the art historian, Ernst Gombrich, style is "any distinctive and therefore recognizable way in which an act is performed and made." Archaeologists and anthropologists have defined "stylistic areas" as areal units representing shared ways of producing and decorating artifacts.

subsurface detection Collective name for a variety of remote sensing techniques operating at ground level, and including both invasive and non-invasive techniques.

surface survey Two basic kinds can be identified: (1) unsystematic and (2) systematic. The former involves field-walking, i.e. scanning the ground along one's path and recording the location of artifacts and surface features. Systematic survey by comparison is less subjective and involves a grid system, such that the survey area is divided into sectors and these are walked systematically, thus making the recording of finds more accurate.

systematic sampling A form of *probabilistic sampling* employing a grid of equally spaced locations; e.g. selecting every other square. This method of regular spacing runs the risk of missing (or hitting) every single example if the distribution itself is regularly spaced.

systematic survey See *surface survey*.

taphonomy The study of processes which have affected organic materials such as bone after death; it also involves the microscopic analysis of tooth-marks or cut marks to assess the effects of butchery or scavenging activities.

tectonic movements Displacements in the plates that make up the earth's crust.

tell A Near Eastern term that refers to a mound site formed through successive human occupation over a very long timespan.

temper Inclusions in pottery clay which act as a filler to give the clay added strength and workability and to counteract any cracking or shrinkage during firing.

thermoluminescence (TL) A dating technique that relies indirectly on radioactive decay, overlapping with radiocarbon in the time period for which it is useful, but also has the potential for dating earlier periods. It has much in common with *electron spin resonance* (ESR).

thin-section analysis A technique whereby microscopic thin sections are cut from a stone object or potsherd and examined with a petrological microscope to determine the source of the material.

Three Age System A *classification* system devised by C.J. Thomsen for the sequence of technological periods (stone, bronze, and iron) in Old World prehistory. It established the principle that by classifying artifacts, one could produce a chronological ordering.

trace element analysis The use of chemical techniques for determining the incidence of trace elements in rocks. These methods are widely used in the identification of raw material sources for the production of stone tools.

tree-ring dating See *dendrochronology*.

tribes A term used to describe a social grouping generally larger than a *band*, but rarely numbering more than a few thousand; unlike bands tribes are usually settled farmers, though they also include nomadic pastoral groups whose economy is based on exploitation of livestock. Individual communities tend to be integrated into the larger society through kinship ties.

type A class of artifacts defined by the consistent clustering of *attributes*.

typology The systematic organization of artifacts into types on the basis of shared *attributes*.

underwater reconnaissance Geophysical methods of underwater survey include (1) a *proton magnetometer* towed behind a survey vessel, so as to detect iron and steel objects which distort the earth's magnetic field; (2) *side-scan sonar* that transmits sound waves in a fan-shaped beam to produce a graphic image of surface features on the sea-bed; (3) a sub-bottom profiler that emits sound pulses which bounce back from features and objects buried beneath the sea floor.

Uniformitarianism The principle that the stratification of rocks is due to processes still going on in seas, rivers, and lakes; i.e. that geologically ancient conditions were in essence similar to or "uniform with" those of our own time.

uranium series dating A dating method based on the *radioactive decay* of isotopes of uranium. It has proved particularly useful for the period before 50,000 years ago, which lies outside the time range of *radiocarbon dating*.

varves Fine layers of alluvium sediment deposited in glacial lakes. Their annual deposition makes them a useful source of dating.

Wheeler box-grid An excavation technique developed by Mortimer Wheeler from the work of Pitt-Rivers, involving retaining intact baulks of earth between excavation grid squares, so that different layers can be correlated across the site in the vertical profiles.

zooarchaeology See *archaeozoology*.

Illustration Credits

15 Wiltshire Archaeological & Natural History Society; 16 *The London Sketchbook;* 18t F. Catherwood, *Views of Ancient Monuments in Central America, Chiapas and Yucatán,* London 1844; 19t The St. Louis Art Museum, Eliza McMillan Fund; 20a Courtesy the Peabody Museum, Harvard University; 20bl A. Pitt-Rivers, *Excavations in Cranborne Chase,* 1893–1898; 20br A. Pitt-Rivers, *Excavations in Cranborne Chase,* 1893–1898; 21a Petrie Museum of Egyptian Archaeology, University College London' 21bl Archaeological Survey of India; 22tl Courtesy the Peabody Museum, Harvard University; 23 The Royal Commission on the Ancient & Historical Monuments of Scotland; 32bl Courtesy of Mrs Mary Allsebrook, Oxford; 32br The Principal and Fellows of Newnham College, Cambridge; 33tl University of Colorado Museum; 33b Jen and Des Bartlett and Bruce Coleman Ltd.; 33tc P. Dorrell, Jericho Exploration Fund; 33tr Courtesy the Peabody Museum, Harvard University; 38–39 ML Design (after A. Sherratt (ed.) *Cambridge Encyclopedia of Archaeology,* 1980, fig. 20.5); 42l, 42r Iva Ellen Morris (courtesy Lewis R. Binford); 42 Sue Cawood; 44 Annick Boothe (adapted from W. Rathje & M.Schiffer, *Archaeology* 1982, fig. 4.11); 50b Ian Bott; 50al, 50ar Griffith Institute, Oxford; 51 After Rudenko; 52 Tracy Wellman; 65 Annick Boothe (after Flannery (ed.) 1976, figs. 3.2, 5.2); 67 Cahokia Mounds State Historic Site; 68 Cambridge University Collection of Air Photos (photo J.K. St Joseph); 69a R. Agache, Service des Fouilles; 69br Annick Boothe (after Oxford Archaeological Unit); 70 Danebury Trust (from B. Cunliffe, *Danebury* 1983, fig. 64); 72 Jet Propulsion Laboratory, National Aeronautics and Space Administration, California; 73 Tracy Wellman; 75 René Millon; 76 Courtesy Mandy Mottram 96–97; 77 Drazen Tomic adapted from information supplied by Mandy Mottram; 80 University of Miami, Japan Division; 82 Andrew David, English Heritage; 85 Drazen Tomic (after M. Carver, *Underneath English Towns* 1987, fig. 2); 87b Sutton Hoo Research Trust, photos Nigel Macbeth; 87t Courtesy Robin Coningham; 88 Lewis Binford; 89 Annick Boothe (after *The Courier,* Unesco Nov. 1987, p. 16, drawing by M. Redknap); 90a Annick Boothe (after *National Geographic,* supplement Jan. 1990); 90bl Canadian Parks Service (photo Rock Chan, Denis Pagé); 90br Canadian Parks Service (by P. Waddell & J. Farley); 91 Museum of London; 93 Annick Boothe (after J. Deetz, *Invitation to Archaeology,* Natural History Press/Doubleday & Co., New York 1967); 100 Wheeler, *Ancient India* 3 Jan. 1947; 101, 102 Annick Boothe (after Rathje & Schiffer, *Archaeology* 1982, fig. 4.17); 103 ML Design; 110 Simon S.S. Driver (information from Bannister & Smiley in *Geochronology,* Tucson 1955); 112 Annick Boothe; 113 Annick Boothe (113l after Hedges & Gowlett in *Scientific American* 254 (1), Jan. 1986, p. 84); 115 After Gordon Pearson; 116 After Gordon Pearson; 118 David Hurst Thomas & the American Museum of Natural History; 124 Drazen Tomic (adapted from R. Foley & R. Dunbar, *New Scientist* 14 Oct. 1989, p. 40, with addition by P. Winton); 126–127 Simon S.S. Driver (with amendments by Drazen Tomic); 133 Igor Astrologo; 139 After C. Renfrew & E.V. Level in C. Renfrew & K.L. Cooke (eds.), *Transformations* 1979, figs. 6.11, 6.12; 140 Tracy Wellman (after Isaac); 143 From B. Fagan, *In the Beginning* (6th ed.)1988, fig. 16.4 (after Winter in Flannery (ed.) 1976, fig 2.17); 147 Charles Higham; 148a Mary Ellen Miller; 148b Simon S.S. Driver (after Renfrew); 150 Paolo Matthiae; 151 Hirmer Fotoarchiv; 153bl, br Lewis Binford; 156 U.S. General Services Administration; 157 Chester Higgins; 158 Courtesy Landesdenkmalamt Baden-Württemberg-Archäologische Denkmalpflege; 160 Drazen Tomic after Lois Martin; 165r Lucy Maw; 168l Annick Boothe (after Shackley 1981, fig. 4.3); 168r Annick Boothe (after Scarre (ed.) 1988, p.107); 169 Philip Winton (after Piperno and Ciochon, *New Scientist* 10/11/90); 170 Philip Winton; 173 H.J. Deacon; 176 After A. Marshack, *The Roots of Civilization* 1972, fig. 78b; 180 Annick Boothe (after J. Greig, Plant Foods in the Past, *J. of Plant Foods* 5 1983, 179–214); 183 After Mangelsdorf; 186 Pat Shipman & Richard Potts; 188 Netherlands Institute for the Near East, Leiden; 196 Peter Bellwood; 197 Annick Boothe; 198a Simon S.S. Driver; 198b Brian Fagan; 201 Oriental Institute, University of Chicago; 205al Museum für Völkerkunde, Vienna; 205ac British Museum; 205ar By courtesy of the Board of Trustees of the Victoria & Albert Museum; 205c National Archaeological Museum, Athens; 205bl Musée des Antiquités Nationales, St-Germain-en-Laye; 205b, br Werner Forman; 209 ML Design (after Peacock 1982, fig. 80); 211 ML Design (after Renfrew); 213 Annick Boothe (after Pires-Ferreira in Flannery (ed.) 1976, fig. 10.16); 214a George Bass/Cemal Pulak, Institute of Nautical Archaeology; 214b ML Design (after Bass); 215 George Bass/Cemal Pulak, Institute of Nautical Archaeology; 222 British Museum; 223 Reproduced by permission of Chris Henshilwood, African Heritage Research Institute, Cape Town, South Africa; 224l ML Design; 224r After M. Ruspoli, *The Cave of Lascaux* 1987, p. 200; 225 Eurelios/Ministère de la Culture, Paris (photo Jean Clottes); 226l British Tourist Authority; 226r Philip Winton; 227 Colin Renfrew; 230 Musée des Antiquités Nationales, St-Germain-en-Laye; 232a Annick Boothe (after Burger); 232cll Annick Boothe (after Burger); 232clr Richard Burger; 232bl Richard Burger; 232br Wilfredo Loayzo L.; 235 Agora Excavations, American School of Classical Studies at Athens; 237 Annick Boothe; 238 British Museum; 239 British Museum; 240a Annick Boothe; 240b Annick Boothe; 241l British Museum; 241cl Staatliches Museum für Völkerkunde, Munich; 241cr Nationalmuseet, Copenhagen; 242t John Prag; 242br British Museum; 250a Annick Boothe (after Kirch); 250b Annick Boothe (after Gelb); 251cr R.D.K. Hadden; 251bl ML Design (after Garlake); 260 University of Pennsylvania Museum, Philadelphia [493]; 261 University of Pennsylvania Museum, Philadelphia [493]; 270a Tracy Wellman; 270b Photo Josephine Powell; 272 Toni Schneiders; 273 Hirmer Fotoarchiv; 274 Paul Bahn; 275 Photo Katz Pictures; 278tl Iraq Museum, Baghdad, Director General of Antiquities, Iraq; 278tr Courtesy Dr John Curtis; 280ar Colorado Springs Fine Art Center – Taylor Museum Collection; 280bl Werner Forman; 282 Christopher Peebles; 284t Museum of Fine Arts, Boston; 284b Antalya Museum; 285 By courtesy of the Trustee of the Marquess of Northampton 1987 Settlement; 286 Hiroshi Kasiwara; 288 Hiroko Koike

Index